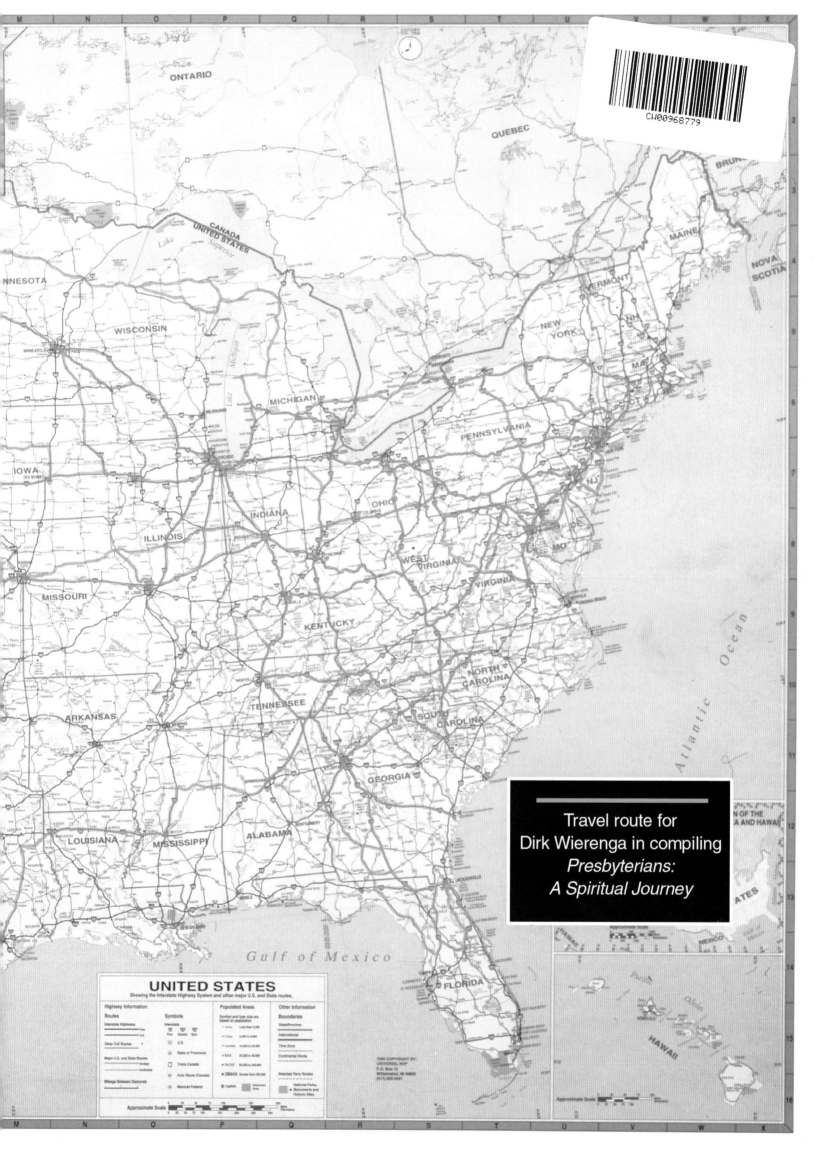

Travel route for
Dirk Wierenga in compiling
*Presbyterians:
A Spiritual Journey*

PRESBYTERIANS
a spiritual journey

PRESBYTERIANS
a spiritual journey

DIRK WIERENGA

GENEVA PRESS

LOUISVILLE, KENTUCKY

Book design by wk studio

First edition
Published by Geneva Press
Louisville, Kentucky

PRINTED IN HONG KONG.

00 01 02 03 04 05 06 07 08 09 – 10 9 8 7 6 5 4 3 2 1

Library of Congress Cataloging-in-Publication Data

Wierenga, Dirk.
   Presbyterians : a spiritual journey / Dirk Wierenga.
      p. cm.
   ISBN 0-664-50116-8
    1. Presbyterians--United States. 2. Presbyterian Church (U.S.A.) I. Title.

BX9220 . W54 2000
285'.1--dc21   00-026165

CONTENTS

FOREWORD

I first met Dirk Wierenga in mid-1997 when I received an e-mail titled "Growing Our Church." Since issues pertaining to church growth have been a passion of mine ever since I assumed the presidency of Louisville Seminary nearly twenty years ago, I felt compelled to check out this message from a stranger.

In the e-mail, Dirk told me a little about himself and his personal faith story. He is a third-generation Presbyterian who left the church while in college and didn't return for over fifteen years. Although he had grown a successful business that specialized in providing writing and graphic design services to an impressive list of nationally known businesses, his life felt empty for years. Then he returned to the church, and his life was transformed.

Dirk was proposing an idea: What if he were to travel by car across the country interviewing Presbyterians about their faith? Once he had found the stories, he would hire a team of photographers to follow in his path and capture the images for inclusion in a book about the church.

The idea was intriguing, so we agreed to meet. I wanted to see how committed he was and determine if he had a true sense of call. When we sat down in my office, Dirk enthusiastically shared his vision. He also told of how this idea had come to him: He was about to start a new project that would change the focus of his business. The business plan was written, and the bank had agreed to finance it. Then the night before he was to make the commitment, he awoke in the middle of the night with a strong sense that he was to abandon his plans and write a book about the church.

I was now convinced that not only did Dirk have a passion for this book project but he also had a strong sense of call. This prompted me to arrange a series of meetings with Gary Luhr from the Office of Communications at the General Assembly Council and Tom Long who had just taken the position as director of Geneva Press for the Presbyterian Publishing Corporation. After each met Dirk and saw his vision for this book, they asked how they could help make the book a reality.

Gary agreed to commission a study on the feasibility of such a book while Tom took the idea to his editorial team. I took on the role as fundraiser, knowing that to make the book affordable a sizable amount of its development costs needed to be underwritten by various foundations and organizations. The book you are holding in your hand is the result of an incredible series of actions of faith and hard work. During his eighteen months of travel Dirk crisscrossed the country by car, often away from his wife, Anne, for six weeks at a time. To keep costs down he stayed in low-priced motels and picked up food from the salad bars of countless supermarkets.

He logged over ninety-two thousand miles and spent nearly 220 nights in motels. Over two hundred people were interviewed and approximately eighty are included in this book.

Along the way Dirk and I stayed in constant contact. His stories from the road were inspiring. Countless Presbyterians agreed to take time out of their busy schedules to spend a day with him. They showed him true Christian hospitality. They opened up their hearts and told about what God was doing in their lives. I challenge everyone to read these stories. They will truly touch your heart.

The Presbyterian Church, along with many other churches, has endured over thirty years of membership decline. The reasons are due to both changes in our society and the mass exodus of many baby boomers who for one reason or another have left the church. Studies are showing that, like Dirk, many of these people are now returning to the church. What they are finding on their return is a vital church that is doing the work that Jesus asked of his disciples.

As you read these wonderful stories and view the dramatic pictures I'm sure you will join me in celebrating the resurgence of the Presbyterian Church in this country and around the globe. I hope these stories both inspire you and challenge you to answer God's call.

DR. JOHN M. MULDER
President of Louisville Presbyterian Theological Seminary

ACKNOWLEDGMENTS

The author and publisher wish to thank the over two hundred people who agreed to give up their valuable time to be interviewed for this book. All those interviewed had wonderful stories to share. Unfortunately, because of space restrictions only half those interviewed are included in these pages. The selection process took many hours of discussion and prayer. We hope to use the other interviews in future works.

This book would not have been possible without the gifts and grants from the following:

Lilly Endowment, Inc.
Board of Pensions of the Presbyterian Church (U.S.A.)
General Assembly Council, Presbyterian Church (U.S.A.)
Presbyterian Church (U.S.A.) Foundation
The Independent Presbyterian Church Foundation

We also thank the following who served as advisors to the publisher:

Dr. John M. Mulder
President and Professor of Historical Theology
Louisville Presbyterian Theological Seminary

Dr. Dorothy Bass
Director of the People in Faith Project
Valpariaso University

Dr. Milton J Coalter
Professor of Bibliography and Research and Director of the Library
Louisville Presbyterian Theological Seminary

Dr. James H. Costen
President Emeritus of the Interdenominational Theological Center
Atlanta, Georgia

Dr. Richard J. Mouw
President and Professor of Theology
Fuller Theological Seminary

Dr. Syngman Rhee
Professor of Evangelism and Mission
Union Theological Seminary in Virginia

Dr. Thomas Long
Director of Congregational Resources and Geneva Press
Presbyterian Publishing Corporation

Mr. Gary Luhr
Director of the Office of Communications
Office of the General Assembly Council
Presbyterian Church (U.S.A.)

A portion of the proceeds from the sale of this book are being given to the Presbyterian Church (U.S.A.) Office of New Church Development with the hope that enough funds can be raised to assist in the building of new churches.

While standing in the checkout line of a supermarket in San Bernadino, California, I overheard a conversation. The woman behind me had just run into an acquaintance, a young man probably in his mid-twenties who was having trouble with both his marriage and the law. The woman asked the man if things in his life were improving. He said they weren't; his wife was leaving him, and a warrant was out for his arrest. This wonderful woman, whom I'll call Rose, responded by saying, "You gotta go to church, 'cause if you do and you put your faith in God, good things will begin to happen." Rose's strong faith so moved me, I turned to her after the young man left and said that I couldn't help overhearing what she had said and that I was humbled by her faith. Suddenly here we were, two strangers in a grocery store talking about our common bond: our faith in God. When I turned to leave, she grabbed my arm and simply said, "God bless you." This is just one of the many faith encounters I was blessed to have during my travels as I interviewed people from around the country for this book, a book that shows how God is working through individuals, congregations, and the larger church.

This book is called "Presbyterians: A Spiritual Journey," not because Presbyterians are to be lifted up above other denominations but rather because I have chosen to explore the spiritual journeys of people today through the lens of the church I know best: the Presbyterian Church (U. S. A.). Presbyterians recognize the ministry and sacraments of all churches confessing Jesus Christ as Lord and Savior.

A vast majority of Americans repeatedly tell pollsters that they believe in God, and Americans are thirsty for spirituality and community. With fewer than a third of the population actually attending church on a regular basis, however, it is understandable why this thirst remains unslakable. To justify the lack of regular church attendance, many people point to the busyness of life. Yet the thirst for spirituality and community persists. In my travels, I encountered many people who had placed faith on the back burner due to busy careers and others who were jarred into faith only by personal crisis.

When I checked into a small motel in Statesville, North Carolina, the housekeeper, whose name is Ginger, was still cleaning my room. We started to talk. She asked where I was from, and after I told her she exclaimed, "Michigan! What in the world are you doing here?" I explained that I was a writer. "What is your book about," she asked. "I'm interviewing people about their faith," I said. "Oh," she replied, "I don't think about that much, it's not a big thing in my life." Ginger turned away and went back to her work.

The next month I found myself checking into the same motel. As I walked down the hallway I heard a familiar voice. "Dirk," she exclaimed, "I'm so glad you're back." It was Ginger. "Do you have a second? I need to tell you something. Last night my boyfriend beat me up. He also beat up my daughter. I'm leaving him, and I'm scared. Tell me more about your faith; I need all the support I can get." After we talked she said something that nearly brought me to tears. Ginger asked me to pray for her daughter and herself. The next morning I slipped her a note of encouragement. After she read it, Ginger said, "I'm not a Christian. In fact, I don't know what I believe, but if your faith is as compassionate as you say, I think I'll have to try going to a church some day."

Another time, during a trip to New York City, I was standing on the platform in Stamford, Connecticut, waiting for the commuter train to Manhattan. Being a visitor, I wasn't sure which train to take. A man who looked to be in his mid-thirties was standing next to me. He was reading his newspaper and was oblivious to what was going on around him. I decided to engage him in conversation. "Excuse me, I'm not from around here. In fact I'm from the Midwest. We don't have commuter trains where I live, so this is new to me. Is this the train to Grand Central Station?" He grunted, "Yes," never taking his eyes off his paper. Then I asked him if he lived nearby. Again he grunted, "Yes." This time he turned away from me. But I persisted, deciding to ignore his body language. "Do you take the train every day?" Again a terse, "Yes." Now he looked perturbed. I asked him yet another question. "What do you do for a living?" He snapped, "I'm an investment banker." As he responded he glanced at me briefly before returning to his paper. All of a sudden he seemed to warm up and he looked me in the eyes and asked, "What brings you to the city?" I told him I was writing a book on faith.

The train arrived and he stood a couple of feet from me in the crowded car. During the trip, we would exchange brief conversations from time to time. At one point I introduced myself, and he said his name was Bob. Before long the train arrived and we disembarked, with everyone hurriedly rushing to get to work. Bob was way ahead of me. Then something happened. He stopped and turned to me. "Where did you say you were going?" he asked. I told him I was going to Fifth Avenue Presbyterian Church. "Let me take you there," he offered. So together we walked the mile or so down Fifth Avenue. All the while he was asking me about my faith and sharing his story. At one point he said, "When I was growing up, my family went to church, but nowadays I never go. Life is just too busy and I need the weekends to unwind and play a little golf." I asked him if weekends ever seemed like two Saturdays in a row and he said they did. I shared that weekends were at one time that way for me. Then I started to go to church and now Sunday has become a special day. As we arrived at the church, Bob said he'd think about what I'd said. I thanked him for his help, and we parted ways.

The opportunity of telling these stories has had a profound influence on my own spiritual life. It is my hope that others will be touched by the stories and will be motivated by them to get involved in the work that Jesus began. If one person is inspired by these journeys in faith and does something for another of God's people, then the book will have accomplished its purpose.

Organization of Book

The organization of this book is a typical faith journey that many of us have taken, from a personal discovery of the gift of faith to involvement in a church to an understanding of the role of the larger church.

In the first part, "Stories of Faith," individuals tell how faith has impacted and transformed their lives. The second part, "Spiritual Communities," shows how communities of believers are called together through their churches in order to do the work that Jesus expects of us all. The final part, "Connectional Bodies," illustrates the importance of the larger church and how, through a connectional structure, the church reaches out to those involved in mission, education, social justice, the chaplaincy, and other global and national ministries.

1 | Stories of Faith

The Christian movement began two thousand years ago when a man named Jesus, who lived in

Galilee, began to call people to follow him into a new way of life. He gathered disciples, preached

good news, and gained a reputation as a compassionate healer and a daring teacher. However,

his radical message and his ministry with outcasts made him a threat to the established powers.

When he arrived in Jerusalem to  the cheers of the crowd during

the Passover festival, those powers conspired to have him arrested,

tried as a criminal, and sentenced to execution on a cross. This much

historians can verify—a man named Jesus lived, was nailed

to a cross, and died. What happened next is a matter of

faith. Jesus' followers proclaimed how Jesus had been raised from

the dead, appeared to them, and sent them into the world as

witnesses, promising to be with them always. These early follow-

ers boldly set out to tell this story and continue the ministry of Jesus. Many who heard them

believed. People were healed, sins were forgiven, lives were renewed, and the Christian move-

ment spread throughout the world. The stories that follow are about ordinary people—

Presbyterians—who have been touched by this movement and transformed by the Christian faith.

OUT OF HIS COMFORT ZONE

As a young man Ken Crowe asked God to place him in a situation that was outside of his comfort zone—he found it in South Korea.

When Ken Crowe was commissioned in the army, he asked God to place him in a situation outside his comfort zone. His prayers were answered after basic training when he was given a year's assignment in South Korea. "I grew up on our family farm near Greenville, South Carolina, with parents who had strong Christian beliefs," Ken recalls. "I always tried to be a good kid, which is easy when you live in a small rural community."

To spare his parents the expense of college, Ken enrolled in R.O.T.C., and after graduation, he began to fulfill his four-year military obligation. "The first person who really influenced my faith was my army captain during my three years of R.O.T.C. at Furman University. He never pushed his religious beliefs on his soldiers, but you could tell that he had a faith that was strong just by the way he lived his life. I decided that when I had the opportunity to lead a group of soldiers, I would follow his example."

Ken's opportunity came when he left Fort Knox and became the leader of a platoon—sixteen men and four tanks. "An incredible amount of teamwork is required," Ken reports. "Each tank has four soldiers, and every team member has a totally different responsibility. If one team member isn't doing the job, the tank can't function. Since tanks are always deployed in multiples of two, the safety and effectiveness of the entire unit can be compromised."

Ken's platoon was assigned to South Korea. "We were definitely out of our comfort zone. We didn't speak their language and didn't understand their customs. The men in my platoon had left their families and country behind and everything was completely different from the standard of living they were used to. That left many of the men feeling that there were just two things to do on their leave time: either face loneliness in the barracks watching videos or go out on the town and drink. The result was a lot of alcohol abuse."

"I would respond that there is one universal God.
The same God that is back home is also in Korea."

Ken Crowe and members of the "Bridges" Young Adult Class from First Presbyterian Church of Colorado Springs work on mission projects and enjoy each other's fellowship.

Searching for a way to lead his soldiers spiritually by his own example, Ken was able to get involved in a fellowship of Christians sponsored by several denominations, including the Presbyterian Church. "It was a chance to live a complete Christian life where I could work with, live with, and have fellowship with the same people. The mission provided school for the children of Americans and conversational English training for Korean children. Many of us from the base volunteered our time working with the Koreans, and it was a very satisfying experience."

Several times soldiers would approach Ken and ask him how he could be at peace with himself when they were so lonely and needed an escape from reality. "I would respond that there is one universal God. The same God that is back home is also in Korea. You can drink to your heart's content, and God will still be with you and will never leave you."

When Ken's tour of duty was over in Korea he was reassigned, first to Fort Stewart in Georgia and then to a six-month stint in Texas. During this time, Ken stopped attending church because he was reluctant to form new relationships and then have to leave. While taking a training course in Fort Leavenworth, Kansas, Ken ran into someone from one of his earlier assignments. The soldier had been struggling at that time, and Ken had tried to counsel him. Now Ken was in need of spiritual encouragement. The soldier told Ken that his words of faith had stayed with him. He went on to say that Ken had planted a seed and that after some time, that seed had blossomed. "His words were the trigger I needed to get back with Christ."

Ken's current assignment is in Colorado Springs. A friend invited him to attend the First Presbyterian Church, and he quickly became involved in "Bridges," which is geared to single people in their twenties and thirties. "It is an incredible program for singles," Ken explains. "We worship together, sing praise music, have discussion groups, study the Bible, and have fellowship." The people involved in Bridges go on retreats, take ski trips, play basketball, and enjoy the outdoors together. "I've enjoyed being a part of an active group of young Christians who are able to have fun and worship in the name of the Lord." ∎

". . . your God . . . will not fail you or forsake you."
(Deuteronomy 31:6)

THE **HOMEMAKER**
AND **THE HOMELESS**

Mother of three reaches out to homeless people and learns that one person can help make the difference in rebuilding their lives.

After a life of hopelessness, Louie Regalado is now on the road to self-sufficiency and recovery.

Lori Gonzalez, an active member of Glenkirk Presbyterian Church in Glendora, California, has worked as a volunteer at her church's homeless shelter for several years. "During my first few years at the shelter," she says, "I kept the homeless at arm's length. Then one day they asked me to serve the gravy in the food line, and I was touched by the people I met. Soon I found myself praying for them, and I felt touched by the spirit of God telling me that I had to know their names. I realized that these were people who others kept their distance from. Getting to know their names and hugging them meant a lot. That day I found my calling."

Louie Regalado, a homeless man, first met Lori at the shelter in the winter of 1997. They formed an immediate bond. When the weather turned warm, though, Louie vanished into the streets. The following year, Louie came to the shelter again, and Lori worked hard to deepen the friendship she had tried to build the year before. "Something was troubling him deep down," Lori recalls, "and the closer I got, the more he pulled back. After he disappeared the year before, I felt a deep sense of loss. So I was determined to get to know him better."

The youngest of seven brothers in a troubled home, Louie was never accepted by his parents or siblings. By the time he was eleven, Louie started hanging around with a group of local teens. "I was looking for role models," Louie remembers. "I just wanted to find people who liked me for myself. Instead the group I chose was into drugs and alcohol, which I started to use in order to be accepted." By the time Louie was eighteen he had been arrested numerous times for drug use. "I was on a downward spiral," he says. "To pay for drugs, I shoplifted, robbed people, and committed burglaries."

"In an instant my life was transformed into a love affair with a most seductive lady, heroin."

One day a friend offered him heroin. "In an instant my life was transformed into a love affair with a most seductive lady, heroin." For the next thirty years Louie was an addict, spending time in and out of prison. "Thankfully, most people will never know how mentally and physically addicting heroin is. Your life becomes a continual search for the drug. When my mother was dying, I never visited her. I was too busy looking for my next fix. You know what you are doing is wrong, but you feel powerless to change."

One skill Louie learned well in prison was how to survive. "If another inmate senses that you have a weakness, they lean on you. So you learn how to keep your feelings to yourself and never show vulnerability." Louie moved in with a friend in El Monte, California, and began selling drugs. The friend was arrested, however, and Louie found himself broke and homeless. To feed his heroin addiction, he began to beg for money on the street. Then, one day, someone came up to him and offered shelter at Glenkirk Presbyterian Church in nearby Glendora. As he made his way to the church, Louie remembers thinking that "it was strange going to a church. I always believed in Christ, but never felt worthy of his love. Here I was a bum, who could accept me like this."

When he arrived at the church, Louie met Lori, a homemaker and mother of three who enjoyed volunteering at the shelter. "We connected right away," Lori remembers. "He was such a nice man. So caring and kind." But Lori was also aware of Louie's need to hide. We'd be talking, then all of a sudden he'd get this look on his face that said, 'Stay back.'"

Louie recalls thinking,
"What does this lady see in me?
Doesn't she know who I am?"

Louie recalls thinking, "What does this lady see in me? Doesn't she know who I am?" When the cold season ended, Louie returned to the street life of El Monte. Lori missed seeing him, however, and wanted to get back in touch. "I had this photo of him, so I went from motel to motel in El Monte asking if anybody knew where he was. Finally one man told me that he had seen Louie. 'Your friend is a heroin addict and he's wasted,' he told me. I remember feeling shocked," Lori says. "But then I thought, so what if it's true? It doesn't matter. He's still my friend."

Lori and her children, Shelbie, Kortni, and Skyler, have been moved through their work with the homeless.

What Lori didn't know was that Louie was doing his best to avoid her. "I just didn't want her to see me in that condition," Louie said. It wasn't until the next cold season that Lori saw Louie again at the shelter. "He saw me as I approached him," Lori said, "and before I could say anything, he started to run away. I yelled, 'Hey Louie!' and he stopped. Then we hugged each other."

As Louie recalls, "Knowing that she knew about the heroin made it difficult. Finally I said to her, 'Yes, I do heroin. This is the kind of person I've become.' When that drug grabs hold of you, your values get lost. One day, when I was living on the street, this young lady came up to me and handed me five dollars saying that God had told her to give the money to me. Of course the first thing I did was spend it on drugs. But you know something? To this day, I still think of that lady. So sometimes things don't change right away, but people really have an effect. I believe now that was a message from God." Another time a woman came up to Louie and gave him a piece of paper with "Jesus Loves You" written on it. To this day he still carries it with him.

> "My goal is to mature in my relationship with Christ and to use my faith to guide me in making the right decisions."

After seeing Lori again, Louie finally decided to get help. "The day I was to go into rehab, I was waiting for the bus. Somebody I knew came up to me and gave me a beer. One thing led to another, and I decided to have one more fix. I don't even remember the bus ride to the shelter; all I remember is walking in and announcing in a loud voice, 'Hey, I'm here!' They simply took me aside, said a prayer for me, and put me to bed."

That was the last time Louie took drugs. Louie spent the better portion of a year in rehab. Through withdrawal, therapy, and prayer his addiction ended, and he was prepared for a new life. Now living in his own apartment for the first time in years, Louie is employed full time and spends weekends doing maintenance at Glenkirk Church. "I still struggle a lot, and each day is a challenge," Louie says, "but I'm getting stronger every day and life is much better now. Every single day when I wake up I thank the Lord for keeping me alive all those years. My goal is to mature in my relationship with Christ and to use my faith to guide me in making the right decisions."

Lori and her husband now think of Louie as a member of their family. "One day we hope to start a shelter for the homeless, and we want to name it 'Louie's Place' because he has had such a wonderful impact on our family and on others he meets." ∎

". . . Just as I have loved you, you also should love one another." (John 13:34)

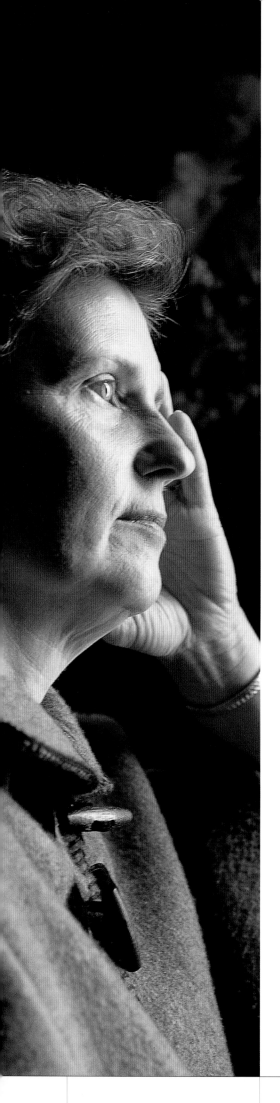

Faith comes to different people at different times, for Hendrickson family suffered their inexplicable loss,

Sue Hendrickson grew up attending a Methodist church, but in college she "got too busy." With work and study, she claimed, there wasn't time for other things. While in college she married Ron, a farmer's son, and gave birth to two daughters, whom they raised while she worked part-time as a substitute teacher. "Our life together was full," she said. "Church was not a priority."

One day, while visiting a nursing home with her daughters, then three and six years old, Sue received a sort of "bolt from the blue." She explained, "A minister, who was also visiting the home, thought it would be nice to treat the residents to a song. He asked my daughters and me to join him in singing 'Jesus Loves Me.' As we sang, I realized my daughters were not singing along. When the song ended, I asked them why not. 'Because we don't know the song, Mommy,' was their response."

Sue realized that by being "too busy" for church, she was denying her daughters the rich and wonderful part of their childhood that being part of a church had given her. Soon thereafter, she and Ron began attending the Presbyterian church in South Range, Wisconsin, where they enrolled their daughters in Sunday school.

Years later, Ron's sister, her husband, and two young children flew in from San Francisco in their own plane to celebrate the holidays with the Hendrickson family. "We had a glorious time together," Sue reminisced. "A couple days after Christmas, they left to fly back home. We all hugged as they boarded the plane and promised we'd get together again the following year."

That night, the phone rang. Ron picked it up, thinking it would be his sister telling them they had arrived home safely. But instead it was devastating news. The plane had crashed, and Ron's sister and her family had perished.

"It's funny," recollected Sue. "To this day, I remember the phone ringing, but I don't remember the call. I guess I was in such shock I've blocked it from my memory. I hold on instead to the memory of hugging those babies for the last time as we lifted them onto the plane."

Sue explained that Ron's family did not have any close church connections, so Sue and Ron decided to bury his sister and her family near

**different reasons. In the years since the
their faith has grown and flourished.**

South Range. "I called our minister and asked if he would handle the funeral. That is when we discovered the meaning of the church as a community of believers. It was like a great machine, and someone had thrown the switch, bringing it to life. Our brothers and sisters in the church helped us plan the funeral, prepared food for the reception, and stayed by our side the whole time. After the funeral and for weeks following, members continued to bring meals, take care of our children so that we could see to the details of the estate, and perform countless other acts of kindness for us. Every time we turned around it seemed someone was asking, 'What can we do for you?' They didn't nourish us with just food for our bodies, but also with love, tenderness, and sympathy to heal our wounded spirits. For weeks it seemed as if we were held in a loving embrace. It definitely helped us recover and go on."

A trunk containing family mementos sparks fond memories of the family that Sue and Ron lost.

Reflecting on that time, Sue mused, "Here we were a family the church hardly knew. We had attended only occasionally and never participated in the life of the church. But that didn't matter. We were a family in need, and our needs were met with grace, kindness, and understanding. They say the word 'evangelism' has 'angel' in the middle for a good reason. Well, the people of our church reached out to us like angels. Their help and loving concern meant everything to us."

"Church is now a place for worship, fellowship, rejoicing, and caring."

In the years since the Hendrickson family suffered their inexplicable loss, their faith has grown and flourished. Sue said, "We don't just 'attend' church now; we are truly involved. We look forward to sharing in the love of the Holy Spirit with the people who made such a difference in our lives. To us, church is now a place for worship, fellowship, rejoicing, and caring. It's about getting involved and reaching out to others, like that minister did that day long ago when his simple hymn made me sit up and realize all we were missing. I don't know what I would have done when we lost our family if we hadn't had our family of the faithful." ■

"My grace is sufficient for you . . ."
(2 Corinthians 12:9)

DEAR GOD

Rachel began to keep a journal and started every entry with a short prayer. As her faith deepened, her entire entry became a prayer.

Like so many others her age, Rachel Harris has to cope with the frustrations of being in high school. "Most of the kids I know just want to get on with their lives," Rachel says. "They get down on school and spend most of their time thinking about what others think. They get so fired up about off time, being free, and getting away from their parents. Not that there is anything wrong with their parents, they just want to get on with things."

For Rachel being involved in the youth group of her church, Memorial Drive Presbyterian Church in Houston, Texas, has helped her cope with the pressures of daily life. "When I first joined the youth group in the sixth grade it was hard. I didn't have any friends in the group and didn't know if I would fit in." But Rachel kept attending, and soon she had made new friends and felt part of a Christian community. "Most of my friends at school didn't believe in God. So I felt stupid trying to act like a Christian around them. The friends I made in youth group help me deal with the pressure and keep me from doing some of the bad things that happen in school."

Rachel Harris with members of her youth group participated in Bible study at Memorial Drive Presbyterian Church in Houston, Texas.

Youth group is a way for young people to get out of the house, have fun, relax, and participate in Christian fellowship.

While in the ninth grade, Rachel began to keep a journal. "At first I started each entry with a short prayer followed by what I did that day." Over a period of months, the entire entry became a prayer as Rachel's faith began to deepen. "I begin each entry with, 'Dear God, this is what you did for me today,' and then go on to pray for others and ask for guidance." Rachel's journal has become a testament to her faith and allows her to express her joy and concern each day. "I have learned to turn to God first, and through faith I have found strength in everything I do. God always has the right answer, and when you pray, everything gets better."

When Rachel faces hard times, she reaches out to God. "I like to leave notes for myself on the bathroom mirror," Rachel explains. "One says, 'Lord help me to shine for you.' Others say things like 'Help me to have patience,' 'It isn't my stuff, it's yours,' and simply 'pray.' Just looking at those notes in the morning as I'm getting ready for school helps me feel better and keep God at the center of my life." ■

". . . Christ will shine on you." (Ephesians 5:14)

Nurse practitioner reaches out to the poorest of the poor in the once proud shoreline community of Asbury Park.

Kathleen and her staff of medical professionals take great pride in providing exceptional medical services to the residents of Asbury Park, New Jersey.

He was a lonely figure sitting on a park bench near the courthouse in Freehold, New Jersey. After noticing him for several days, a local social worker became concerned. The cold of winter was ahead, and this man seemed to be homeless. But whenever the social worker tried to communicate with him, he ignored her. Frustrated, she called Kathleen Knight, a nurse practitioner and executive director of the Visiting Nurse Association's Community Health Center in Asbury Park. Every day Kathleen made the trip to Freehold and sat next to the man. Gradually he became comfortable with her presence. After a month, he finally began to open up and share his story. He was alone and homeless, and his only possessions were the clothes on his back. At night he slept under the steps of the courthouse. Kathleen could tell from his labored breathing that if something were not done soon he would eventually contract pneumonia. He needed immediate housing and physical care. Kathleen knew of a boarding house that would take him if he were made presentable. The problem was finding a place for the man to bathe, and a local YMCA provided the solution. Even though he would not be allowed to use the indoor facilities because of a concern for contamination, he could use an outdoor shower near the pool. There he showered, got his hair cut, shaved his beard, and was given clean clothes to wear. Later that day the boarding house accepted him, and a local clinic gave him medications. For the first time in years the man enjoyed Thanksgiving with others and was befriended by a local Presbyterian pastor, who provided him with a new church home.

This is one of the happy endings that keeps Kathleen energized. Originally from Long Island, Kathleen describes herself as "a third-generation preacher's kid." Her father was a Presbyterian pastor, and her interest in healthcare came from her grandfather, a Presbyterian minister who served the poor in the hospitals of New York City. While studying nursing at Cornell University, Kathleen met her future husband, Donald, who was then in the army. They married, and after his military service ended, Donald went on to seminary. In the mid-1970s, the family, which now included two sons and a daughter, moved to Belmar, New Jersey, where Donald is pastor of the local Presbyterian church.

The once bustling Asbury Park shore-line is littered with empty hotels and amusements, which stand as testaments to earlier times.

Kathleen's life was transformed when she attended a church retreat called "Faith and Healing," which was geared to people in the health profession. Kathleen found in this retreat what she had always wanted: a way to merge her faith with her profession as a registered nurse. Now she felt called to join her faith and her work by serving the underprivileged. In order to do this Kathleen felt that she needed more education, so she went to graduate school to become a clinical specialist in community health. After finishing her graduate work, she found her calling in nearby Asbury Park, New Jersey, an area with stagger-ing needs. The city had fallen on hard times and hopelessness was everywhere. A once proud shoreline community that had been home to some of the finest

Victorian hotels, beachfront amusements, and a wonderful boardwalk in earlier times was now a shadow of its former self. From the shoreline to the downtown, unemployment and devastation had spread like a cancer. Most buildings were empty, crime was high, and housing conditions were deplorable.

Many of the hotels that had once served the rich and famous were now occupied by the poor, mentally ill, and sick. Local health officials were powerless to care for the residents of these hotels because the owners of the buildings did not want outsiders to see the terrible conditions in the buildings. In order to reach out, Kathleen knew she needed to get inside somehow. Incredibly, she became a chamber maid in one of the larger dilapidated hotels. For an entire summer she worked incognito doing the dirty, thankless jobs, while ministering to the needs of the residents. Kathleen learned firsthand of the awful living conditions in these facilities and deepened her awareness that the residents were not just statistics but living, breathing people who needed love, encouragement, and nurturing. As she cleaned their rooms, she got to know these people, learned their names, and was able to check their medications. Often she found they had been misdiagnosed and were taking the wrong drugs. For example, a man with tremors who was taking medications for paranoid schizophrenia was later found to have Parkinson's disease instead.

One day, while having lunch with a supervisor from the Visiting Nurse Association, Kathleen blurted out, "Do you know what is really happening in the boarding houses?" The supervisor was shocked at what she heard. As they talked, they realized that the doctors and nurses in the local clinics had tunnel vision. They were exposed only to the people who could physically get to the clinics and had no idea that so many others needed care. The supervisor was able to secure a grant that would allow Kathleen to bring health care to the people at the hotel where she had worked. However, before Kathleen could get this program going, the hotel burned to the ground, and all the residents were displaced, spread across the area. This apparent setback turned out to be an opportunity. Because the former hotel residents were now living in several hotels around the city and Kathleen knew all their names, she now had access to several of the hotels that had previously been off limits. Now she could reach out to an even larger number of residents. "It is my belief that God works in many ways, and this fire happened for a reason," Kathleen states. "It actually was a gift."

In the late 1980s, Kathleen returned to school once again. This time she wanted to become a nurse practitioner, so she could have the authority to diagnose and treat common illnesses and prescribe medications. Today Kathleen is executive director of the Community Health Center for the Visiting Nurse Association of Central New Jersey and works out of an abandoned storefront in downtown Asbury Park. She and her staff now help over 11,000 patients a year. ■

Sitting on the steps of one of the hotels where Kathleen Knight once worked is one of its elderly residents.

*"And the Word became flesh and lived among us . . ."
(John 1:14)*

A WINNING SPIRIT

From child preacher to stockbroker to Presbyterian pastor,

Stockbroker Danny Murphy sat in the office of the head of his investment firm and made a startling announcement. "This may sound crazy, but I'm going into the ministry."

His boss looked up and said simply, "Dan, you are crazy."

Raised in a non-church going family in Milwaukee, Danny, when he was seven years old, was invited to attend a Pentecostal church by the mother of a friend. Soon Danny's parents followed, first joining a Baptist church and then, when Danny was fourteen, a nondenominational church. It was there that Danny first started to feel the call to ministry, and by the time he was seventeen, he was playing the organ and preaching on occasion.

One day an evangelist, Kenneth Bacon, came to the church. In need of an organist for his upcoming evangelistic meetings, he invited Danny to join the tour, and for the next three years, Danny traveled the country with the Kenneth Bacon crusade. During this time, Danny not only played the organ but also conducted the afternoon youth services. When he left the crusade, Danny, now twenty, began preaching in area churches.

Wanting to become an ordained minister and needing to further his education, Danny enrolled at the Milwaukee Theological Institute. He became acquainted with Ernest Glenn Jr., who served both as president of the school and pastor of the Christ United Presbyterian Church. One day after class, the Reverend Glenn offered Danny a part-time position in ministry at his church, and Danny poured himself into local mission projects and Bible study classes for adults. He also became a Presbyterian.

Eventually Danny veered away from ministry. He married Judy and took a job with an investment firm. Danny and Judy had two children, and Danny was, by all accounts, a shining success as a stockbroker. His list of clients was growing, he was earning a six-figure income, and he and his family had all the trappings of success. "But I just wasn't happy," Danny explains, "and my wife, Judy, knew why. She said, 'You're unhappy because you haven't followed the path that God has called you to do—to continue your ministry.'"

So Danny resigned his position at the investment firm and enrolled at Johnson C. Smith Theological Seminary in Atlanta. But the transition would not be smooth. From the time he made the decision to go to seminary,

Danny Murphy is a very determined man.

Reverend Danny Murphy believes in the power of learning. In spite of financial challenges, he always found a way to further his education.

one setback after another happened. As Danny recalls, "We thought we had saved enough money for seminary. However, just before we left, Judy became sick, and because the hospitalization insurance had temporarily lapsed, all of Judy's medical expenses had to be covered from our savings. Thankfully Judy got well; however, our savings was gone, and we had just enough money left over to move to Atlanta."

When the family arrived in Atlanta, it had only one hundred and fifty dollars left after paying the movers. "I called the seminary," Danny says, "and they gave us directions to our housing. However, we were shocked to discover that there had been a mixup and the house was already occupied. Since it was a weekend and the seminary was closed, I had to talk the drivers of the moving van into waiting until Monday so that we could work out the problem." That cost Danny his final penny. With no place to stay, Danny called an old friend he had gotten to know while touring with the crusade and who lived in Atlanta. The friend had an extra room, and Danny and his family were welcome to it.

The following Monday, Danny called the seminary and found there had indeed been a mistake. In fact, there was no housing available at all. For the next eight months, Danny, his wife, and two children lived in a single bedroom at his friend's home. "I felt as if God was telling me that I was not supposed to go to seminary," Danny remembers. "Four of us living in a single room was not fair to my family, so I didn't go back to the seminary and instead got a job to make enough money to move back to Milwaukee. My plan was to return to my old job at the investment firm. Things were pretty bad, so I prayed about it: 'Lord maybe the ministry is something I want to do but is not in your plan because every decision I have made seems to be wrong and nothing has worked out.'"

However, just before Danny and his family left Atlanta, his telephone rang. It was the pastor of the First Presbyterian Church of Oostburg, Wisconsin, who said they had some money they wanted to send for his seminary education. The amount was ten thousand dollars per year, which was exactly what Danny needed to go on with seminary. The pastor told Danny that a man who lived in an old, rundown house and who was thought to be quite poor had recently died. The pastor had visited him regularly, even though the man was shunned by others in the community. After the man's death, it was discovered he had been wealthy and had given a significant portion of his money to the church. This church decided to use the interest derived from investing the money for mission projects.

The people of the Oostburg church had met Danny and knew he was in seminary. To qualify for the money, Danny needed only to be enrolled in the seminary, but Danny had withdrawn from the seminary and, consequently, was not officially enrolled. By now, it was almost midterm, and the chance of being admitted late was remote. "I met with the head of admissions the next morning," Danny remembers. "After I explained what had happened, he simply said, 'I'm sorry, we can't do anything for you.' I persisted by assuring him that I had the money, but he kept turning me down. Finally he said, 'I told you that I can't let you in and that is final.' So I looked at him and said, 'I'm not leaving this office until you let me in.' Still he turned me down. I assured him that I was a good student and only wanted a chance to prove that I could handle it. But, he still wouldn't let me in. I decided to stay there until he changed his mind."

That entire day, Danny sat in the admissions office as the director went about making phone calls, doing paper work, and dictating letters. Still Danny persisted. The director left for lunch, and Danny was there when he returned. He left for afternoon meetings, and when he returned, Danny was still there. As the day stretched into the evening and the director passed by his office, he noticed Danny had not left.

"I'll never forget my first Sunday. There were nine people in the church, and five of them were in the choir."

Finally, the director went into his office, looked Danny in the eyes, and said, "OK, I'm going to let you in. I like your determination, so I'll give you a clean slate, but you have to make the grades on your own." Not only did Danny catch up to the other students, he ended up graduating with the highest honors in his class. "I think of this experience," Danny says, "as a lesson from God. You just can't see things as they are. You have to envision things as they could be and then constantly work toward making your vision into reality. Too many people run into an obstacle and, instead of facing it, they give up. This is why God gave us faith, so we could tackle our problems and move beyond them."

During his final semester at the seminary, Danny served as an intern pastor at Calvary Presbyterian Church in Winnsboro, South Carolina, which meant driving four hours each way from Atlanta. After graduating in 1988, he was called to be the pastor at Calvary. "I'll never forget my first Sunday. There were nine people in the church, and five of them were in the choir. It was a church that refused to die and instead wanted to grow. Even though there were no young people in worship, they still had a Sunday school program for youth. At first, my two children doubled the youth ministry of the church, but soon they were joined by others."

Gradually over the next few years, membership began to grow, and in May 1992 the church applied for a redevelopment grant from Trinity Presbytery, the Synod of South Atlantic, and the General Assembly in order to add new programs that would reach out into the community. A youth ministry was started in the community with projects such as a mission trip to Mexico and a "Friday night at the movies" film and discussion. A gospel choir was formed, and its music has attracted many new members. As Danny explains, "When I first arrived, the congregation had a very low self-esteem. At first I didn't recognize it. New ideas kept being suggested, but after discussion, they were always being turned down. Then it occurred to me that our members had suffered greatly through loss of members and failures of earlier programs. Their self-esteem was so low that rather than try something new, it was more comfortable to do nothing and avoid failure."

Danny decided to try a new approach. "Why not experiment before making permanent changes, thereby insuring that if something new failed it was just an experiment? Nothing ventured, nothing gained." It worked, and soon everyone in the church was suggesting changes. "This allowed us to discover both our strengths and our weaknesses," Danny reports, "and we could then channel our programs to our strengths. Soon we started experiencing success, and one success led to another. That was the turning point for our congregation. Before long, it wasn't uncommon to hear people saying, 'Let's experiment by doing this.'"

Calvary Presbyterian Church has been transformed from a dwindling church to a vibrant growing church, making a difference in its community. Danny puts it in perspective: "When I was fourteen, a wonderful woman named Mother Jones helped to nurture my faith and build my self-esteem. Now one hundred years old, she continues to pray for me each day. It's people like her who have made a difference in my life, and every time I have a challenge, just knowing that she's praying for me helps lift me up." ■

". . . For I will restore the fortunes of the land . . . ,
says the LORD." (Jeremiah 33:11)

The future of the church can be seen in the eyes of its young people such as Sophia Dick, Jabari Hollins, Medina Martin, and Tekia Hollins.

Calvary Presbyterian Church is now a growing congregation with many young people including Kenya and Iloka.

Loaded to the rooftop with the tools of his trade, a craftsman brings his workshop on wheels to wherever God is calling him.

While driving on a freeway near his Los Angeles area home, Tom Bartlett had a vision. "I saw myself behind the wheel of a semi truck. It was such a strange idea that I tried to put it out of my mind, but the vision kept returning."

Tom grew up in a family that didn't attend church. "I'm convinced that my parents had a strong faith," Tom remembers, "but we just didn't go to church while I was growing up." In the early 1970s, Tom married and together he and his wife raised a son. "My wife was Catholic, but I never joined the church. I just couldn't understand why Communion was closed to nonmembers." After over twenty years, the marriage broke down, and the couple was divorced. "The divorce was devastating to me," Tom remembers. "I couldn't function and was feeling depressed."

One day, Tom's next door neighbor suggested that he attend a divorce recovery workshop at St. Andrews Presbyterian Church. "I agreed to go and thought it would be a group of depressed people sitting in a small circle commiserating with each other. Instead almost four hundred people were gathered in a large hall." Leading the workshop was Dr. Bill Flanagan, minister of Missions and Singles. "Immediately I knew that I was not alone and that many others were facing the same challenges." The six-week program had such an impact on Tom that he enrolled again. "It was great," Tom remembers, "not only did I appreciate the workshop, I also joined a Bible study and a singles group."

When the workshop started again, Bill asked Tom to be a small group leader, and over the next four years, Tom led nine different groups. "I was astounded at the change it made in my life and how much I changed. The darkness in my life suddenly disappeared, and I began to discover my faith." During this time, Tom worked in his own tool and die company. "In spite of my other problems, my business kept chugging along. I was making a good living, and I was getting by just fine." However, the more his faith grew, the more the business started to decline. "God was trying to get my attention and get me to do something else with my life," Tom believes. "So, over a three-year period the business slowed down to a trickle." Tom decided to close down the company.

Tom Bartlett and volunteers from across the nation build and repair homes in the coal country of rural Kentucky.

Beautiful vistas mask the everyday struggles faced by the people in the coal country of southeast Kentucky.

"The vision was so clear, so precise, that I immediately driving school and, after graduation, became a long-haul

It was during this time that Tom had the vision of the truck. "The vision was so clear, so precise, that I immediately enrolled in truck driving school and, after graduation, became a long-haul truck driver." However, after one cross country trip, he decided it wasn't the kind of life he wanted and quit his job. "Here I was, unemployed for the first time in my memory," Tom remembers, "and I didn't have a clue about what to do next." One evening Tom attended a potluck dinner at St. Andrews. "I sat down with Bill Flanagan and told him about my dilemma. He turned to me and said, 'Tom you need to go on a mission trip. Pick one and go.' The next day I looked into what mission trips were available and chose one working at the Sheldon Jackson College in Sitka, Alaska."

While on the mission trip, Tom again had the vision about the truck. This time he could see that the truck was outfitted with machines for use in mission work. "What I envisioned was being a traveling mission worker, building houses and repairing churches from a fully outfitted workshop in the truck." Tom met with Bill, and he asked him, "Am I crazy? Does this idea sound sane?"

Bill looked at Tom and said, "You are ready to go, now. We need to find a program willing to accept your idea." They contacted the Presbyterian Worldwide Mission program, and the offers started to arrive. However, because Tom insisted on bringing not only a semi but also his pet Chow, few opportunities presented themselves. Finally, H.O.M.E.S. Inc. of Fleming-Neon expressed interest and indicated they had room for the truck and that his dog was welcome.

enrolled in truck
truck driver."

"It was the sign I needed," Tom recalls. "Now I needed to acquire the truck." To pay for it, Tom sold his house and placed the money in a trust to be handled by the church. Soon Tom located a truck and trailer and began to outfit it. "People I knew were shocked," Tom remembers, "they couldn't believe that I would sell my home and venture off to do mission work. They asked, 'What if it didn't work out?' and 'How could I return if I had nowhere to live?' I told them that I felt called to make a leap of faith. If I didn't sell the house and instead rented it out, then it wasn't much of a leap."

During the first week of October 1998, St. Andrews church commissioned Tom and his truck, and the next day he was on his way. His first assignment was in Fleming-Neon, Kentucky. "It took me five days to cross the country. When I arrived in Fleming-Neon it was like I was in another world—a world of extreme poverty contrasted with the incredible beauty of the Appalachian mountains."

Within six months of his arrival, Tom had already been involved in the construction of a half dozen homes and countless remodeling projects. "God is using me to do his work," Tom affirms. "This is what I am called to do and God will tell me when my time on this site is finished and where my next call will be. I have never been happier." ■

"... *Here am I; send me!*" (Isaiah 6:8)

A LIFE
OF SERVICE

Beulah Travis began her faith journey more than ninety years ago at the First Presbyterian Church of Chili, New York.

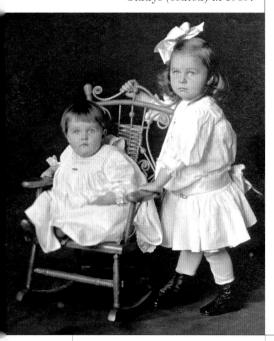

Beulah Travis with her sister Gladys (seated) in 1909.

Beulah Travis recounts her earliest memories with startling clarity. "I was four years old. I remember being lifted into the pew with my sister. We wore our best dresses and bonnets, white silk stockings, and gloves. Through the big open windows I could hear the birds singing and the trees rustling. I took in the wonder of it all—the organ music, the singing, the preacher's voice speaking. All my life I have carried the feeling of peace and love . . . and a kind of mystery . . . that I experienced that day."

At sixteen years old, Beulah was confirmed at Emanuel Presbyterian Church in Rochester, New York. "I was so overcome by the ceremony, I nearly fainted," she said, explaining that the commitment she made to her faith that day was as meaningful to her as the vows she would take on her wedding day some years later. "It was sort of odd for me to react that way, though," she added. "I was such a happy-go-lucky, fun-loving person."

Beulah Travis, in her customary sneakers, visits with "Exploring Your World" students at the McConaghy Youth Center.

A Test of Faith

In 1982, Beulah's daughter, Anne, was killed by a drunk driver. A graduate of the Union Theological Seminary and a Mission Counselor for the Synod of The Northeast, Anne was on her way home after leading a Presbyterian Women's Retreat when the accident occurred.

When asked how the death of her daughter affected her faith, Beulah replied, "It happened and I couldn't undo it. I had to deal with it, so I picked up my life the best I could."

She explained that the driver who killed her daughter was only nineteen. He had been given drinks by a co-worker, and he had no memory of the accident.

"I forgave him and moved on. My faith tells me to forgive and, because I did, I never had to carry that burden with me."

As a young bride, Beulah moved to Syracuse with her husband, Van, and joined First Presbyterian Church United. She and her husband raised a family together, and she become a Sunday school teacher. Several years later she was asked to fill in temporarily for the Christian Education Director, who had resigned. Her "temporary" assignment lasted nineteen years.

"During that time, I became concerned about our church neighborhood, which was beginning to decay. The majority of homes were owned by absentee landlords and occupied by families with only one parent. I knew we needed to find a way to reach out to the kids living there, many of whom had little supervision and often lived in an atmosphere of neglect, drugs, and sometimes abuse. Our church had a building, the McConaghy Youth Center, that was occupied only on Sundays, so we used it to create an island of sanity, safety, and learning for the kids in our neighborhood the rest of the week."

Launched in 1970, the "island" in a troubled neighborhood was named "Exploring Your World." Initially a summer program only, it was so successful that within two years it expanded to include a year-round preschool and after-school program. Neighborhood children received instruction in basic educational skills and social skills and were given the opportunity to explore the world around them through field trips to the library and the zoo. Nearly thirty years later, "Exploring Your World" is still going strong, attracting an annual enrollment that averages three hundred students.

"I was a young sixty-three when 'Exploring Your World' began, and I continued working as its full-time director into my nineties. People are always asking me where I get my energy, and I just tell them it's not my nature to keep still. I have to be busy," said Beulah. "I also love kids. I think they're nuts, but so am I. I know it's an uphill battle to reach a kid whose home life is full of negative experiences. But every so often, we do get through to someone, and the joy of watching that one life bloom helps make up for the ones we can't help. I have always been a positive person, and I never say something can't be done. Instead I figure out how to make it work. This I attribute to my faith. It keeps me going and never lets me down." ■

> "I was a young sixty-three when 'Exploring Your World' began, and I continued working as its full-time director into my nineties."

"Your word is a lamp to my feet and a light to my path." (Psalm 119:105)

DANCING
TO THE
DRUM

Clayton M. Sylestine, First Chief Alabama-Coushatta Tribe of Texas, finds spiritual comfort in the worship service at the Indian Village Presbyterian Church.

Pastor blends her Christian faith with her Native American

When Martha Sadongei was deciding which seminary to attend, Austin Seminary in Texas or San Francisco Seminary in San Anselmo, she agonized over her choices. Both are excellent and equally distant from her Phoenix home. So she based her decision on a surprising factor: "You can predict a tornado but not an earthquake, so I decided to go to Austin."

Martha Sadongei's father is a member of the Kiowa tribe from Oklahoma while her mother is Tohono O'odham, a second-generation Presbyterian. "As a child," Martha remembers, "Saturday was cartoon day, and Sunday was church day." Martha attended a Native American church until she was a young adult and then became involved in an Anglo church. When it was time to consider a career, Martha thought about the ministry, but chose instead to pursue a degree in education. Upon graduation, she became an elementary teacher in Phoenix. "Just as church had been a major part of my life while growing up, it was also important to me as a young adult."

"Since the white man first brought the
our people were told that they had to
Native American beliefs. I believe

While a member of Palo Cristi Presbyterian Church in Phoenix, Martha was ordained an elder and attended the meeting of the General Assembly in Milwaukee. "John Fife was elected Moderator of General Assembly that year and spoke of the need for racial diversity in order to make it a colorful church. I thought to myself at the time, 'Yeah, we could do that but the pulpit also needed to reflect the same diversity. Not just people of color serving ethnic churches but also serving Anglo churches as well.'" As a result of Martha's experience in the church and a deep sense of call, the seed was sown for her to consider the ministry again. She took a year's absence from her teaching position to enter seminary as an inquirer.

roots at the Alabama-Coushatta reservation in Texas.

During her first semester at Austin, Martha caught the attention of Ellen Babinsky, a professor of church history, who one day asked to speak with her after class. Ellen asked Martha to accompany her to a Presbyterian church on an Indian reservation in east Texas. "I kept thinking to myself, 'OK, why is this professor wanting to take me there. Has she just discovered Native Americans? Is she truly interested or is she trying to make conversation?' After all, here I was, just another first-year student. Why was I being singled out?"

That spring, Ellen got in touch with Martha again and said that she had made arrangements for them to drive together to the Alabama-Coushatta reservation to observe a worship service. Martha thought, "Now I've got to spend hours in the car with a professor. What are we going to talk about?" Martha had always felt that Christianity and Native American spirituality were traveling on parallel paths. "Since the white man first brought the scripture to the tribes, our people were told that they had to choose between Christianity

Martha provides pastoral care and counseling in a local care facility.

scripture to the tribes, choose between Christianity and there is room for both . . ."

and Native American beliefs. I believe there is room for both and that the road is not that narrow. It is wide enough to allow for two paths down the same road."

While studying her Christian roots, Martha learned that the early Presbyterian missionaries had several motives in bringing the gospel to the tribes. The missionaries saw the Native Americans as unclean and uncivilized. They told the tribal members that their traditional ways were wrong and that they needed to learn to act more like the white man. In order to be Christian they had to choose either God or their Native culture. "This disturbed me." Martha recalls. "Why did it have to be either-or. Why not both-and?"

A Proud Tradition

The Alabama-Coushatta reservation is located on a fifteen-square-mile site in east Texas and has a population of approximately one thousand. The majority of the residents are from two tribes: the Alabama tribe, which migrated to Texas over a hundred years ago, and a smaller group, the Coushattas, who live mostly in Louisiana.

Because the Alabamas supported the Confederacy during the Civil War, Sam Houston gave them their land. One day a Presbyterian pastor named S. F. Tinney was on his way to a presbytery meeting in Beaumont, Texas. En route he became lost in a heavily wooded area on the reservation, and by the time he was found by the Alabamas, he was sick. During the next few days, he was nursed back to health by tribal members. Once he completed his journey, he felt the call to establish a Presbyterian church on the Alabama-Coushatta reservation. Today, it is still the only church located on reservation property.

When the women arrived at the Indian Village Presbyterian Church on the Alabama-Coushatta reservation they were warmly received. Martha was surprised when she was asked to preach during the worship service. "At first, I was filled with anxiety. After all, I had been involved in an Anglo church and it had been awhile since I had gone to a Native American worship. However, during that worship service I was filled with the Holy Spirit and on the drive home decided that I wouldn't mind coming back."

"I've always believed that you can be both Indian and Christian. To me the two beliefs are parallel. So I began to preach about accepting both their heritage and their beliefs."

Indeed, she did go back. Two years later after graduating from seminary, Martha received the call to be the pastor of the Indian Village church. "I was honored that they accepted me and called me to be their pastor." Martha moved into a home on the reservation and soon discovered that the church was reluctant to honor Indian traditions. She also found out that she was the first Native American pastor in the church's 115-year history. "They struggled with the feeling that their own traditions were not compatible with living a Christian life. However, I've always believed that you can be both Indian and Christian. To me the two beliefs are parallel. So I began to preach about accepting both their heritage and their beliefs."

One traditional practice that Native American Christians often avoided was the powwow. Younger Native Americans, seeking to recover their heritage, take pride and find great joy in attending powwows, and as result, often stop attending church services. However, Martha likes the powwow and soon was asked to deliver the opening prayer at the tribal powwow. "Many of the older members had always been taught that the powwow was wrong. But I love to dance, and I also enjoy the music and fellowship of the powwow. To me the powwow represents an opportunity to reach out to new generations living on the reservations who never miss the powwow but have a difficult time coming to church." Martha feels that one of her roles as pastor is to bridge the gap between generations by celebrating both her Christian beliefs and her native culture. ■

"... my house shall be called a house of prayer for all peoples." (Isaiah 56:7)

Former athiests learn to open their hearts and minds to the awesome power of God.

Steve Nelson and Jamie Vreeland have always had much in common. Both were raised in Glendora, California, both were the products of Lutheran families, and both became anti-Christian during college. When they were married, they insisted that the ceremony be performed outside the church and that no mention of God be used in the ceremony. They were married in a beautiful historic mansion by a friend who was a federal judge.

"When we were in college," Jamie remembers, "we learned to question and to rely on facts instead of mythical teachings to guide us in our studies. Good research is based on using credible sources." Steve adds, "We used science and logic to get to the cold hard truth. Life is far more complicated than the simplistic answers Christianity seemed to provide." Jamie agrees, "After all, when we attended church with our families we were too young to make up our own minds, so the people in the church tried to brainwash us into following what they believed."

So, both Steve and Jamie left the church and began their careers— Jamie as a teacher and Steve as a historian. As Jamie viewed it, "We were not bad people, we both had helping jobs, we didn't hurt others, so we must be OK." Adds Steve, "I made a pact with myself that since I didn't believe in God, I would not draw on a God that I didn't believe existed. To do so would be hypocritical. In fact while in college I became very antagonistic toward

The first time Steve and Jamie went to church they sat

Christians who would visit our campus in order to reach out to students. For entertainment I would watch evangelists on television. In my mind they were evil people who were taking advantage of others. Yet I also found them to be hilarious with some of their rather bizarre behavior. Look, I would say, here's science, here's the logical explanation, how can these people deny it. At the time I didn't realize they were coming from a different perspective than what I had."

Over the next few years events occurred that tested Steve and Jamie. Steve was offered a dream job in Houston, Texas, and after struggling with the choice, Steve and Jamie decided that the job was too good to pass up. So Jamie took a leave of absence from her school, and she and Steve moved to Texas—prepared to return to California if things did not work out. While happy for Steve, Jamie was depressed about having to give up her own teaching job and being so far away from her family. During their time in Houston, Jamie's mother had heart bypass surgery and Jamie rushed to her mother's side. "While I was waiting for the results of the surgery, I found myself drawn to the hospital chapel. I kept asking myself, how can I go into a chapel, I don't believe in God. Finally I went inside and said a few words to the life force, whatever it was."

"Here was my friend and mentor . . . and he had killed himself. Is this how I would also end up?"

After living almost a year and a half in Houston, Steve and Jamie faced another test. Jamie's leave of absence from her teaching position was coming to an end, and they had to decide whether to stay in Texas and make the leave permanent or to return to California. It was a hard decision, but they ultimately decided to move back to California. Steve resigned from his dream job, and even though Steve was able to get employment right away, he felt that leaving Houston was a real loss. Adding to Steve's burden were the deaths of three close friends, among them a college professor who had been his mentor. Steve was shocked to discover that his old professor had committed suicide. "Here was my friend and mentor, the man I turned to for all the answers, and he had killed himself. Did he really have all the answers? Is this how I would also end up?" Steve fell into a deep depression. "I was turning into a pile of mush, convinced that my fate would be the same as my mentor. Soon I was overtaken with panic attacks. My heart would race and I was convinced that I was having a heart attack." Steve's depression soon made it hard for him to get out of bed, and he sought the help of a psychologist. "I decided to accompany Steve to the psychologist," Jamie said, "because I had heard that he was

in the back so they wouldn't be noticed.

a Christian and I didn't trust him to keep his beliefs to himself." Indeed, in the first session Steve told the psychologist, "Look, I know you are a Christian but don't bring your beliefs into these sessions. Don't bring anything spiritual in. Just help me work on my problems." Though the psychologist did not discuss his own faith in Steve's treatment, Steve and Jamie found out later that he is a member of the Glenkirk Presbyterian Church.

Still feeling depressed, Steve woke up one day and announced that he wanted to go to church. Jamie was shocked and asked if they could have a week to think about it. "I kept asking Steve for more time in order to prepare myself. I felt like the walls would cave in if we went to church. Here we were, two heretics, two nonbelievers, going to church." But Steve insisted. He wanted to go to church right then. "There was no way that I was going to let him go to church without me," Jamie remembers. "I was afraid that once they got a hold of him that he'd be different, like a cult member." So together they went to Glenkirk Presbyterian Church since a couple of their friends had spoken highly of the church.

Jamie Vreeland and Steve Nelson in the sanctuary of Glenkirk Presbyterian Church in Glendora, California.

Steve and Jamie sat near the back so they wouldn't be noticed. "We didn't know if we belonged in church," Jamie remembers, "but the service touched our hearts and the message was very relevant. As a child I couldn't appreciate the church. Now we could." Glenkirk's pastor, Walter Ray, called them to see if they wanted to come in and talk. Steve recalls, "Here is this pastor of a large church calling us and wanting to meet. That really impressed me." Steve and Jamie have continued to attend the church, and their faith journey has been a time of discovery. As Steve sees it, "My outlook on life is different. Things that used to bother me don't get to me like they used to. Things that used to seem too simple now become focal points. Just sitting in a comfy chair watching my nephews play is something I can now enjoy. We're learning that life is more about relationships than getting things done." Jamie is also noticing changes. "The scripture is starting to make sense to me. I find myself humming hymns and thinking about God. I also seem to be purchasing a lot of spiritual books, which is something I never would have considered doing before."

"We feel like we're just beginning our spiritual journey."

"We feel like we're just beginning our spiritual journey," Steve says. "We find ourselves questioning many things, because when you are on a journey or path, you're changing all the time. This is a lifelong process, and we are enjoying every minute of it and our hearts have been opened." ■

". . . God, who is rich in mercy . . . made us alive . . ."
(Ephesians 2:4-5)

LIVES TURNED UPSIDE DOWN

When Margaret Gurecky reflects on the early years of her life, the word "easy" comes to mind. Growing up in a small central Texas town, both Margaret and her future husband, Milton, were raised in Christian homes and had comfortable childhoods. "We were both baptized in our small Presbyterian church, confirmed as twelve years olds, and married there. After college, Milton got a job with the Texas Department of Transportation, and I worked in school administration. All our lives we had been nurtured by our church."

So when Margaret and Milton became the proud parents of a baby boy, he was baptized in their church. "The baptism was such a meaningful event in our lives. We gave our child to God, and the congregation promised to be there for him always. It was such an important time."

"When our son Matt was four, Milton had accepted a job transfer to Dallas. We built a home together in a suburb of Dallas, and I was hired by the local school district. Matt grew up in a spiritual home and was a happy, well-adjusted child. Life for us continued to be easy. We just didn't have the struggles that others had." Margaret remembers that they were lulled into a simplistic view of life. "By following the rules of society and doing the right things then everything would work out right."

As a teen, Matt continued to be a joy to raise. "He was never in any trouble and his grades at school were good. He was just perfect." While in junior high school, however, Matt's behavior began to change. As Margaret remembers, "Matt was always a little quiet, but gradually he began to become withdrawn. We could still talk, but he was beginning to spend more time alone in his room. I thought it was just a phase. I'd ask him if anything was wrong and he'd say he was fine. Still, I couldn't help but wonder what was bothering him."

After graduation, Matt decided to work for a year before going to college. Still living with his parents, Matt took a job in a local store. One day Matt started bringing home empty boxes from work and storing them in the attic. Everyday he would bring home more boxes. When his mother asked him why, he said, "Oh, I don't know, maybe I'll need them someday." Margaret thought it was a little strange but justified it by thinking that maybe he was going to store some of his books and CDs because Matt was always very organized.

One morning, as Margaret was walking by Matt's room, he asked her to come in. "I have something I need to tell you." As Matt spoke, his mother's heart sank. "Mother, I'm gay." Margaret remembers having several feelings at once. While upset and disturbed by Matt's words she was also relieved. "There had been this cloud hanging over him for the past couple of years. Now, finally, maybe it was lifting. So I just hugged him and told him I loved him."

"Here he was, our own son, thinking that we would cast him aside just because of his sexual orientation."

All that day Margaret kept the news to herself. She couldn't even talk to her husband, Milton, about it. "There was a pit in my stomach. I knew that our easy life had ended and nothing would ever be the same." The following night, Margaret tossed and turned and could hardly sleep. When she arose the next morning, Milton was sitting in the sun room in an old wicker chair that he had been rocked in as a baby. "I'll never forget how he took the news, he just doubled up and began to weep."

"We started to see our world differently and wanted to keep our news from others and even stayed away from friends and family," Margaret says. It was a time when we really needed our faith, yet we felt that others would shun us, so we stopped attending our church." This was especially difficult for Milton since he was an elder and very active in the church. "I kept thinking of Matt's baptism," Margaret remembers. "The church promised that they never would leave him. Yet here we were at our time of need, and we didn't feel our church would be there for us."

One day the newspaper from the Presbyterian synod arrived. A classified ad caught Margaret's attention. It was about a support group for parents of gay and lesbian children. She called the number and left her name. That evening, a woman named Jane Loflin, who also had a gay child, called. "She was so compassionate," Margaret recalls, "it was as if a huge burden was lifted from my shoulders. In our conversation Jane told me that it had always been her dream to form a pastoral care ministry within the Presbyterian Church where parents of gay and lesbian children could reach out to one another, share their pain, learn about homosexuality, and ultimately bring healing to families. We were comforted to know that a Presbyterian congregation in north Dallas would willingly permit this ministry to meet in its parlor. To know a church's doors were still open for parents like us who felt so isolated from the church family was consoling. We attended the first meeting and were surrounded by parents from other Presbyterian congregations who were also hurting and afraid. It was a safe place where we could share our faith, hold hands, and begin to wipe away the tears."

A couple of years after Matt shared his feelings about his sexuality with his parents, his mother was cleaning the attic when she came across the boxes Matt had put there. "I called him up and asked if he still needed the boxes. 'No mom,' he said. 'Go ahead and throw them out.' I then asked why he had put them there, and he said, 'Remember the day I told you I was gay? I thought you would throw me out.' I just sat there in the attic and cried," Margaret remembers. "Here he was, our own son, thinking that we would cast him aside just because of his sexual orientation. Even today, whenever Milton and I talk about it, we can't help but get emotional. To think a parent would actually throw a child out. But they do, and often they use scripture as their reason. It's so sad." Margaret adds, "God created our son just as he is for us to love unconditionally. He is a gift from God." ■

"[Love] bears all things, believes all things, hopes all things, endures all things." (1 Corinthians 13:7)

RESHUFFLING THE DECK

Popular Lieutenant Governor John Hager is in demand as a speaker throughout Virginia.

Dealt a bad hand, this former executive changed his life focus through faith and determination.

As a hard-charging businessperson, John Hager felt that his life was extraordinarily full. Only in his mid-thirties, he had just been promoted to executive vice president of a large, multinational corporation. His wife had recently given birth to their son, Jack, and they were selling their home to move to New York. Then one day, John fell while jogging. Thinking nothing of it, he resumed his run. One evening, several days later, as he climbed the stairs to the bedroom, he suddenly lost the use of his legs. An ambulance was called and he was transported to the hospital.

At first the doctors thought the discs in his back were out of alignment, however the treatment they provided had no effect. Assuming at that point that John had a tumor, they operated and found that the surgery was not effective. John's legs remained paralyzed. Later, tests revealed a shocking diagnosis: John had contracted polio from his young son, who had just received his vaccination. Against one-in-six-million odds, the antibodies from the vaccination had transferred to John, and his paralysis was permanent.

"My faith was one of the things I relied upon during this period in my life," John maintains. "Even though I had always been a believer, these events strengthened my faith and helped me get through it. I also received a lot of support from my church, First Presbyterian of Richmond, in prayer, visitation, and words of encouragement. Along with my family and friends, the church was there for me."

After recovering almost ten weeks in the hospital from the effects of the surgery, John was transferred to a rehabilitation center in New York to learn how to function without the use of his legs. When he returned to Richmond over two months later, John found that his company had reversed the promotion he had worked so hard to earn and, in fact, was requiring him to start all over again in a near entry-level position. "This is when I discovered that there was more to life than the business world," John recalls. "In my heart, I knew I could still be productive, so I decided that since my responsibilities at work were decreased, I had more time for other things."

Initially John sought more involvement in his church, eventually becoming a deacon and chairing several committees. Then he branched out into civic and political organizations, serving on over thirty boards and commissions, usually as chairperson or in other leadership roles. John remembers how his involvement in the church and community built his inner strength. "With the support of my friends and people at the church," John remembers, "my self-confidence was restored, and I began to view my disability as an opportunity rather than a disadvantage. Don't let this fool you though; I still wish the polio never happened. But wishing would not change the reality that I wouldn't walk again. The wheelchair doesn't change who I am; it's just an inconvenience."

After several years, John had worked his way back up the corporate ladder to the position of senior vice president. Then, in another sudden reversal, the company was sold, and all the executives, including John, were forced into retirement. He may have been out of a job, but John had no intention of slowing down. "I felt that there were three options," John recalls. "I could get another job, continue doing civic work, or start on a new path. I chose the latter."

With all his experience in community volunteering and involvement in statewide organizations, he decided to try politics full time. He first ran for state party chairman, losing in a close race. Then in 1996, after having served as treasurer of his party, John decided to run for lieutenant governor, even

though he had never before held public office and was considered a long shot. In hotly contended races, he narrowly won the party's nomination and was elected in the fall.

In his new role, John Hager is redefining the importance of the position of lieutenant governor. He spends his time traveling the state and meeting his constituents, serving on commissions, performing administrative duties, and appearing at various events, while still maintaining a strong connection with many civic and church groups. "I loved my many years in the corporate world and equally enjoyed the time spent in civic and church organizations," John states. Our faith keeps us strong while the church provides a mechanism for people to get together in worship, to help each other, and to provide the spiritual guidance we all hunger for today."

John has found that through the support of family, friends, and his church, his disability does not slow him down or limit his vision. When John was in the rehabilitation program in New York, he spoke with a man who also was in a wheelchair due to polio. John recalls the man saying, "I have a tip for you that may be useful. Take a nap every afternoon, it will serve you well."

"I told my wife," John says, "that I'll never take another nap as long as I live, and in the twenty five years since, I never have. Would I have been better off taking an afternoon nap? I guess I'll never know. All I know was that what the gentleman said infuriated me at the time, and it made me work harder at keeping my independence and determination. I guess I've never believed in taking the easy way. Instead I dive right in to anything I do. ■

". . . do everything in the name of the Lord . . ."
(Colossians 3:17)

Above:
Lieutenant Governor John Hager in front of the capital building of the Commonwealth of Virginia.

Below:
Always on the move, Lt. Gov. John Hager begins another busy day working for the people of the Commonwealth of Virginia.

WHY ME?

Faced with the death of her husband, Glendora Paul learns

Dr. Glendora Paul relaxes at home beside a photo of her late husband, Prodeep.

On a snowy February morning in 1995, Prodeep Paul had just finished breakfast and was preparing to leave for the college, where he was a professor. He complained to his wife, Glendora, that he did not feel well. "We had just returned from a visit to India," remembers Glendora, "and we felt a little out of sorts on our return." Glendora urged Prodeep to take the morning off and see a doctor, but he insisted on going to work.

Glendora watched him cross the backyard and make his way to the garage—heavy coat, boots, gloves, and his briefcase in hand. "I remember noticing him making fresh footprints in the snow and then entering the back door of the garage." A couple of hours later, she received a phone call from the college dean asking for Prodeep. His students were waiting for class to begin. "I told him that my husband had left a couple of hours ago and was probably in the library. But if he liked, I would be happy to check the garage just in case his car had problems."

Quickly, Glendora put on her boots and made her way to the garage. Prodeep's car was still there, and as she entered, she saw him lying on the floor. "His briefcase was by his side, and the keys were in his hand. Prodeep had a peaceful look on his face and his eyes were wide open as if to say, 'I lift up mine eyes unto you.' I knew immediately that he was dead."

A native of India, Glendora was raised in a Christian home. Her grandfather had converted from Islam to Christianity at age seventeen after hearing the scriptures from a missionary. However, his conversion carried a price. "After he was baptized, he never saw his family again," Glendora says. "In India, when you become a Christian you bring disgrace and dishonor to your family."

Glendora barely knew her father, who died when she was a child. "I understood the importance of education very early in my life," Glendora remembers, "My mother taught school and I attended an English boarding school." Glendora was selected as a recipient of a Fulbright Student Exchange Program scholarship to study math in the United States, and while attending Washington University in Saint Louis, she joined a local Presbyterian church within walking distance of the school. One day she went to a mission fair put on by the denomination and met Dorothy Wagner from Presbyterian Women, the denomination's organization for women. "Dorothy came up to me and asked if I was available to attend a gathering of Presbyterian Women at Purdue University. I was honored, and the experience changed my life. There we were, five thousand women worshiping together. Who wouldn't have been touched by the presence of the Holy Spirit in a gathering like that."

Later that summer, Glendora returned to India to fulfill her obligation for the Fulbright scholarship, which called for recipients to share what they had learned with their native country. "But I wanted to return to the United States and earn my doctorate," she recalls.

A few years later, in 1967, Glendora received a scholarship to earn a doctorate in education at the University of Pittsburgh. However, due to a problem with her visa, her trip back was delayed for three months. "My mother was constantly urging me to get married," Glendora remembers, "but marriage was not in my plan because it would have kept me from completing my education."

One day while visiting her mother, Glendora was introduced to Prodeep, who was a member of their church. She found him attractive and remembers thinking, "I can't get involved at this time; it's not in my plan. I've got to get back to the states for my doctorate." Glendora remembers praying at the time, "God, how do I know if this is the man for me. I need a sign if I'm going to give up my plans and lose everything I've worked so hard for." The next day she received a letter from Prodeep that began with a verse from the Bible, Romans 8:28: "All things work together for good to those who love God."

"It stopped me cold," Glendora recalls, "That was my favorite verse from the Bible." She recalls thinking, "Oh God, what are you trying to tell me. If this is a sign, maybe Prodeep and I can have a life together." They were engaged to be married a short time later. Their plan was for Glendora to leave for the United States and for Prodeep to join her at a later date.

In December of 1968, Glendora and Prodeep were married in the chapel of Pittsburgh Theological Seminary. Prodeep became a college professor, while Glendora took a position as an associate executive in the Women's Program for three synods of the Presbyterian Church. In 1994, after over twenty-two years with the denomination, Glendora decided to leave and get involved in a mission program at Pittsburgh Theological Seminary. "I had always been interested in overseas mission." It was during this time that Prodeep died.

"Our dream was to devote the remainder of our lives to the world mission . . . when he died the dream died."

The overwhelming loss she felt plunged Glendora into deep grief. As Glendora recalls, "Prodeep and I had dreamed of one day devoting the rest of our working lives to world mission. When he died, my dream died with him. I didn't know what to do with the rest of my life and so I became angry and depressed. I had dedicated my life to serving God and now everything had been taken away from me.

Above:
The campus of Pittsburgh
Theological Seminary is
home of the World Mission
Initiative—a partnership
between the seminary and
the Worldwide Ministries
Division of the Presbyterian
Church (U.S.A.).

"I kept thinking of our last morning together," Glendora remembers, "our conversation over breakfast, our morning prayer and Bible reading, Prodeep complaining about not feeling well, and my lack of insistence on taking him to the doctor. Thinking about that morning made me angry with Prodeep for not seeking help and myself for not insisting on it."

In the days that followed Prodeep's death, Glendora was enveloped by the love of her family and friends. She recalls, "I truly experienced what it meant to be a part of a Christian community. The hugs, the support, the letters, and the phone calls. They all helped me get through those early days."

However, after a while Glendora began to feel restless. "I wanted to get on with my life, but I was so upset and depressed that I just couldn't do much more than feel sorry for myself." Glendora also found that her faith was not enough to sustain her during the first few months. "I was so restless," she recalls. "Here I was a woman of faith, but my faith was not enough at that time. I remember getting up one day at two in the morning and getting on my knees and praying that I needed help, that I felt so lonely, and that I didn't know what to do with the rest of my life." The next morning Glendora sought the help of a counselor. "I didn't want to be a burden on the people closest to me. The counselor helped me to say the things that were in my heart."

For Glendora healing came slowly. With the help of the Seminary community, her friends in the church, and the love of her family, she started picking up the pieces of her shattered dream. In July 1995, Dr. Scott Sunquist came to teach at the seminary, and he and Glendora connected immediately. "I felt Scott was the answer to our prayers," she recalls, "and gradually I started sharing with him a dream I had—that everyone who goes to the seminary should have at least some experience in mission before they graduated. Mission is so important. When Jesus died it was with outstretched arms, embracing all of us, not just our local communities or our nation, but the entire world. Scott was a gift from God. He embraced the dream and the result is the World Mission Initiative."

Through a partnership with Worldwide Ministries Division of the Presbyterian Church (U. S. A.), local and regional churches, presbyteries, and synods along with support from the seminary, the World Mission Initiative has become a reality. Still in its early phase of development, classes are already being taught on the importance of mission. In addition, students have been sent to work with Kurdish refugees in Germany, with a border ministry in Mexico, and with the poor in Kenya. Over the next several years, it is hoped that every student will be able to experience mission work around the world.

"Prodeep is not with me in a physical sense," reflects Glendora, "but I feel his presence every day. Even though I will always miss him, through the World Mission Initiative my life has found new meaning. While being a Christian didn't spare me from the pain of his death, I have realized that the Lord is the source of my strength and that I will never be alone." ■

". . . I am with you always . . ." (Matthew 28:20)

A PROTECTIVE BUBBLE

Even though her parents were not supportive, Tracy learned how to excel through faith.

To many young people, the idea of growing up without any rules may be very appealing. But to Tracy Howe, whose parents divorced when she was in the fifth grade, the experience was hurtful. "I remember walking around Boulder, Colorado, until two in the morning with my junior high friends knowing it didn't matter." Tracy, however, wanted more for herself, and when her friends would offer her drugs or alcohol, she said no. "I knew that there was more in store for me."

Tracy soon began to excel in sports and music. Even though she didn't receive much affirmation from home, her friends' parents and her teachers were there to cheer her on. "I always felt like there was a protective bubble around me that nurtured me and kept bad things away. As my Christian faith grew I began to see my protective bubble as God's love for me."

In the summer before her senior year in high school, Tracy took a job working with backpackers at Rainbow Trail, a Christian summer camp in the mountains of Colorado. The experience deepened her faith. "It was an incredible summer," Tracy recalls. "Here was a whole bunch of young people serving Christ and working with kids. It was just a fantastic thing to witness. When I came off that mountain at the end of the season, my faith was like a rock because I was part of a community that was centered on Christ."

It was during that summer that Tracy began to think about her father. Even though she and her younger brother had always spent every other weekend with him, they were not close and didn't fully understand each other. While at camp she decided to move in with her father for her senior year in order to get to know him better. "The first week I was there I became extremely sick with a fever. My father is a Christian Scientist, and I understood his upbringing kept him from using traditional medicine, so I didn't approach him about my illness. What hurt was that during this time he never even asked me how I was feeling, and that further separated us." While Tracy continued to excel in sports and other school organizations, her father didn't encourage her participation or even attend her sporting events. When Tracy decided to investigate colleges, her father tried to discourage her, instead telling her that a community college would be better. Tracy began to become depressed, and her once constant smile began to disappear. To add to her stress, her father's girlfriend moved in, and Tracy no longer saw a reason to stay. "I felt like a failure because my reason for moving in was to get closer to my father and now that his girlfriend was living there it no longer made sense to live there."

Feeling defeated and hurt, Tracy visited her mother and asked about the possibility of moving back in with her. It was then that her mother dropped a bombshell. "I was told that when I was very young and my brother was an infant, my father had beaten him. Even though I had witnessed it, I somehow erased the experience from my memory. The news crushed me. In my mind, the greatest wrong a person can do is to hurt a child. Now I was living with a man who had done this terrible thing. I wanted to scream at him, but instead I kept it inside." Tracy fell into serious depression, and her smile was completely gone. Feeling on the verge of tears twenty-four hours a day, Tracy sought a counselor at school whom she had never met. The counselor told her that it was strange to see her come into his office because in the last few days three people had asked him to keep an eye on her. "I didn't even know this man and yet he was reaching out to me. I believed this was God at work." Gradually, Tracy began to feel better, and her smile started to return. She also moved back in with her mother.

During the Christmas holidays in her senior year, Tracy went back to Rainbow Trail Christian Camp to be with friends. While hiking in the mountains she suddenly had a seizure. Doctors diagnosed her with Graves' disease, which attacks the immune system. This was a setback for Tracy. She was just learning to overcome her depression and was now faced with the possibility of taking medications for the rest of her life. Tracy felt that her health problem was the result of the stress she had been facing at home. It was time to take control of her life and make a decision she had been reluctant to make. She signed the commitment papers for Colorado College in Colorado Springs for the following fall. Tracy had no idea how she was going to pay for her education, and neither of her parents were interested in helping her financially. Unexpectedly the next week, Tracy received word that she had been awarded several scholarships, and everything started falling into place. She recalls thinking, "OK, God's pulling me in the right direction and it's time to follow." Tracy also made the decision to separate from her parents once school began in order to break the bonds of stress. "I knew that my physical and mental health was a direct result of the emotional and social instability at my home."

"God blesses everyone with gifts whether it's a particular talent or passion. I've been blessed with the gift of faith."

Tracy spent her summer before college as a counselor at the Rainbow Trail Camp. The day before she left for camp her father called to tell her that he and his girlfriend were expecting a child. "My heart began to sink," Tracy remembers. "All the feelings of my father's abuse began to come back." They had originally decided to put the baby up for adoption. However just before their baby son was born, they decided to keep him.

One day after college began, Tracy's father visited. "I took him around the campus and showed him where I lived, studied, and practiced karate. He told me that he was proud of me and that my decision to attend Colorado College was a wise one. Finally he had said the words that I had prayed for him to say. I knew it was the beginning of me being a daughter and him finally being a father to me. Now I feel as if my life is complete. I have two younger brothers that my father has dedicated his life to, and my father's wife is wonderful. I've embraced them and they've embraced me and through faith I was able to grow back into the family. It is truly a testament to God's presence and his continuous love in my life as well as their's."

While at Colorado College, Tracy was invited to go on a mission trip to Mexico with a group from First Presbyterian Church of Colorado Springs. Upon returning, she became involved in several groups within the church and began serving on the contemporary worship team. First Presbyterian Church of Colorado Springs reaches out to the students in the community and has attracted a growing number through ministries focused on their needs. "Once I started coming to church I jumped in with both feet. Here is a place that I can use the gifts that God has given me in order to praise God and share the Word. It has been an incredible door that God's allowed me to pass through." ∎

"In the day of trouble, I seek the LORD . . ."
(Psalm 77:2)

Pregnant and unmarried, a young woman turns a difficult situation into an incredible gift.

When Heather Noce woke up she was in a strange house and partially dressed. Lying next to her was a young man in the same condition. "I was terrified, so I jumped up from the floor and just walked out. I tried to walk home, but I was completely disoriented and emotionally distraught." Finally a police officer pulled up alongside her, checked her identification, and drove her home. "I didn't know what had happened at that house and didn't want to know. I felt dirty, ashamed, and vulnerable, so I showered, went to bed, and tried to forget about it."

Heather was born into a family of non-Christians. When Heather was young her parents fought a lot, came close to divorcing, and ultimately sought help from a marriage counselor. They had been attending First Presbyterian Church in Boulder, Colorado, for the sake of their children but realized they needed God in their lives. With the grace of God and help from the counselor, they slowly began to change and the marriage began to heal. "As a child watching my parents go through the healing process, I was convinced that God was real and I became a Christian."

While she was in high school, Heather went on a mission trip one summer with International Servants. It was a life-changing event. "I learned what it meant to have a relationship with Christ and came home wanting to be a missionary. However, I soon learned that when you are a high school senior the most you can hope for is being a youth advisor for junior high kids in a church. At first I disliked junior high students, because they can be so mean to each other. But gradually God taught me to love them, and we began to enjoy our time together."

Prior to her junior year at the University of Colorado, Heather worked as a summer camp counselor in Durango at Cross Bar X Youth Ranch with low income youth. It was during that summer that she met her future husband, Jeremy, who was also working as a counselor. Since he was a student at New Mexico Tech, they carried on a long distance relationship during the following school year. The next summer Jeremy came to live in Boulder as a full-time intern at First Presbyterian Church, and Heather volunteered at the church and waited tables at a local restaurant. Often after work, Heather was invited to go out drinking with the other waitresses. She always resisted; however, after Jeremy went back to school in the fall, Heather decided to join them in order to get out of the house and relieve her loneliness. "We went to someone's house," Heather recalls. "It felt safe, and a lot of people were there. I wasn't used to drinking and must have passed out. I didn't know if the guy who I woke up next to had put something in my drink that night, but when I was unconscious, he must have raped me."

As Heather remembers, "I was in my last year of college, and after graduation I was planning a two-year mission trip to Romania. It was an exciting time. Then one morning, I started feeling sick. I figured it was stress related

Heather Noce and members of her
junior high youth group enjoy an
Atlanta Braves baseball game.

to school, so I ignored it." When the sick feelings continued, Heather went to
a doctor, who told her she was pregnant. "Why me? I had no idea what to do.
The only thing I knew was that I couldn't have a baby. Not now, not when so
much was happening in my life. How could I tell my parents? What would the
parents of the kids at church think? What would Jeremy think."

Heather felt her only solution was to get an abortion and not tell anyone.
"But I had to tell someone, so I told my roommate who called another friend."
Heather eventually went to a counselor, who gave her three options: get an
abortion, give the baby up for adoption, or keep the baby. "The counselor told
me to keep the news to myself and not tell Jeremy so that my decision wouldn't
be unduly influenced. So of course the first thing I did was tell Jeremy. I asked
him not to hate me because I was thinking of having an abortion. He said he
loved me no matter what I decided to do."

Next Heather phoned her parents. "At first they responded with anger,
asking me how I could have let such a thing happen. I said I really don't need
this right now. I just wanted their love and support." Later that evening, her
parents called back and told her she was right, and they began discussing their
options as a family. "We made a family decision to go ahead with the abortion,
and we made an appointment." Then, unexpectedly, five different friends called
Heather, including a friend who had been adopted. They asked her to reconsider.
"I believe that God speaks to us through people, so I knew that I needed to
stop and pray about it. Knowing that only God creates life, I chose, through
prayer, to have the baby."

Heather Noce is director of junior
high ministries at Peachtree
Presbyterian Church in Atlanta.

A friend made an appointment for Heather at the Caring Pregnancy Center, which is supported by many churches, including First Presbyterian. At the center they comforted her with prayers and listening ears and arranged child-birthing classes and a doctor's appointment. "They were awesome," Heather recalls, "they even connected me with the adoption agency." During the ensuing pregnancy Heather was sick much of the time and the hormonal changes were having an effect on her body. Heather was also receiving judgment from several people, many of whom were from her church. "Even though I physically felt awful, God used me and my situation to do ministry. For the first time in my life I knew beyond a shadow of a doubt that I was doing God's will. I found comfort in God's love and learned to lean on him and believe in myself." During Heather's pregnancy she continued to work with the youth of the church. She was allowed to share her faith story with the church youth group along with her two-hundred-member college fellowship group and some kids from a local high school.

At the same time Jeremy was also experiencing criticism, both from his parents and his friends. Through it all, Jeremy was able to stand up for what he believed in and also share his faith. According to Heather, "it was amazing to both of us that in the midst of our pain, our faith brought us closer. God took control, and we were comforted by his promise."

Prior to the delivery of a healthy baby boy, Heather spoke with her pastor. He said he knew a couple who wanted a child but were unable to conceive. After she was assured that they were Christian, she decided through prayer to give the baby to this couple. After the adoption process, Heather went away for a week to recover, and during that time she wrote two letters. The first was to the baby explaining the reason she had given him up for adoption and telling him how much God loved him. The second letter was to the man who had raped her.

"A couple who couldn't conceive got a child, Jeremy stood by me, and through God's grace my faith deepened."

"I told him that I forgave him. This was difficult, but I knew if I didn't forgive him I would carry my hatred with me and I needed to let it go. Even though this was a terrible experience, good came out of it," Heather explains. "A couple who couldn't conceive got a child, Jeremy stood by me, and through God's grace my faith deepened."

Heather completed her college education, married Jeremy, and moved to Atlanta where she is director of junior high ministries at Peachtree Presbyterian Church. ■

"We know that all things work together for good for those who love God, who are called according to his purpose." (Romans 8:28)

NURTURED BY FAITH

Separated from her parents, a young girl develops a special bond with her aunt.

When Shenny Carlson was eight, her parents immigrated from Guatemala to the United States, leaving Shenny and her two brothers, Ivo and Jubert, in the care of their grandmother. Their plan was to find jobs in America, get established, and send for their children in about a year. Little did they know that the marriage would not survive the transition and, instead of one year, it would take seven long years before the children would come to the United States. During the seven-year separation, Shenny's mother would visit her children once a year at Christmas. "It was all she could do for us," Shenny remembers. "My mother was working in a job with little pay, and she just couldn't afford to bring us back with her."

Shenny has a special fondness for her aunt Angela, who took a special interest in Shenny during the time that her parents were away. Angela had two daughters of her own, and she felt it would be good for Shenny to visit them

Calvary Presbyterian Church is located atop a steep hill in the Pacific Heights neighborhood of San Francisco—just a short cable car ride from the Golden Gate Bridge and Fisherman's Wharf.

on weekends in order to be around other girls. Angela also took Shenny to church. "If my aunt hadn't taken me to church with her family, I doubt if I ever would have had the church in my life. Church for me became a secure place. I enjoyed everything about it: the worship, the Sunday school, the sense of being at home. Now that I look back on it, I think the church for me became my family. A place where I felt wanted, safe, and good about myself."

Finally, Shenny and her brothers were able to rejoin their mother in the United States. Her mother had remarried and started her own beauty salon just south of San Francisco. Shenny enrolled in the local high school, but struggled because she didn't speak English and didn't understand the culture or the lifestyle. "Kids in Guatemala are still kids at fourteen," she says. "In the States they are young adults, interested in clothes, the latest music, and boys. It was a big shock for me, and my immaturity showed." However, because she was so outgoing, Shenny was able to make friends easily and soon became fluent in English. After she finished her education, Shenny began working for the City of San Francisco as an accounting clerk, and it was there that she met Robert, who also worked for the city. Eventually Shenny and Robert married and decided to start a family. When Shenny and Robert were expecting their first child, they moved into a one-bedroom apartment in the Pacific Heights neighborhood of San Francisco. Often they would pass by the Calvary Presbyterian Church during their evening walks. Shenny recalls saying to Robert, "What a beautiful building! It looks more like a museum than a church, sort of European in design. We should check it out sometime and see what it's like."

One evening the church was open for an event, so they decided to go in and look around. "It was so intimidating," Shenny says. "People were dressed formally and not very friendly. All I could think was that I would not fit in, and it kind of turned me off." Shenny remembered comparing it to the church she attended in her native Guatemala, a friendly place where everyone knew each other.

Undaunted, however, by their first experience, Shenny and Robert decided to attend worship one week and returned several more times over the next few months. After the birth of their son, Robert Jr., the Carlsons purchased a condominium in a neighborhood close by. "We got to know a gentleman named Ed Currie who lived next door," Shenny says. He kept talking about his church and how wonderful it was. He'd say, 'You've got to come to my church. You'll love it.' We asked him which church, and he told us Calvary Presbyterian. Ed kind of took us under his wing, introducing us to other members and getting us involved. He was a true godsend." Soon the Carlsons became members, and as Shenny puts it, "The more we got involved, the smaller and more friendly the church became."

Always warm and friendly, Calvary Presbyterian Pastor Laird Stewart has helped guide the Carlsons during their faith journey.

"When you move to this country at a young age you quickly become an American."

Shenny resigned from her job in order to be a full-time mom. "I didn't want our kids to grow up without their mother around," she states. "My mother always said that she missed not being able to be with us when we were younger. I didn't want someone else to enjoy raising my babies." The couple now has two children who are school age. Shenny has begun a new career as a Spanish teacher in a private school. She enjoys cycling and recently completed the "AIDS Ride," a 570-grueling mile bike ride from San Francisco to Los Angeles. Her team raised over $100,000 for AIDS services and support. Along the way, she passed many fields where migrant workers were at work. "When you move to this country at a young age you quickly become an American," she reflects. "But as I peddled through the farming country, I was reminded of my Latin heritage. Most of the workers were also Latin, and I could see that the lives they lived were difficult. What really touched my heart were the little children with their big brown eyes and great smiles. They were standing by the edge of the road with baskets of strawberries for us to enjoy. I couldn't get their soiled, yet smiling, faces out of my mind. There they were, giving us nourishment and encouragement along the way, yet the challenges they face are so immediate. I remember sobbing as the taste of that sweet fruit fed my soul." ■

". . . you are no longer strangers . . . but . . .
members of the household of God." (Ephesians 2:19)

Transformed by the wonderful power of faith.

From her earliest memories, Susan Forshey had an awareness of God's presence. While in the second grade her parents sought to enroll her in a private Christian school. During the initial visit, Susan wondered into the chapel. "It was like I was home," she remembers, "the light cascading into the sanctuary gave me peace, and I felt as if a seed of faith had been planted." To encourage her faith journey, Susan's parents gave her a children's prayer book and Bible. They encouraged her to choose a church to attend when she was old enough to understand the options. For years she can remember reading and asking a lot of questions about God and the church.

When Susan was entering sixth grade, her father, a military officer, received a new assignment in Germany. "Germany was a great place to discover my faith," Susan says. "The cathedrals were magnificent. I've always been a visual person, and I especially liked the Catholic churches because of the wonderful religious symbols and art they used."

At age twelve, Susan decided she was ready to choose a church. "I chose to join the Catholic Church because of its rich history and traditions." Though her parents were not Catholic, they supported her decision to join the church and joyfully attended her Baptism and First Communion.

In her ninth-grade year, Susan's father was transferred to Tacoma, Washington. Susan looked for a church to attend but was disappointed at the options. "I was used to this small church in Germany, which was rooted in history and tradition. The nearest church in Tacoma was large, and it just didn't feel like my other church." Susan stopped attending church but did continue to read her Bible and pray.

After graduation from high school, Susan chose to stay in Washington to attend college while her parents returned to Germany on assignment. "I was feeling a little bit afraid," Susan recalls. "I prayed that God would lead me to other Christians on campus. When I moved into the dorm, I was feeling a little low. I distracted myself by playing a Christian music CD while I sat alone in the room. All of a sudden, my next door neighbor burst into the room without even knocking. 'You are a Christian!' she exclaimed. 'You've just got to come to my church.' Later that day when I met my roommate for the first time, she was sitting on the bed reading her Bible. I felt my prayers had been answered."

When Susan attended church with her next door neighbor she was exposed to a different style of worship than what she was used to in the Catholic church. "This was a Protestant church that worshiped to loud, amplified praise music as the congregation stood with their hands raised in the air. All I could think was, 'God, what have you gotten me into?'" Susan enjoyed experiencing the Christian practices of bible study and charismatic prayer, but she still yearned for the liturgy and contemplative prayer she had loved so

"God, I don't believe you exist, but I'm not going to leave you."

much in the Catholic Church. So, in addition to worshiping in the Protestant church, she also attended a Catholic church on campus. "I felt like I was walking on a balance beam between two totally different traditions," Susan recalls. "Then to make things more confusing, I started to attend a Presbyterian fellowship group on campus."

Just prior to her graduation, Susan woke up one day to the realization that she no longer believed in God. This was a shattering experience because it meant not only a loss of faith but also of vocation, since Susan planned to do religious work after graduation, perhaps even attend seminary. "I was terrified," Susan remembers. "What was the meaning of my life if God wasn't here? It was awful; I had lost everything and it was extremely hard for me to function. My spiritual rug had been pulled out from under me."

Susan faced feelings of mortality that led to uncontrollable panic attacks and anxiety. "I had dealt with panic attacks for years, and my faith had given me the courage to face them. Now they all hit at once, and nothing seemed to help." Late one night while taking a campus bus, Susan found herself saying, "God, I don't believe you exist, but I'm not going to leave you." She remembered Psalm 73, "Nevertheless I am continually with you; you hold my right hand. You guide me with your counsel, and afterward you will receive me with honor" (vv. 23–24). As Susan recalls, "It was as if I were being told, 'I'm here and will take you into glory with me, like it or not.' And from that time on, the anxiety and panic were gone, and my faith was restored. It was an incredible revelation for my life, and the new freedom I felt was amazing."

Susan graduated from college and moved to Seattle, where she began looking for a church home. One Sunday, she attended the worship service at Bethany Presbyterian Church and was moved by the inclusion of a prayer from the Catholic Mass and the use of contemporary praise and worship choruses. "It was as if I was finally home," Susan relates. "Bethany also offered a group called the Post-College Fellowship (PCF). Once there, Susan and her friends began an intentional community of single adults committed to living together as Christians.

For the past three years, Susan has lived in a house near the church with three other women. Unlike roommates who merely share space and ignore each other, Susan and her friends are committed to being there for each other—both spiritually and emotionally. To facilitate this community, a trained spiritual director meets with the women once a month. According to Susan, "It is both wonderful and difficult. You learn a lot about yourself when you are living with three other people. You learn to love, and you learn to trust God." ■

Susan Forshey stands by a display of her art at New Horizons Ministries.

"I was glad when they said to me, 'Let us go to the house of the LORD . . .'" (Psalm 122:1)

Post College Fellowship nurtures the faith of young adults in Seattle.

Kathryn Moser relaxes in her Seattle apartment.

Like Susan, Kathryn Moser is part of PCF. While a freshman at Seattle Pacific University, Kathryn went on a mission trip to an Indian reservation in Canada. During the fifteen-hour drive, a friend invited her to come to Bethany Presbyterian Church. "I never thought of myself as Presbyterian," Kathryn recalls, "but when I attended a worship service the sermon, biblical teachings, and the music touched me. When you are a student at a Christian college people assume that you understand your faith and have no doubts. But I think the opposite is often true; students in a Christian school are there because they do have doubts."

During her last year of college, Kathryn needed to find some new friends who she could trust. Her two closest friends had deceived her—a traumatic experience that not only caused the loss of the friendship but also made her less willing to trust others. Kathryn felt that the best place to look for new friends would be in church, and indeed, she found fellowship and friendship through Bethany's PCF.

"After I graduated from college I was looking for a Christian organization that would nurture my faith," Kathryn recalls. "PCF has provided a grounding for me as I moved from job to job the past few years. It's great to be part of a group of people who are both trustworthy and Christ-centered. When I first got into the workforce, I needed to keep my career as a healthcare worker in perspective by finding an organization that gave me more than what my job alone could provide. To be able to go to PCF's Monday evening meetings after work and think of spiritual things and sing praise music is great. It shows me that work is not all that life has to offer."

Kathryn thinks a great deal about the relationship between her faith and her career. "As a Christian in the science field, I really do believe that science and the Christian faith are both correct and that science is a gift from God." According to Kathryn, "My generation grew up not knowing what to believe. Being a member of the Post-College Fellowship has helped nurture my faith while providing spiritual growth." ■

Native Oromo starts a new church in the United States after being pressured to leave Ethiopia.

After completing his B.A. degree in biology in the United States, Gemechisa Guja moved back to his native Ethiopia in 1977. He was warned that the political climate was becoming dangerous. The Socialists had ousted the emperor, Haile Selassie, after a forty-two-year reign, and freedom of religion was being challenged. Still, Gemechisa felt obligated to return. After all, the Presbyterian Church had helped him to secure his scholarship with the understanding that he would come back once his schooling was finished. He felt called to help work with community development projects, which included spring protection, clinic building, bridge building, literacy programs, and the farmers' association revolving fund program. All were under the leadership of Western Wollaga Bethel Synod of the Ethiopean Evangelical Church Mekane Yesus.

One Sunday, two years after Gemechisa returned, he was attending worship in his church, sitting near an open window, when he heard a commotion outside. A policeman, gun drawn, was approaching the church. He came directly to the open window and ordered Gemechisa to leave the building. Gemechisa arose slowly, walked down the aisle, and left the church. Every eye was on him as the police forced him into a truck filled with church officials and ministers, who had also been arrested. After a long trip, the prisoners were placed in a small jail cell, already crowded with thirty other captives. "I remember that room as if it were yesterday," Gemechisa says. "All day, we had to stand, because there was no room to move. At night, we slept on the floor, and when one person wanted to roll over, we all had to change positions at the same time. It was a horrible place."

To pass the time, the prisoners would recite scripture from memory. "We used it as a time to get to know each other, tell our favorite Bible stories, and pray," Gemechisa remembers. "Even though the prison guards prohibited Christian practices, we found a way to celebrate Communion silently. One prisoner would take a piece of bread and break it. Then without saying anything, he would pass the loaf, and each of us would take a piece. Then we would pass a cup in the same way, with each of us taking a drink. It was a way to practice our faith in a place where, if caught, we would have surely been punished severely."

Above:
Gemechisa Guja and the congregation of the Oromo Evangelical Presbyterian Church.

Parents tend to their children during worship and pass the Oromo language and heritage to the younger generation.

Worship at the Oromo Presbyterian Church is conducted in the Orominga language.

After two months of captivity, Gemechisa was released. "I was one of the lucky ones," he states. "Many others were imprisoned for much longer, some for several years." After his release, he tried to resume his work, however, the new government had taken all the synod's equipment. The churches had been closed, and everything was taken by the government, including pews, pianos, music, and Bibles. The buildings had become government-run community centers. Christians were forced to go underground, meeting secretly in open fields and private homes. "It was amazing: the more the government cracked down, the stronger Christians grew in their faith," Gemechisa recalls. "When believers saw each other in different places, we comforted each other by sharing our favorite scripture passages. Even in public, when two or three Christians met, we repeated and shared scripture verses without military or government officials knowing it."

As facilities and equipment were taken over by the government and as it became impossible to do work, Gemechisa decided to move his family back to the United States and further his education. After two years of waiting, they were granted permission to go to the United States. They moved to Philadelphia in the early 1980s. "I thought we would be in this country only for a short time," Gemechisa says. "However, God had other plans for us."

"We praise God that we are able to gather together and worship in our native language."

In 1990, Gemechisa, his wife, Rahel, and their four children began to meet for prayer in the home of another Oromo-speaking family. Soon, other families joined them. What began as a few families meeting in each other's homes grew into a house church. Today, the Oromo Evangelical Presbyterian Church is a congregation that holds Sunday worship in the building of Summit Presbyterian Church in Philadelphia. The Presbytery of Philadelphia is working alongside this newly developed Oromo congregation as one of its new church development projects.

Now that his children are grown, Gemechisa has decided to follow his calling into the ministry. He has enrolled at Princeton Theological Seminary with the dream of leading the Oromo Evangelical Church into its own sanctuary. Oromo natives from Ethiopia have started churches in several North American cities, including Minneapolis, Washington, Seattle, Atlanta, Columbus (Ohio), and Toronto. "Having our own Oromo Evangelical Church here in Philadelphia is wonderful," Gemechisa says. "We praise God that we are able to gather together and worship in our native language." ■

". . . in our own languages, we hear them speaking about God's deeds of power." (Acts 2:11)

THE PASTOR OF **BUFFALO MOUNTAIN**

Farm and home of Bud and Cora Sutphin. Their son, Marvin, attended Presbyterian Mission School at Buffalo Mountain and Presbyterian College in Maxton, North Carolina.

Bryan Childress lives with his wife, Paulene, on top of Buffalo Mountain in western Virginia. Buffalo Mountain is the tallest peak of the Blue Ridge Mountains, which span from southern Pennsylvania through the Carolinas. Bryan was born thirty miles away but spent his early adulthood on the mountain, and now, it is where he has chosen to retire.

To the casual observer traveling southwest of Roanoke along Interstate 81 or across the Blue Ridge Parkway, the rounded, tree-covered Buffalo Mountain provides a spectacular view of a countryside that has seen little change in decades. Living in the midst of the isolated beauty of the Blue Ridge are rugged individualists who have managed to survive countless economic hardships through sheer determination, often bending the law in order to feed their families.

"My dad was from a nonreligious family mountains in extreme poverty, living

The fourth of eight children born to Bob and Lelia Childress, Bryan grew up in the shadow of his legendary father, whose life was chronicled in Richard C. David's book *The Man Who Moved a Mountain*. "My dad was from a nonreligious family and grew up in these mountains in extreme poverty, living in a cabin with dirt floors," Bryan relates. "The family made its living selling moonshine, which was not that uncommon in those days.

Growing up, his dad lived the worst kind life—he was a drunkard who spent his time drinking, fighting, and being immoral. Then one day he went to a tent revival meeting and became a Christian. He changed his ways, got married, started his own blacksmith shop, and was soon blessed with a son, followed by a daughter."

His dad's life changed again when a traveling Presbyterian minister named Roy Smith arrived and started a church. He got Bob involved in the church, and soon Bob felt called to the ministry. But there was a problem: Bob had never completed high school. So, every day he would ride by horseback to the local school with one child on the front of the horse and the other on the back. As Bryan remembers, "During the flu epidemic of 1917, my dad's first wife died. Soon after that he met my mother, and over the next several years they had six more children." After completing high school, Bob enrolled in Davidson College in North Carolina and worked his way through college selling apples and doing other assorted odd jobs. From college he went to Union Seminary in Richmond, Virginia, and after three years, he graduated.

Bryan recalls what came next. "Dad was in his thirties when he graduated from seminary. Dr. Peter Clark, who was the executive of the Presbytery

Bryan Childress' family lives atop Buffalo Mountain in Virginia.

Mountain," continues his father's heritage.

of Montgomery, got hold of dad and said, 'Childress, we've got some work on the mountains, enough work to kill you. We'll give you a living while we're killing you.' Dad took the call, and beginning in the spring of 1927, he started a church in a school that the presbytery had begun a few years earlier." In 1929, a rock-sided church, which is still in use, was constructed on Buffalo Mountain. But Bob wasn't finished yet. Over the next twenty years, he built five more rock-sided churches throughout Floyd county. This was no easy task, since very few roads existed in the area, and to get from one to another, he had to maneuver his Model T Ford over unpaved paths and through streams. In order to help solve the problem of how to get the people from their homes to the churches, Bob became involved in the politics of the county and was instrumental in getting the county to build better roads.

Above:
Standing in front of the rock-faced Buffalo Mountain Presbyterian Church built by his father, Bryan Childress recalls growing up in the mountains of Virginia.

Below:
Lacy Kemp is a charter member of the Buffalo Church.

and grew up in these
in a cabin with dirt floors,"

Every member of the Childress family was involved in the church, and each one chose to stay active, with the two youngest sons going into the ministry. Bryan was the exception. "I was very shy, and even though my faith was strong, I chose to work at a variety of other jobs, finally working at my own sawmill." Then in the early 1950s, Bob suffered a series of strokes. He asked Bryan to help out by doing some of the preaching. "The most I'd ever done was to teach Sunday school," Bryan recalls. "I told him that I couldn't preach, but dad insisted by saying, 'Maybe you can't preach, but you can read scripture and you can also pray. You can fill in the rest of the time with hymns.' So while he recovered, I helped out, and soon I felt the call and decided to follow my father into the ministry."

However, in order to become an ordained pastor, Bryan needed to go to seminary. Now in his thirties, Bryan had not gone to college, so he sold all his possessions, including his home and the sawmill, and enrolled in King College. After college, he followed in his dad's footsteps and went to Union Seminary, where he graduated in 1957. A year earlier, however, his father had died from complications of the strokes that had afflicted him.

After Bryan was ordained, he became the pastor of the churches his father had started. Five years later, he took a call to be a pastor of a church in West Virginia, and then served a church in Virginia for twenty-one years until his retirement in 1986. Bryan and Paulene moved back to the family home on Buffalo Mountain when he retired. Soon he was asked to be the supply pastor at two of the churches his father had started. It is a role he continues to fill today. ■

"LORD, you have been our dwelling place in all generations." (Psalm 90:1)

The legacy of Bob Childress, "The Man Who Moved a Mountain."

Bob Childress's son, Bryan, relaxes in the sanctuary of the Buffalo Mountain Presbyterian Church.

Bryan Childress remembers a time when his father burst in the door of their house saying that there was an elderly man living nearby who was sleeping on a bed of hay. The man was sick and near death. "Dad ran up to his room and took his own mattress off his bed and brought it to the man. As he brought it out to his car he said, 'I'm not going to allow that man to die like that. He at least deserves the dignity of dying on a mattress.' That was the kind of man that dad was, he would literally do anything for people in need."

Another time, one of the girls in the choir got pregnant and left the community for a Salvation Army shelter in Roanoke. She gave birth there and decided to give up the baby for adoption. As Bryan remembers, "She was back in church the next Sunday and sang in the choir. After the worship service, one of the choir members cornered dad saying that the girl was not worthy of being in the choir and that she couldn't believe that my dad would let her sing. My father turned to the lady and said, 'You know, I thought the same thing. But then I turned around and looked at the other choir members and remembered what some of them had done. Then I thought about some of the things

John and Catherine Sutphin raised five daughters on their farm. John served as an elder at the Buffalo Church for nearly fifty years.

I've done, and I realized that if I told her to leave I'd also have to tell the rest of the choir to leave. I'd have to leave myself, and soon we'd have no choir or minister. So I decided to leave it alone.' After he said that, nobody ever suggested that the young lady leave."

Bryan also remembers the time his father and a couple of friends from Roanoke were out hunting. "Dad was a good shot and usually came home with something for the family to eat. Often he would come across a still, but would never disturb it. On this occasion, they came across someone's still, and one of the fellows hunting with my father suggested calling in the authorities. Dad told them that it was not their place to judge. So they left it alone. A few days later, a man came up to my father and said that he appreciated not being turned in. Dad asked where he was hiding, and the man said, 'Oh, I was behind a tree, and I had my rifle cocked.' My father told him that he didn't approve of the fact that he was making whiskey and that he needed to know that there was a better way. It wasn't long after that the man stopped making whiskey and started to come to church. That was the kind of effect my dad had on people." ∎

Called to Dinwiddie

Bob Childress was once asked to preach to a congregation that was worshiping in a school in Dinwiddie, a small community in Carroll County, Virginia. At the end of the service, the people took a "love offering" in order to pay him for his travels. Bob refused to accept it, saying, "I don't want your money. I'm surprised at you folks, with the cars you drive and the homes you own, here you are worshiping in this school. Why don't you take this money and put it toward building a church." He left, and a few days later he received a letter from them saying, "You made us mad when you refused our money, but you also got us thinking. We'll take that money and start building a church if you'll help us."

Bob met with them several times, and soon they built their own rock-faced church. Bob often preached at the church until he became sick. As Bryan remembers, "Dad was getting older when he took on the Dinwiddie church. We told him he was taking on too much, but he insisted 'This is what the Lord wants me to do,' and that was that. Dad had a very strong will, and once he decided to do something there was no talking him out of it. But part of his legacy is that because he took on that task, the church in Dinwiddie is still a vital congregation."

A RUDE AWAKENING

Life in the fast lane is detoured to a music ministry after the discovery of a brain tumor.

"David, you have a brain tumor. We operated and took out what we could. But we got the lab report, and it's cancerous. You have probably a year to live."

That was the terrible news David Bailey received from the surgeon when he awoke from the anesthesia on July 4, 1996. Two weeks before, David had complained to his wife, Leslie, of a bad headache. While Leslie was concerned, the doctor passed it off as stress. After all, David had recently taken a new job with a computer software company that required a move from Virginia to Massachusetts, and the couple was trying to sell their home while negotiating for the purchase of another in Boston. The concern about housing prices, the demands of the new job, and the weekly commute to Boston were all weighing heavily on their minds.

David had recently taken a trip to Boston that guaranteed to add to the stress. He drove instead of flying and stayed in Boston for two weeks before coming home. When he arrived at the hotel in Boston, he hit the ground running. Breakfast on the go, a full day on the job, back to the hotel in the evening, then working through the night on his portable computer—David worked flat out with little regard for rest. It was always his formula for success. It was easy to understand, then, why David had a headache as he got in the car for the eleven-hour trip home. He took a pain reliever, and soon the headache went away.

David Bailey has recorded several CDs, which help support his music ministry.

Providing Support for Others

Every four months David is tested at Duke Medical Center. The testing procedure charts David's progress in battling the cancer. Sometimes the news is good, and other times additional testing is needed. He has endured four different types of chemotherapy, radiation treatment, and four surgeries. Right now his disease is stable and there is no visible sign of the tumor. However, there is significant "necrosis," commonly known as "dead or scar tissue."

David and Leslie have become active in providing support to other people who have brain tumors, and they often spend hours on the phone listening, counseling, and praying with people facing the same challenges they have. At times, things turn out well, but other times they don't. According to Leslie, "Sometimes the phone will ring, and it's in the evening. We're trying to get the kids to bed, and we're tired. Maybe we had a brain tumor call the night before and we're emotionally and mentally exhausted, and now someone else is calling and we're drained. But we take the call and spend as much time as needed. Maybe we can't tell them anything new, but we can at least be there for them."

"All it takes is to remember what those first few days were like for us," David adds, "how desperate for information we were, how scared we were, and how alone we felt. Just remembering that gives us strength and helps us to be there for others."

"David traveled a lot," Leslie recalls. "When he wasn't on the road, he was sitting at the kitchen table working on his computer. I had to care for Kelcey, who was a very active toddler, and Cameron, who was an infant, and that responsibility alone was a full-time job. I'd be at my wit's end with the kids, and yet David was working in the next room. I felt like a single mom."

David's new job promised some degree of relief. David would be traveling less and able to spend more time with the family—a change both David and Leslie desired. In the prior year, the family had gotten more involved in their church, Summit Presbyterian in nearby Stafford, Virginia. Leslie was active in Presbyterian Women and sang in the choir. "It was my way of being more involved; it was a chance to get out of the house and have some adult interaction," she remembers. "David was also becoming more active and actually took the time to be a youth group leader. I think in his heart he knew that he needed to become a little less career-minded. He was beginning to put things in a better perspective."

The son of Presbyterian missionaries Kenneth and Ethel Bailey, David was born in Pittsburgh but spent most of his life in the Middle East—first in Egypt, then twelve years in war-torn Beirut. "When you are growing up in a predominately Muslim country," David says of his days in Lebanon, "the issue of what it means to be Christian is significantly outlined. It was an important part of my earlier years that until now I didn't fully appreciate." Despite the war, David enjoyed his time in Beirut. "I remember after the shooting stopped, several of my friends and I would get onto the rooftops of some of the buildings and collect spent bullets. It was a fun thing to do at the time and shows how you can adapt to a bad situation."

In 1982, when the Israelis invaded the country and tensions reached a boiling point, David and his family were evacuated to Cyprus, and David was sent to Germany to complete high school. While in Germany, David, who played the guitar and wrote music, formed a rock band with some local musicians. A missionary heard the band and arranged for a summer tour behind what was then known as the Iron Curtain: eastern Europe and the Soviet Union. "It was a special memory," David recalls, "singing in the churches of those very oppressed countries."

After high school graduation, David returned to the States and attended Grove City College near Pittsburgh, where he met Leslie. Two years

predominately Muslim country, Christian is significantly outlined."

later, they were married. According to David, "that first year we were very poor, but looking back now, those were very special times." In late 1988, they moved to the Washington D. C. area, where Leslie began work in an economic consulting firm and David eventually became established with a small software firm. As the company grew, so did David's responsibilities, and soon he found himself traveling across the United States and to overseas countries. "It is so easy to be pulled into that corporate world," David observes. "It's a real ego thing, playing the role of the successful professional, climbing the corporate ladder."

On the day David returned from his two-week stay in Boston, he had another headache. This one was more intense than the last one, and he managed the long drive home by taking large doses of pain relievers. A few nights later, David awoke with yet another terrible headache, this time with even worse pain. All night long, he sat up in bed applying pressure to his head, but the pain would not go away. In the morning he got out of bed, became nauseated, lost his balance, and fell. It was time to call the ambulance.

"This is nuts," David recalls thinking as he got into the ambulance. "Nobody calls an ambulance for a headache." The emergency physicians decided that David's condition was caused by a reaction to the pain medication and were about to conduct more tests when David suffered a grand mal seizure. A CAT-scan disclosed a mass the size of a baseball in his brain. They immediately transferred David by helicopter to a hospital in Fairfax, where surgeons operated the next day.

"It was a very dramatic way for God to get my attention."

David awoke from surgery to receive the grim news that his days were numbered. "I look at that date, July 4, 1996, as my personal independence day," David recalls. "It was a very dramatic way for God to get my attention. I wish God had found a way that was slightly more gentle, but in my case, I don't think it would have worked. I was on a career train and had no intention of getting off. This kicked me off; it made me reevaluate everything about my life—what is important and what isn't. When you're looking at such a short space of time you start figuring things out really fast."

Cameron, Leslie, David, and Kelcey Bailey are living one moment at a time, but are enjoying life.

Not long after the surgery, David and Doug, a musician friend, sat in David's backyard and talked. A thought occurred to them: "What if we give all our music to God—the songs, the guitar playing, the singing? What if we said, 'Here they are God. Let us know what you want. Let's see what God can do with two guitars and a brain tumor.'" We asked, what can two guys from Virginia do to make a difference in people's lives? The answer came very quickly: yes, we could make a difference, one heart at a time. So I began to write and write and write, and slowly invitations came in for us to perform. First it was around the corner, then an hour away and then around the country."

The pair decided to call themselves "Not By Chance" because they saw that David's illness was for a reason. David now performs as a solo artist and has recorded three albums in addition to the two recorded as a duo. He tours constantly, sharing his songs and message in concerts at churches, colleges, conferences, and coffee houses. Looking back he says, "I think in retrospect that God was standing there saying, 'David, if you will turn everything over to me, I'll give it back to you.' I did and God did. Even though there are setbacks sometimes, I am blessed to be here, living life to the fullest." Now each morning when David rises he proclaims, "Hallelujah! I've got one more day." ■

"What shall I return to the LORD? . . . "
(Psalm 116:12)

Suffering from the pain of depression, a man's heart is opened to God by his three-year-old niece.

At the family's Christmas gathering, Jon Oberg was dressed as Santa. But Santa was crying. Two weeks before, Jon's second wife had left him, and he was in no mood to celebrate. All evening long, he tried to get into the holiday spirit, but the harder he tried, the more his sadness became apparent. "I just kept thinking," Jon remembers, "'Why am I here? What's going on in my life? Why won't this pain go away?' It was just a terrible time."

Just then, Jon's three-year-old niece Sara came over to him with a folded sheet of paper in her hand. "This is your friend from God," Sara said. "God sends you a friend." Jon looked at her blankly. She insisted, "This is your friend from God." This time, Jon took the folded sheet of paper and opened it. It was just a series of colored scribbles with no particular form. "But when I looked at it," Jon remembers, "I just collapsed into tears. Here was this little child, who wasn't even old enough to read, telling me that God cares about me, God knows I need a friend, and God has a place for me."

When Jon returned home, he stuck the sheet of paper on the refrigerator. "For months afterward," Jon says, "every time I walked through the kitchen, I couldn't help but look at that picture." Still depressed and feeling sorry for himself, he started talking to the picture. "I'd say things like, 'Thank you Lord for giving me another day' or 'Please, God, help me with my pain.' One day, I found myself just standing in the kitchen, staring at the picture. I always believed in God, but had seldom attended church. Then it occurred to me that any church teaching my niece the kind of love she expressed to me was where I needed to be."

The next week, Jon accompanied his brother Danny and his family to the worship service at their church, First Presbyterian of Grand Island, Nebraska. Within weeks, his life began to change and a new inner peace began to take hold inside. Not only did Jon join the church but he became a member of the praise singers for the contemporary worship service, started volunteering to help cook at church breakfasts, and began sharing his experiences and reflections about divorce with young people.

"You know I probably wouldn't have become active in the church if it hadn't been for the Reverend Roxie Davis," Jon relates. "I like to say that Roxie drives a bulldozer for God. The first time I attended, Roxie came up to me and introduced herself and then immediately asked me if I knew how to sing. When I said I did, she got me into the praise singers. Then, when I didn't show up for worship for a couple of weeks, Roxie called me and got me to come back. Like I say, Roxie drives a bulldozer for God."

Jon's life was filled with troubled memories. When Jon was quite young, his family went with another family to a cottage for a vacation. One morning everyone except Jon, his father, and the wife of the family friends left for town to shop. "I remember pushing a toy truck around the cabin," Jon recalls. "As I pushed it around the couch and into the living room I remember looking up and seeing my father kissing the other lady. Since I was so young, nothing appeared wrong. I just looked at them with accepting eyes." However Jon's father jumped up and started to slap him. The slap was so hard that it opened up a cut on Jon's face, and he started to wail. Just then, his father, trembling with rage and fear, clutched his chest and collapsed to the floor with a heart attack.

Jon's father survived, but his parents' marriage did not. Jon and his brother moved with their father to Kansas while Jon's sister stayed with their mother. The family's distress was not over, though. Jon's mother battled mental illness, and when Jon was fourteen, his father died in an automobile accident. Jon and his brother became the custody of his father's parents. He recalls that as a child, he moved a total of sixteen times.

At twenty one, Jon married and began raising a family of his own. But that marriage ended after thirteen turbulent years. "Had God been a part of my life during that time," Jon recalls, "I can say with some certainty that it wouldn't have ended in divorce. I was married to a wonderful woman, and she put up with a lot." A second marriage lasted only seven years. "Two weeks before Christmas in 1996," Jon recalls, "we got into an argument, and later that day she moved out." It was that Christmas that his niece Sara gave him the picture.

Since that time, Jon's faith has deepened and his life has changed remarkably. As a shop foreman in a boat sales and repair business, Jon often has direct contact with customers, and he admits that his attitude was once one of impatience. "I was often short with some of the regular customers. One man in particular stands out. I just didn't like him, and I was always treating him poorly. Since my involvement in the church, that man now asks specifically for me whenever he comes in. Now before I react to people, I find myself asking, 'What would God expect?' That is a thought that never used to enter my mind."

When Jon thinks of the future he no longer finds himself afraid of what will happen in his life. "If someone special comes along, that would be great, but it's in God's hands, and that gives me peace of mind. Knowing God is there for me has made my life much more meaningful, and I'm truly thankful." ∎

Jon Oberg and his niece Sara and the Reverends Bill and Roxie Davis gather on the steps of the First Presbyterian Church of Grand Island, Nebraska.

"... *Weeping may linger for the night, but joy comes with the morning." (Psalm 30:5)*

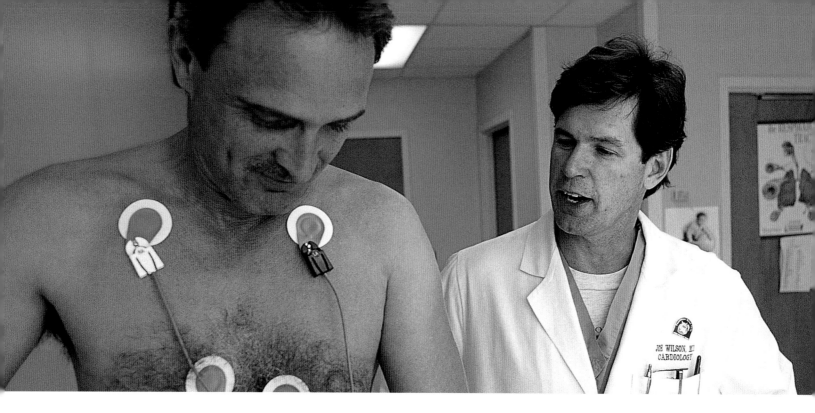

A TIME FOR HEALING, A TIME FOR PRAYER

Atlanta couple makes a difference in the life of their church and community.

"Grandpa, do you have to go to church to be a good Christian?" Joe Wilson remembers asking this question as a child, and he never forgot how his grandfather answered. He said "No, but if you're a good Christian you'll want to go."

All through college and medical school, Joe was driven to succeed. By the time he was in his mid-thirties, he had become a successful cardiologist in Atlanta, but his personal life was not fulfilling. Still single, Joe wanted a family. "Medical training allows a person to remain socially immature," he says. "It is easy to throw yourself into your career and avoid any personal responsibility." While attending a professional medical conference, Joe met Sharon. She was a recently divorced nurse from Birmingham, Alabama, in the process of moving to Atlanta to pursue a new job.

Sharon remembers a religious turning point in her life. "One day a coworker took me aside and asked if I had a personal relationship with Jesus Christ. At that moment, I realized that while I had always thought of myself as a Christian, I had never accepted Christ as my personal savior." Before long Sharon joined Briarwood Presbyterian Church in Birmingham, where she remained a member until her move to Atlanta.

"As soon as I met Sharon, I knew she was special," Joe recalls. "She has a maturity in her beliefs that will never be compromised." Soon Joe and Sharon were talking about marriage. "My previous marriage had not worked," Sharon explains. "I needed to be in a relationship where the two of us were walking on the same path."

"Sharon made it very clear that the rope that would keep our relationship together would be our faith in God."

According to Joe, "After I graduated from medical school I spent a year climbing mountains in New Zealand. As a climber, you are totally dependent on your partner, and the rope is the bond between you. You learn very quickly how important that rope is. You also learn that if you spend your energy wondering whether the rope is going to break, you're in trouble. You've got to have faith in that rope. Sharon made it very clear that the rope that would keep our relationship together would be our faith in God."

The more Joe thought about the things he had depended on in his life, the more he realized that something was missing. "I had always thought of my faith as an intellectual acceptance of God. Through Sharon I was actually starting to experience religion deeply for the first time." Sharon and Joe were married, and before long, they were blessed with two daughters, Katie and Mackenzie. After attending a variety of churches in Atlanta, the couple decided to join Peachtree Presbyterian Church. "We were attracted to Peachtree," Joe explains, "because it is a very dynamic church with a tremendous number of programs. Since we were starting a family, the variety of activities were important."

Soon both Joe and Sharon became quite active in the church. "After we joined," Joe continues, "our lives began to change. We started to look for opportunities to share the gospel and have an impact on the lives of others. I was blessed because my medical practice was successful, and Sharon was blessed with a clear vision of her faith and the time to practice it."

One day in early 1990, Sharon met a man who operated a local shelter in south Atlanta for boys in the juvenile justice system. Like so many other cities, Atlanta is overflowing with kids in trouble. Many of them come from broken families, and their resulting anger and fear lead to disruptive behavior at school and sometimes to trouble with the police. The shelter is a place for caring adults to intervene in the lives of these teens and offer the hope of modifying these kids' behavior.

A Prayer Ministry

Shortly after joining the church Sharon decided to form a prayer group. When only three people came to the first meeting, though, she was very disappointed. "I kept asking myself why in such a large church would so few be interested. When I shared my frustration with Joe, he reminded me that I was not the judge of the success or failure of the prayer group. My call was to be faithful and obedient, and the rest was up to God. His words reminded me of something Mother Teresa had said: 'I'm not called to be successful; I'm called to be obedient.' So I stopped worrying about the number of people and instead concentrated on prayer."

After a year, Sharon added a study dimension to the group. Now, the group not only spends time in prayer but also learns about the nature and importance of prayer. Many of the people who attend begin to understand for the first time what prayer is. As Sharon explains, "It is a true pleasure seeing people growing in their faith and getting closer to the Lord. It has become one of my missions in life."

Katie, Sharon, Mackenzie, and Joe Wilson enjoy a relaxing moment in their suburban Atlanta home.

Compelled by the mission of the shelter, Joe and Sharon became involved as volunteers. However, the program was not having the impact they hoped. "We realized that only a Christ-centered program offered the hope for change we so desired for these troubled youth." The Wilsons decided that they could make a difference.

After a visit to a successful youth program in Sacramento, Sharon and Joe joined with the Metro Atlanta Youth For Christ ministry to begin the program in Atlanta. They hired a talented new director for the program, which also includes anger control classes. A mentoring program will be the next component added, which will match each boy with an adult mentor, many of whom have faced similar challenges in their youth. The program is proving to be very effective. Hundreds of young men have made decisions for Christ and are effectively redirecting their lives. As Joe explains, "When young people are exposed to Christians practicing their faith, the results can be powerful. Lives are dramatically changed every day at the shelter. That in turn enriches the lives of all who are involved, including the staff, volunteers, Sharon, and myself."

Joe goes on to tell how being involved in the church has changed his approach to medicine. "As a cardiologist I have the opportunity to talk with heart patients at a very introspective time in their lives. Often I will sense, as they face death, usually for the first time, they wonder what purpose there is for their life. I tell them that I don't have the answers—only God does. Surgery may provide physical relief, but to truly find peace, they need to look to God. Years ago I never would have talked about my faith at the hospital. Now I feel it is very appropriate and needed." ■

". . . I have made the LORD God my refuge . . ."
(Psalm 73:28)

Former corporate executive recalls alcoholic past.

Bob Dawson had to have a drink. He convinced his wife, Nancy, who had earlier intervened and confined him to home, to let him go to the corner store for a pack of cigarettes. Instead he bought a liter of vodka, drove around the block to a church parking lot, and consumed the entire bottle in less than three minutes. Somehow he managed to drive himself home, but he fell onto the driveway as he got out of the car. The last thing Bob remembers is looking up into the eyes of his four-year-old son, who had pedaled his tricycle up to the car to greet his father.

"I had no pulse, no blood pressure, but luckily God had arranged to have a doctor as my next door neighbor," recalls Bob. "She revived me and had me rushed to the hospital, where they pumped my stomach." Initially, the doctors thought that Bob would not survive, but after a full day unconscious,

he awoke. Standing over his bed was Bob's minister, Angus MacKnight. "I just looked up at him and exclaimed, 'Where is your God now?'" Angus simply replied, "He's here, He's in this room, He's everywhere." This was the beginning of a long recovery process with many ups and downs in the years that followed.

Bob Dawson is the son of a Presbyterian father and a strict Baptist mother. He knew from the beginning that no matter how much fun he had on Saturday night, he would still be in church on Sunday morning. When Bob was fourteen, his father had a stroke. His first instinct was to go to church, but he found the church doors locked. "I'll never forget how devastated I was when I couldn't get in. I've been told that the Vatican with all its treasures is open twenty-four hours a day. But my church in Brooklyn was locked up!"

After graduating from high school, Bob enrolled at Johns Hopkins in Baltimore. During his senior year, he married his wife, Nancy. The church remained a significant part of his life. Unfortunately, so did alcohol. "I always drank socially and gravitated to friends who also liked to drink, but in my mind it was not a problem and it certainly didn't interfere with my job performance." After graduating from college, Bob became a rising star in his company. Soon he was transferred to an assignment in the Middle East. "Here I was, a twenty-three-year-old kid, just out of college and heading for Istanbul, Turkey. I had a great time on that fourteen-hour flight to Turkey. I traveled first class, was waited on by the flight attendants, and drank the entire way there."

Then, Bob and Nancy settled in Brussels, Belgium, where he became assistant manager of international operations. They also started a family, first with a daughter and then a son, and joined Saint Andrews (Presbyterian) Church of Scotland in its Brussels' location. Eventually Bob and his family were transferred back to the United States, where he commuted to New York City from their home in New Jersey. "Drinking was still a big part of my life. I looked forward to the daily trip home where I would meet up with a friend at the Port Authority Terminal to drink. But it still wasn't a problem. After all, I was productive at work and never missed a day on the job. I thought I could handle it. Besides, in those days everybody was doing it."

A few years later Bob was promoted to general manager, responsible for Europe, Africa, and the Middle East. "We were active in the church and had a good home life. But drinking was also important. I remember I always had a vodka bottle in my desk drawer, and I especially drank heavily in my hotel room when traveling on business." However, Bob's life was beginning to spin out of control. "I remember being in a hotel room one night and picking up the Gideon Bible." Two psalms touched his heart: Psalm 69—" you know the one that says I am up to my eyeballs in trouble, and I don't know how to get out of it," and Psalm 46—"Be still, I know I am God." Even though Bob found strength in the psalms, they didn't stop him from drinking. "I knew inside that I had a problem, but I had always been a good kid, been active in church, and was an elder. God wouldn't let this happen to me."

In 1975, a new boss came on the scene and noticed alcohol on Bob's breath. Bob was soon told that he was being transferred back to the United States. It was then that he overdosed on vodka. After the close call in the hospital, Bob began to gain control of his drinking. The family joined First Presbyterian Church in Ramsey, New Jersey, and Bob joined Alcoholics Anonymous, often attending meetings at Fifth Avenue Presbyterian Church in midtown Manhattan during his lunch break. "I've always had a love-hate relationship with God," Bob confesses. "I've had both good and bad moments with Him."

One of the bad moments came when Bob lost his job after a dispute with management. Now for the first time in his life, he was unemployed, and a new job did not come along for eight months. During this time Bob did not drink, but he was mentally devastated. He had to apply for unemployment— a humbling experience for a man used to traveling first class, staying in the best hotels, and eating in the finest restaurants. "I think this was God's way of telling me to slow down. But it was difficult because a man defines his worth with what he does for a living. It was very humbling."

At last, Bob found work and eventually moved to Atlanta. "I no longer was drinking; however, I had substituted a new addiction, prescription medicines. I used tranquilizers and muscle relaxers." Finally when his drug abuse got out of hand, Bob was admitted to a substance treatment program, paid for by his employer. When Bob was released, his boss asked him what he should do if it happened again. "By the grace of God," Bob replied, "I'll be OK. However, if I ever do this again, fire me." In 1991, Bob had a seizure while on a business trip to Japan; the doctors discovered a brain tumor and recommended surgery. Since Bob and his family had just moved to Atlanta, they had not joined a church yet. They attended worship at Peachtree Presbyterian Church. Bob placed a note describing his condition in the collection plate during Sunday worship. By that afternoon, Frank Harrington, the senior pastor at Peachtree, whom Bob had never met, along with several of the staff members, called to offer support and prayers. "This church calls itself the church that cares. They truly demonstrated that to me." Happily, the surgery was a success, and the tumor turned out to be benign. Instead of returning to work, Bob chose to retire early. "I wrote a letter to Frank, and in it I said I didn't know what to do with my life. He responded by getting me involved in many programs in the life of the church." Bob is now very active and has become an elder, a Stephen Minister, and a volunteer in the AA and Metro Atlanta Recovery Residences programs. "I think I've always been a Christian, yet until now, I never had a true appreciation of who Christ is." ∎

". . . we too might walk in newness of life."
(Romans 6:4)

On most days, Bob Dawson can be found at Peachtree Presbyterian Church in Atlanta where he serves as an elder, attends Alcoholics Anonymous meetings, and is a Stephen Minister.

COME, CHILDREN, COME!

Retired teacher begins second career in ministry.

Ethelyn Taylor drove by the Oxford Presbyterian Church every day on her way to seminary. She couldn't help imagining that it would be a wonderful church to serve as pastor once her schooling was finished. Even so, it came as a complete surprise when she received a preaching assignment at the Oxford Church. "I was so excited to get a chance to preach at the church that had caught my attention. So I bounded through the doors and met with the clerk of session." One of Ethelyn's first questions was about the church's outreach mission. She was shocked to hear that the church had fallen on hard times and that membership had dwindled. The clerk of session sadly informed her that the church opened its doors on Sunday mornings, locked them just after the service, and didn't open them again until the next Sunday. Ethelyn was so upset she exclaimed, "Shame on you folks; don't you realize what this church could be doing in the community?"

Anyone who knows Ethelyn would not be surprised by her comment. All her life she has held strong views about her faith. Always active in church, Ethelyn has taught Sunday school, directed the choir, and run summer camp programs. She has also taught in the public schools and at the university level for twenty-five years. One day, she was sitting on her porch contemplating her future and the possibility of retirement from teaching, when she began to pray out loud, "Lord, whatever you want me to do for the rest of my life, I will do for you." Ethelyn felt she had already been to one mountain top, a life-time of teaching that had resulted in many successful students and numerous awards. What could she do now that would apply her teaching skills to her love for the Lord?

"One evening during prayer," Ethelyn reports, "I got the call. Continue the journey that you have already begun, but you must be theologically prepared." So in the summer of 1990, at an age when many would have settled into retirement, Ethelyn enrolled in seminary. "When I turned in my resignation to my principal he asked me what I was going to do, and I told him that I had a higher calling."

This is how it happened, then, that in 1994 Ethelyn Taylor was ordained and installed as pastor of Oxford Presbyterian Church in Philadelphia, a dream come true. "The first thing I did was walk around the community and talk to people. I also met the kids at the school bus stop, asking them if they needed any help with their school work." This led to a tutoring center in the church, which grew so large that pretty soon volunteers were needed to help. Getting kids into Sunday school was also a challenge since, no matter how hard she tried, only a handful of children attended. They decided to change to a "Saturday school." It was an immediate success, growing to over sixty children.

Because of the ministry of Ethelyn Taylor, Oxford Presbyterian Church now vibrates with activity. As a result of the congregation's efforts, as well as the work of many others, the area around the church has begun to flourish again. With its lovely, well-cared-for homes, the neighborhood is viewed as a wonderful area to raise families. "When I came to this church," Ethelyn said, "I realized it had an inward focus and was not reaching out into the community. Once we became involved in the community, the community became involved in the life of the church. Our mission is to be a beacon of light to the people of this community." ■

Above:
The walls come alive with praise, music, and fellowship during an evening youth group revival at Oxford Presbyterian Church.

Below:
Reverend Ethelyn Taylor is surrounded by congregation members of Oxford Presbyterian Church in Philadelphia.

"You are the light of the world . . ." (Matthew 5:14)

YOU CAN
ALWAYS COME HOME

Pastor couple finds peace, faith, and happiness in rural Wisconsin.

David King's first memory of church is when he was five years old and attended a youth event at his family's church in Greenville, Michigan. The program featured a magician, and at the end of the magic show they wanted the kids to come forward for an "altar call." "I was being yelled at because I refused to go forward with the other kids," David recalls. They called me a sinner and said that if I didn't come forward God was going to destroy me. That didn't make sense to me since my parents had always said that God loved me and would never leave me. So, I just sat there as they yelled at me. It was a terrifying experience, but also very empowering because I learned that the people in this church couldn't control the way I thought."

David's parents were people of deep faith, and every day their commitment was evident in the life of the family. David was taught many profound lessons by his parents. They told him that no matter what he did, he could always come home, and they encouraged David to think for himself but also to realize that all choices have their consequences.

During David's pre-teen years, the family moved to Buchanan, Michigan, and made a major change in their church life—they joined the local Presbyterian church. David completed the church's confirmation class but was not entirely at ease with the way Presbyterians conduct baptism. Many Presbyterian congregations sprinkle water on the head of the one being baptized, but David, accustomed to the tradition of where people are plunged completely under the water at baptism, decided he wanted a "full immersion baptism" instead. So, he contacted the pastor of his former church to see if he would baptize David that way. "The pastor agreed to baptize me if I would explain the circumstances and the date on which I was saved. It brought back the memories of having to satisfy someone else's standards in order to be accepted and loved by God. I realized at that moment why I was a Presbyterian."

During his confirmation, David memorized the entire Westminster Shorter Catechism, which includes over one hundred questions and answers about the Christian faith. He found himself internalizing the first question, "What is the chief end of man? Answer: Man's chief end is to glorify God and enjoy him forever." This really touched him because it rang true to what he had learned from his family. "It became my creed," David says. "I knew from that point that no matter what I did in life, it had to include God and it had to be enjoyable. When it came time to pick a college I looked into social work and science. The ministry was far from my mind."

David enrolled in the chemistry program at Lake Forest College and was doing fine in his studies until he failed calculus. Discouraged he turned to his organic chemistry professor for advice. The professor said that he felt there was something bigger than David at work in his life. As David recalls, "The professor, who was an athiest, suggested that I listen to my inner voice, which he described as 'your God.' His advice turned my life upside down. I quickly changed my major to philosophy since it was the only major I could complete without taking an extra year to graduate." After graduation David enrolled in Dubuque Theological Seminary and became an ordained Presbyterian minister.

During his time in seminary, David married, and he and his wife had three children. "Here I was just out of seminary with a youthful arrogance that compelled me to single-handedly save the church. My first call was to two small yoked congregations in rural Wisconsin." However, because of his overly confident attitude and workaholic personality, David could not hold his marriage together. Within three years, his wife left with their three young children. He also lost his ministry and the use of the church's manse.

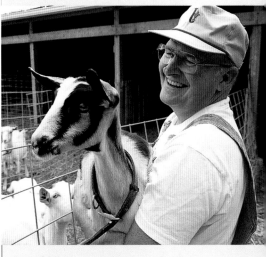

David King grows crops and raises livestock, which provide much of the food that his family consumes.

Tentmakers

One option for smaller churches, which often find it difficult to afford a full-time minister, is to call a part-time, or "tentmaking," pastor. Tentmaking ministers serve as pastors but also work at other occupations, often in non-church-related fields. The tentmaking concept is patterned after Paul's ministry as described in Acts 18:1-3—"After this, Paul left Athens and went to Corinth. There he found a Jew named Aquila, a native of Pontus, who had recently come from Italy with his wife Priscilla, because Claudius had ordered all the Jews to leave Rome. Paul went to see them, and, because he was of the same trade, he stayed with them, and they worked together—by trade they were tentmakers."

David remembers the words of his father, "No matter

Divorced, jobless, and homeless, David remembered the words of his father, "No matter what you do, you can always come home." So, in 1975, he moved back in temporarily with his parents. As David recalls, "During those few weeks together, we had lots of long talks and plenty of hugs, and while this was helpful and supportive, it provided me with few answers. I knew that the only way for me to work out my problems was to go back to Wisconsin to be close to my kids and find a place to live where I could be close to the land and have solitude."

Although David's parents did not have much money, they agreed to do what they could to help him. He borrowed a thousand dollars for a parcel of land in a remote area, and his parents loaned him a small travel trailer in which to live. What followed was two years of personal struggle. As David remembers, "I learned several things while living alone in that trailer. First, it can get very cold in a noninsulated trailer when it's forty below zero. Second, family and friends are very important. Third, I learned the importance of place and discovered that I need to be close to the dirt; it's my place to feel closest to God. Lastly I learned the importance of church. Even though I thought the church had rejected me, individuals from the church reached out in the name of love to me. One was a former presbytery executive who told me that I could leave the church but the church wouldn't leave me. Hearing those words provided me with an image of God hanging on with a grip that couldn't be broken. It awakened my spiritual self and gave me hope for the first time in months."

what you do, you can always come home."

David's chance to revive his ministry came a short time later when an old friend from seminary got in touch with him one day. His friend had just become the interim pastor of a large church in Iowa and offered David the position of interim associate pastor of Christian education. In the meantime, David had worked on his overbearing personality, discovering that he needed balance in his life. While he was in Iowa a small church in Mauston, Wisconsin, offered him the position of part-time "tentmaking" pastor. It was just the position he needed. It allowed him to have both a pastoral life while also having the time to find another part-time job to ensure a livable income. Finally David had the balance for which he yearned. In order to supplement his part-time pastor's income, he has, over the years, worked as a substitute teacher, an installer of vinyl flooring, and now as town clerk. To satisfy his need for being close to the dirt, David purchased a farm, which allowed him to provide much of the food he needed. After taking the call to the church, David met Linda Kuhn, a Presbyterian pastor. Linda is active in presbytery peacemaking efforts, and when she and David met, she was a campus minister at a college a hundred miles away in the same presbytery. "Linda and I met while we were directing a junior high canoe trip," David recalls. "We often joke that our first date lasted a week and that we had eleven junior high chaperones. What attracted me to Linda was that she is an out-of-the-box thinker who has a passion for the church. Her calling is to be an interim pastor for churches in transition. She has the gift of helping churches make the transition from one pastor to another or assisting churches that are seeking renewal."

In 1982 David and Linda were married. They now live with their son, Ben, on a forty-acre farm near Mauston, Wisconsin. ■

> ". . . work out your own salvation with fear and trembling . . ."
> (Philippians 2:12)

FROM RUSSIA WITH LOVE

After the death of a husband, a new life begins.

On a cold, rainy Friday afternoon in May, Andy Skidmore left the school where she taught right on time. She needed to stop by a local auto body shop on her way home to get an estimate for some repairs on her car. However, when she arrived, she found a note on the door: "Closed for Annual Picnic." As she drove away Andy couldn't help but laugh. She remembers thinking, "Who in their right mind has a picnic in May? Michigan weather is too unpredictable." All she could think was that her husband, Marlin, would get a real kick out of her story. She couldn't wait to share a laugh with him when they went out to dinner.

As Andy approached her home, she noticed that both the barn and garage doors were open. This meant that her husband was out with their three dogs. As she drove in, exercising caution in case one of the dogs ran out in front of her car, a movement near the woods caught her eye. The dogs were getting up; they had been lying down next to Marlin, who was lying face down in the grass. Andy rushed to his side, but it was too late. "Here I was excited about having an evening out, and now I found myself telling the ambulance driver which funeral home to take his body to. It was like a bad dream."

Understandably, Andy could not sleep that night. She played the events of the day over and over in her mind. Even though Marlin suffered from heart problems, they had never discussed what to do in case he died, and the thought of making the arrangements for his funeral was the farthest thing from her mind. When she woke up the next morning, however, the entire plan for the funeral was in her head, down to the smallest detail, as if it had been a gift. She called the funeral director and told him exactly

Andy and Abby are adjusting to their new lives.

what to do. He asked if she wanted a minister to conduct the funeral. She did, and since Andy and Marlin had no church affiliation, the funeral director selected a name from a list of ministers.

Two days later Andy met with the minister. "I was in such a state of shock," she recalls, "that the next day I couldn't remember a thing we talked about or even what the minister looked like. However, he did the most wonderful job at the funeral. He spoke as if he knew Marlin personally. After the funeral service, people who had never met Marlin actually came up to me to say that they wished they had been able to meet him because he sounded like a terrific person."

The minister was Mike Fry, the associate pastor of First Presbyterian Church of Grand Haven, Michigan. Two weeks later, Andy looked up the name of the church, and although it had been years since she had been part of a church and despite the fact that First Presbyterian was located several miles from her rural home, she decided to attend that week. "I made sure that my arrival was just in time for the service, so that I wasn't too early or too late. It was important to me that I wasn't noticed so that in case the church wasn't to my liking, I wouldn't feel obligated to return."

Andy sat near the back of the church and looked around. She decided that the church was so large and with so many members that it wasn't a church that she would have likely chosen. "Then an amazing thing happened," Andy remembers. "As I was sitting there, a person came in from the back and sat in the open seat next to me. I looked at her and was as surprised to see her as she was to see me. The woman was my neighbor Kyle Rancourt. I feel it was God calling me to this church, because if Kyle hadn't sat next to me, I probably wouldn't have returned." Instead Andy began to attend the church regularly and soon became a member.

Andy had only one regret from her marriage—she and Marlin had never had a child. A year after his death, she investigated the possibility of adopting a child on her own. She had heard that there were numerous children in Russian orphanages and that many Americans were adopting them. After exploring the process and going through an extensive interview, Andy was added to the adoption waiting list. "While I was waiting for the adoption to proceed," Andy says, "I was very prayerful and was seeing God at work in my life in so many ways. Through my Bible study, my friends, and the church, God was there, shaping and molding me."

In late 1997, word came from Russia that a baby girl was available. However, just as Andy was making travel plans, the adoption fell through. "I was pretty disappointed," Andy remembers, "but luckily I had learned a lot about Russian adoptions and knew that these things happened. I would have to wait for another child." Then, in the spring of 1998 Andy was contacted by the adoption agency. Another baby girl was ready for adoption. She received some photos and a short video of the child, who was three months old at the time.

Three more months passed, and another video arrived. This time the child was being held up to the camera, but she did not seem able to support her head. A care worker kept holding her head up so that her face could be seen. Andy was concerned because she knew that at six months a baby should be able to support its head.

"For the next three months, the only information I had on the child was this short video showing a person nudging the girl's head upward so her face could be seen," Andy recalls. "I didn't have any health information, nothing about her size or weight, just this video, which I played over and over."

In October, Andy received word that the adoption was on and she was to travel to Russia. "I was still concerned about her health," she remembers, "but I decided if God meant for me to adopt this baby, everything would work out for the best." When Andy first walked into the orphanage, she was accompanied by another couple from the United States who were also there to adopt. As they walked into the waiting room, two children were inside. One was seated, and the other was standing next to a chair with a happy look in her eyes. The couple turned to Andy and said, "We recognize ours, so yours must be the one standing."

The little girl was a radiant and healthy child. "I was so relieved," Andy says. "This child reminded me of myself. Very active and not wanting to sit still. Here I was with big saucer eyes, falling in love with this little child who has this glowing, playful personality."

Before the adoption could be completed, Andy had to appear before a court to gain custody. "The people of Russia love children," Andy states, "and it is very important to them that these kids are placed in good homes. When it was my turn I was asked many questions. I was suddenly aware of my own status as a single, widowed woman." The judge asked how, as a single person, Andy was going to raise this child and if she had arranged for day care when she was working. When the judge was finished with the questioning, Andy was asked if she had anything to say. Through an interpreter, she said "I will love this little girl with all my heart. My family, friends, and church will all be there for her."

The judge turned to Andy and said, "God bless you," and the adoption was granted.

"Hearing the judge say, 'God bless you,'" she remembers, "was so uncharacteristic for a judge in Russia to say, yet so appropriate given my own transformation over the past two years. Since Abby has arrived, my life has totally changed. Before I could do pretty much what I wanted to. Having a young child totally dependent on you means being completely unselfish. Now there is someone else who takes priority in my life and what I do always depends on her schedule, not mine. Abby is a gift from God, and she has been entrusted to me. The important thing is that I love this child with all my heart and that I guide and teach her with the Christian values that will shape her future." ■

"You have put gladness in my heart . . ." (Psalm 4:7)

Connected through faith: Andy and Abby Skidmore with Kyle, Amanda, and Samantha Rancourt.

"The only information I had on the child was a short video showing a person nudging the girl's head upward so her face could be seen. I didn't have any health information . . . just this video, which I played over and over."

2 | Spiritual Communities

When the risen Christ appeared to his followers, he called them out of their ordinary lives and

sent them on a bold mission: "Go . . . make disciples of all nations," he told them (Matthew 28:19).

Thus they ventured out to spread the gospel to others and extend the ministry of Jesus throughout

the whole world. These early followers were known by various names. They were called "Christians,"

because they were disciples of Jesus Christ and believed that he was the Son of God. They were

called "people of the Way," be-

cause of their distinctive way

of life, characterized by love,

prayer, hospitality, and the sharing

of possessions. They were called

"the body of Christ," because they

shaped their life after the pattern

of Jesus Christ, teaching as he

taught, healing as he healed, welcoming the poor and rejected as he did. And they were called

"the church," which translates *ekklesia*, meaning "called out," because they had been set apart

for this daring ministry. The stories that follow show how one part of the Christian church—the

Presbyterian Church (U.S.A.)—continues to serve as people of the Way and the body of Christ,

WHEN DISASTER STRIKES

After a devastating flood, church begins rebuilding process.

It's called a five-hundred-year flood because the chances of its happening
are so remote.

The Red River flows from south to north, separating the Dakotas
from Minnesota. On its western bank stands the community of Grand
Forks, North Dakota, and across the river is East Grand Forks, Minnesota.
Even though the Red River has a strong current, its shallow depth and
high banks can make it seem harmless. Every decade or so, some minor
flooding occurs. In 1979 the river flooded a portion of Grand Forks, so a
levy was built to protect against future flooding. In the spring of 1997, the
warning of a potential flood due to an extremely heavy snow melt took
residents by surprise.

Legions of volunteers set to work sandbagging, and at first it
seemed their efforts would hold the water back. But, as the river rose above
the twenty-eight-foot flood stage to an unimaginable fifty-four feet, the
levy burst. Surging waters engulfed communities on both sides of the river.
More than fifty thousand residents were evacuated to emergency centers
across the region for what officials believed would be a couple of days.
No one could have predicted that the waters would not recede for more
than a week.

In an ironic turn, historic downtown Grand Forks caught fire.
Emergency crews, unable to get firefighting equipment to the site, watched
in horror as an entire square block of the city was destroyed.

Left:
Viewing the scene of Grand Forks, North Dakota, from a helicopter,
President Clinton said, "Every one of those little houses is a life story."

"Try to imagine murky water throughout your house, backed-up sewers, contaminated drinking water, and no electricity. We desperately needed help."

Days later, as the water began to recede and residents returned, the full extent of the damage was revealed. Landmark buildings were destroyed. Homes closest to the river were gone, and virtually every basement in town was flooded to its rafters. Presbyterian churches in both communities—First Presbyterian of Grand Forks and Mendenhall Presbyterian in East Grand Forks—sustained extensive damage. One member recalled, "We were all just in shock and didn't have any idea of where to begin. Almost everyone in the area lost a significant portion of their belongings, and the enormity of the damage defied description. Try to imagine murky water throughout your house, backed-up sewers, contaminated drinking water, and no electricity. We desperately needed help."

Emergency help and survival supplies came from the federal government and organizations such as the Red Cross and Salvation Army. A team from Presbyterian Disaster Assistance, located at the Presbyterian Center in Louisville, Kentucky, and directed by Stan Hankins, was immediately dispatched to assess the damage, link Presbyterians across the country for relief, and assist in developing a disaster response plan. The Mendenhall church, while heavily damaged, was salvageable; but the historic First Presbyterian Church was flooded beyond reasonable repair. A nationwide appeal went out to Presbyterian churches for both monetary contributions and volunteer workers to help rebuild and replace the damaged church buildings as well as to provide ecumenical aid to all area residents struggling to recover from the flood.

Presbyterians across the country responded with an outpouring of help. Contributions from individuals and a grant from One Great Hour of Sharing (a denomination-wide yearly offering) provided much-needed financial assistance. Volunteer work teams from churches throughout the United States arrived within days to help with the massive cleanup. Members of First Presbyterian Church of Fargo, for example, spent days sorting and cleaning the thousands of items damaged in the church basement. Al Kellogg, a Presbyterian from New Jersey, spent his entire summer helping with the cleanup. Another church took up an offering to replace all the lost choir robes.

During the flooding, church members were scattered far and wide across the region. Their personal stories serve as testimony to the bonds of faith. Pastor Gretchen Graf of First Presbyterian in Grand Forks rounded up a group

First Presbyterian Church found a temporary home in the Fine Arts Center of the University of North Dakota.

of church members (along with several pets) and took refuge in the fellowship hall and Sunday school rooms of the Gilby Presbyterian Church some thirty miles away. For more than five weeks, the Gilby church provided shelter in its fellowship hall, a place to worship, and temporary offices for the church staff. From this "command post," volunteers worked tirelessly to locate the displaced church members. As Reverend Graf exclaimed, "It's incredibly disorienting not to know the whereabouts of your congregation. The task of ministering to their needs and providing assistance is next to impossible."

Pastor Gretchen Graf and Sharon Rask, a member of the congregation, inspect the architectural model of their proposed new sanctuary.

> "It was so wonderful to come back together in worship, see the people you missed, and give thanks. . . . It showed us more than ever that the church is not a building, it's the people."

So, a week later when the congregation worshiped together for the first time after the flood at the Gilby Presbyterian Church, the importance of the church as a community of believers was apparent. As one member put it, "It was so wonderful to come back together in worship, see the people you missed, and give thanks. The service was very emotional. People were hugging each other, asking if they could be of help, and inquiring about homes and loved ones. It showed us more than ever that the church is not a building, it's the people."

Local church members at first focused on their own homes, since virtually everyone had extensive water damage. Said one, "We had all we could do to begin functioning again. All our energy had to be focused on our homes. We felt numb." Another member recalled, "A car pulled up across the street, and who should emerge from it but our minister, Gretchen Graf, in her overalls asking, 'Do you need any help?' Now there's a person who takes her work seriously. She was helping us when her own house was underwater!"

As time passes and the cleanup progresses, people are finally able to look forward and begin to rebuild their lives. It will be years before the ravages of the flood are behind them, but the faith shown every day by the people of Grand Forks is a testament to their beliefs. Through hard work and the gifts of many, Mendenhall Presbyterian Church has been repaired and First Presbyterian Church in Grand Forks is moving forward with plans to build a new sanctuary across town. As one member said, "Our faith is the key to our recovery, and our new sanctuary will be a fresh beginning." ∎

". . . they cried to the LORD in their trouble . . ."
(Psalm 107:13)

SANCTUARY IN THE CITY

The dramatic sanctuary of First Presbyterian Church United is a reminder of the grandeur of the city in the early twentieth century.

City church reaches out to neighborhood youth.

First Presbyterian Church United of Syracuse, New York, reaches out to the world beyond its doorsteps. As the neighborhood around the venerable church deteriorated, the people of First Presbyterian United found a way to create a safe haven of education and recreation for the neighborhood's children. They established a neighborhood education and child-care program known as "Exploring Your World."

Church member and education director, Beulah Travis, who founded the program and served as its director for nearly thirty years, commented, "We looked around and saw children growing up in poverty, turmoil, and neglect. Many of them were falling prey to drugs and violence and not succeeding in school. We wanted to give them a safe place to go and something worthwhile to do during the summer. Our church had built a beautiful Christian education center, which was being used only on Sunday. So we opened our doors the rest of the week and invited our neighbors in."

Since the 1960s, Exploring Your World has stood as a citadel of safety, education, and fellowship in a changing—and sometimes hostile—neighborhood.

Since the 1960s, Exploring Your World has stood as a citadel of safety, education, and fellowship in a changing—and sometimes hostile—neighborhood. Today more than three hundred children are enrolled in its programs annually. Its original mission of providing a six-week summer program for needy neighborhood children has expanded and diversified to include a program for children with disabilities. Parents who work in local businesses, schools, and government also take advantage of the quality pre-school and after-school programs offered there. Through the generosity and service of many, Exploring Your World has been able to keep all programs free of charge. All parents whose children are enrolled, however, donate time to help operate a concession stand at Syracuse University, the proceeds of which help support the program.

Monique Kelly, age 7, is a member of the After School Youth Program at Exploring Your World.

According to the program's director, Mary Bundy, former students
have gone on to college, the military, and teaching careers. "Even though the
failures sometimes outnumber the successes," says Mary, "the successes make
it all worthwhile. Many times these
kids are caught up in a vicious cycle
of drug abuse or unemployment
that goes back generations. When
they grow up and make something
of themselves, we take comfort in
knowing we helped to guide them."

"Many times these kids are caught up in a vicious cycle of drug abuse or unemployment that goes back generations."

Mary points out that not all
their stories have happy endings:
"Just last week, one of my boys was
arrested for pulling a gun on someone.
I had such high hopes for him; he
was one of the brightest kids in his
class. It broke my heart. But, as
Beulah would say, 'We have them only a few hours each week. You can't change
their situation in that time. You can only hope to influence them and, occasionally,
save a life.'"

"From the beginning, we opened our arms and said to the neighbors,
'You are welcome here. It is your community center. It doesn't matter who you
are, you are welcome.'"

Organized by early settlers involved in the building of the Erie Canal,
the church has some of the most influential people of the region as its members.
Its present Gothic sanctuary was built in 1909, and its campus includes the
historic James Belden house, which was once owned by a U.S. Senator, and the
McConaghy Center, named for a well-known former pastor who was active in
the Civil Rights movement of the 1960s. ■

"Let your gentleness be known to everyone."
(Philippians 4:5a)

STANDING TOGETHER

For more than fifty years, the churches of Pioneer Parish have served God in worship and mission.

The Reverend Duane Aslyn will tell you that providing pastoral care over a sixteen-hundred-square-mile area requires planning, patience, good maps, and a well-maintained vehicle.

A member of Pioneer Parish said it best: "Being Presbyterian means you and I can disagree on a given issue, yet still share the same pew. If we ever say that because we disagree we don't belong in the same pew, we cease to be Presbyterian."

This acceptance of diversity is nowhere more evident than in Pioneer Parish, a cooperative venture between eight small churches spread over a sixteen-hundred-square-mile area in northwest Wisconsin. Each church has fewer than one hundred members. Faced with extinction due to the costs of maintaining a church and a pastor, these eight churches came up with a creative solution that let them keep their doors open while allowing their own unique characters to remain intact. For more than fifty years, the churches of Pioneer Parish have shared pastoral and office costs in order to serve God in worship and mission. While the members of the parish churches don't always agree on specific issues, their commitment to maintaining their cooperative effort has met the test of time. It is a commitment that calls for imagination, flexibility, and understanding between the member churches and their congregations.

A pastor's day may include hospital region, various meetings in separate in between to prepare sermons and

The Reverend David Heyser pays a visit to the home of a member of Itasca Presbyterian Church of Superior, Wisconsin.

In Pioneer Parish, each member church maintains its own identity, building, budget, membership, and session. A parish council made of up three session members from each church orchestrates parish efforts such as hiring and directing three full-time pastors, maintaining a joint office and staff, and sharing the cost of mission common to all eight churches. The member churches support Pioneer Parish through a funding formula based on a per capita and a per church contribution.

and home visits across the churches, and finding time handle administrative details.

The logistics of conducting Sunday worship in eight churches scattered across a large geographic area are challenging indeed. Each Sunday the three pastors rotate among churches, leading worship in two churches each. Several volunteer lay ministers take turns leading worship in the remaining two churches. Pastors must drive as many as forty thousand miles a year. A pastor's day may include hospital and home visits across the region, various meetings in separate churches, and finding time in between to prepare sermons and handle administrative details.

The strength-in-numbers solution that Pioneer Parish has developed through fifty years of cooperation has helped preserve the small church tradition of rural America. At the same time, the people of the parish have built a strong foundation for financial stability and provided themselves with excellence in pastoral care. ■

The Small Church Challenge

Nationally, 30 percent of Presbyterian churches are small congregations having one hundred or fewer members. The members of these small churches experience a unique form of spiritual intimacy and the bonds that can be formed only in a small, close-knit community.

As costs have increased while memberships have stabilized, however, small congregations face monumental challenges in raising the funds required to attract full-time pastors and provide outreach to their communities.

Will small churches go the way of small businesses and farms in America? Not if the faithful, like those of Pioneer Parish, create cost-effective solutions to preserve treasured traditions.

". . . be united in the same mind and the same purpose." (1 Corinthians 1:10)

A HOME
AWAY FROM HOME

AWAY FROM HOME

Above:
The Reverend James Chi gathers
with members of the Taiwanese
Student Christian Fellowship.

Taiwanese church reaches out to visiting Taiwanese college students in Saint Louis area.

When the Reverend James Chi became the pastor of the Taiwanese Presbyterian Church of Greater Saint Louis he was excited. The church had just completed construction of its new worship center, the membership was growing, there was a large population of people of Taiwanese origin in the community, and the local colleges had a large number of Taiwanese students. James anticipated a congregation filled with local residents and college students. However, as he began his ministry in St. Louis, he could not help but notice the notable absence of college students. He began to wonder how the church could reach out and assist these students.

"It's like sowing seeds. We are making disciples while the students are here, and they blossom when they return to Taiwan."

James understood the experience of Taiwanese students in America. Indeed, he himself had come to the United States to further his education. Born in Taiwan into a Christian family, which from an early age encouraged him to enter the ministry, James graduated from the Taiwanese Presbyterian Seminary in 1974 and became a pastor of a Presbyterian church in Taiwan. Two years later, he immigrated to the United States, where he continued his education at the Pacific School of Religion in Berkeley, California.

James also understood that Taiwanese students today, unlike those of his generation, rarely stay in the United States after their education is complete. Most Taiwanese students are in this country for two to five years and then return home for jobs in Taiwan. These students, far from home and separated from friends and family in Taiwan, yearn for a sense of community.

Therefore, James one day invited a group of local Taiwanese students to his home for dinner and fellowship. Soon other members of the church followed his example and began to invite students to their homes. After a few months, the church decided to invite the students over for a monthly gathering that included Christian education, worship, dinner, and fellowship—a program that became so successful the meetings were soon moved to weekly. Many of these students now take part in the life of the church by worshiping with the congregation on Sunday and by singing in the choir. James recalls, "I always knew that if we could make the student fellowship meaningful in their lives, they would travel to the church in order to take part."

The percentage of Christians in Taiwan is only around 5 percent of the population, but even though the percentage is low, the number of Christians is increasing every year. The remaining population is split between Buddhists, Confucianists, and non-believers. Today the overwhelming majority of Christian missionaries and evangelists at work in Taiwan are native Taiwanese, many of whom received their education in the United States.

Even with a yearly turnover rate of up to 50 percent, the Taiwanese Student Christian Fellowship at James's church continues to grow. The students develop close relationships with each other and with members of the congregation, and they keep in touch when they go back to Taiwan. Some who have returned to Taiwan have formed their own fellowship and refer students planning to attend universities in the Saint Louis area to the fellowship at James's church. "It's like sowing seeds," James says. "We are making disciples while the students are here, and they blossom when they return to Taiwan." ∎

". . . a sower went out to sow." (Mark 4:3)

Above:
Children and young people keep the ministry of the Taiwanese Presbyterian Church energized.

Below:
Worshiper listens to instant translation of service.

Bible studies are available in Taiwanese and English.

THE
SLIPPERY
SLOPE
TO PURGATORY

At ten thousand feet, this chapel in the sky offers spectacular views of God's creation.

One by one the members of the wedding party ascend the mountain on the ski lift singing "Here Comes the Bride." Waiting patiently at the top are the groom and best man wearing tuxedos over their ski gear. Standing next to them is the Reverend Dan Straw. Finally the bride arrives, wearing a white wedding gown, white hat and scarf, and white boots and skis. Once the vows are exchanged, the wedding party skis down an expert-rated slope, celebrating all the way. Dan quietly skis down to his truck with the marriage license in hand. Just another day in the life of the slope-side ministry at Purgatory Resort in Colorado.

For the past twelve years Dan Straw has headed the ecumenical slope-side ministry at Purgatory Resort. Assisting him are three other clergy—a Methodist, an Episcopalian, and a Lutheran—and each Sunday during the ski season, they take turns conducting an ecumenical worship service at mountaintop. As Dan explains, "Talk about a chapel that's close to heaven—it's here. It's very spiritual on the mountain with the clean crisp air, a mountain view that overlooks natural wilderness for as far as the eye can see, coupled with the beauty of fresh powder snow." For some, this worship service is a highlight of their vacation, and over the years, the resort has received a stream of letters saying how much the service is appreciated. Dan is also on call to provide pastoral counseling in time of need.

Besides his work at Purgatory Resort, Dan is the pastor of Pine River Calvary Presbyterian Church in Bayfield, Colorado, and the Florida Presbyterian Church near Durango, Colorado. Although the two churches have a combined membership of only two hundred, they are very diverse congregations

The slope-side chapel services provide a spectacular opportunity for people from this country and abroad to gather for worship.

of ranchers, teachers, businesspeople, students, seasonal residents, and retirees. "This is a very special place," Dan observes, "a place where several cultures meet. Native Americans were here first and are an important part of the community. They were followed by the ranchers who own much of the land. Then over the past couple of decades people have moved here from all over the country in order to get away from the busy lifestyle of large cities."

Raised in a Disciples of Christ church in the farming community of Carlisle, Kentucky, Dan felt an early calling to ministry and made a confession of faith at a Baptist revival meeting at age twelve. In high school, Dan was senior class president and captain of the football team. He then entered the University of Kentucky and studied pre-law. But the call to ministry was still there, and upon graduation from Georgetown College, Dan enrolled in the Southern Baptist Seminary in Louisville. For several years, Dan was pastor of various Baptist churches, including one with over one thousand members. In the summer of 1983, Dan attended Princeton Seminary and became a Pres-

byterian pastor in 1984. He was called to the Pine River Calvary Presbyterian Church, which at the time had only seventy-three members and no full-time pastor. To make ends meet, Dan worked various part-time jobs. According to Dan, "Church members Dennis and Becky Hillyer were instrumental in calling me to Bayfield, and when they saw I was struggling financially, they provided me with work at their tractor dealership." After several years, he became pastor of the Florida Presbyterian Church, which combined with the Bayfield church to provide a full-time pastoral position.

One of the things that Dan looks forward to every year is the tradition among the local cowboys of attending worship on Christmas. Many of these cowboys seldom attend church, but they always come on Christmas. "A few years back," Dan explains, "we started serving Communion at the holiday service. We figured if they won't come any other time, at least we'll make sure they take part in the sacrament." ∎

The youth group from both churches gathers around the fireplace at Dan Straw's home.

"For as the rain and snow come down from heaven . . . so shall my word be . . ." (Isaiah 55:10-11)

ARMS OF HOSPITALITY

Andries Coetzee joins with first-generation West African members clothed in traditional dress for a celebration of African heritage.

South African welcomed by West African members of culturally diverse congregation.

Bringing Andries Coetzee to Houston from Africa to be the assistant to the pastor at Saint Paul Presbyterian Church seemed like a great idea. After all, nearly 15 percent of Saint Paul's members are from West African countries. The only problem? Andries is white, and, moreover, he is from South Africa, at one time the most repressive nation on the African continent. Would he be accepted? Would he be welcome? Would he fit in with the congregation?

Saint Paul Presbyterian Church was founded in the height of the baby boom in the Sharpstown area of Houston, then a pleasant suburb filling up with young families. The city grew, however, and the church gradually became enmeshed in the tangle of urban sprawl. As the neighborhood around Saint Paul Church changed in the 1960s and 1970s, the membership also changed. The founding core of older members remained, joined by several younger families.

Then, in the 1980s a group of first-generation West African families began to move into Sharpstown. Many were graduates of American universities and, equipped with their degrees in engineering, science, and healthcare, were drawn to Houston's bustling economy. A large percentage of these West Africans had grown up as Presbyterians in such places as Cameroon, Nigeria, and Ghana. So, when they were looking for a church to join, they arrived on Saint Paul's doorstep.

From the beginning, the West African families were welcomed by the church. Far from resenting the African culture of these newcomers, the congregation embraced it. Several times a year, special celebrations of their African heritage are observed, including an annual African Sunday featuring the liturgy and worship led by native Africans and the Calabash choir, all dressed in traditional garments singing and dancing to West African music.

Saint Paul's minister, Lynn Johnson, was reluctant to bring in Andries without seeking the advice of several of the African members. Lynn was pleased to learn they had no reservations and were eager to welcome Andries with open arms as a fellow African. Indeed, on the Sunday that Andries arrived, he was greeted with the South African national anthem. Andries was touched by the reception. "In Africa, white people are viewed as Europeans or settlers. They don't see us as belonging. But here, they acknowledge me as African. I feel proud."

Several times a year the congregation's African members worship in the dress of their former countries.

"Apartheid . . . never made sense to me. I always wondered how God could let it happen."

Andries grew up in a small South African town, and as a child during the final years of apartheid, he remembers his father leaving home one evening with a rifle to stand guard at the food processing plant where he was employed. "I was very scared," Andries remembers, "there was a lot of unrest, and people were trying to protect their homes and places of work." He remembers that only white children and people from other countries were allowed to attend his school. Stores always had two lines, a short line for the whites and a long one for blacks. "As a child you never questioned the way things were. It seemed normal, a part of life."

After Andries graduated from high school, life in South Africa began to change. Nelson Mandela was released from prison, and apartheid ended. "My first vote was on the issue of apartheid," he observes. "Like many other whites I voted to end it. Apartheid, even though it was a part of our life, never made sense to me. I always wondered how God could let it happen. God is always with us and loves us all. It doesn't matter if we are suffering or crying, God is there for everyone."

Andries served a mandatory year in the military, went on to college, and then, sensing a call to ministry, spent three years in theological seminary. While on an archaeological dig in Jordan, he met Andrew Dearman, a professor from Austin Seminary in Texas, who was so impressed by Andries that he offered him a chance to come to the United States. An opportunity to serve as assistant to the pastor at Saint Paul Presbyterian Church opened up, and Andries jumped at the chance. "It is a tremendous learning experience. I'll be here for a couple of years and then I will either go back to South Africa and become a pastor of a congregation or stay in the United States and become an ordained pastor with the Presbyterian Church."

Since coming to Saint Paul, Andries has been regularly involved in worship, getting to know the members of the church and starting a young adult Sunday school class. "We're looking forward to a summer African Awareness Month," he said, "where African members of our congregation will take turns teaching the class. It will be a wonderful opportunity for sharing African spirituality and philosophy with the rest of the congregation."

A white South African minister in a congregation with many black West Africans? At Saint Paul Presbyterian Church, they are living out the truth that "God is always with us and loves us all. God is there for everyone." ∎

". . . all of you are one in Christ Jesus."
(Galatians 3:28)

PUSHED TO THE EDGE

Toni Mitchell pulls food and other staple items for a client from the well-stocked food pantry of Broad Street Presbyterian Church of Columbus, Ohio.

Church addresses the root causes of poverty.

The members of Broad Street Presbyterian Church in Columbus, Ohio, have long been committed to reaching out to those in need. Alert to their strategic location in the middle of a declining neighborhood, the church established a food pantry in 1971 in partnership with the nearby Bethany Presbyterian Church. The pantry provides a safety net for people under financial duress. According to Elizabeth Stevens, the manager of the food pantry, "These are people who are often called the working poor. They are hard-working people who live on the edge of poverty and are unable to cope financially with the unexpected, such as a medical condition that prevents them from working or the loss of a job. In these households their rent and utilities are necessities for living. The only discretionary money that they have goes to purchase food, and when they have an unplanned expense these are the only funds available to them."

"A typical client is an unemployed person, an elderly person on a fixed income, or a recently released prisoner. . . . We treat everyone who comes to us with respect and without judgment."

Toni Mitchell and Elizabeth Stevens, food pantry manager, help the Broad Street Food Pantry serve over nine thousand individuals a year.

Margaret A. Watson, COMPASS's director, and volunteer Jean Gregg lead COMPASS in dealing with the root causes of poverty.

The Broad Street Food Pantry distributes over two-and-a-half tons of food a week to over nine thousand individuals per year. To handle such a huge quantity of food requires dedicated volunteers. Each Monday, food arrives in a church-owned truck and is unloaded by volunteers. Most of the food is purchased from the non-profit Mid-Ohio Foodbank at a nominal cost, with additional supplies from food drives at local churches. A typical client is an unemployed person, an elderly person on a fixed income, or a recently released prisoner. "We are required," Elizabeth says, "to follow government guidelines and to provide food to people who are at or below the poverty level in terms of income. Because we are a church, we feel called to help all those who are in need with no strings attached. We treat everyone who comes to us with respect and without judgment."

A staff of over forty volunteers unloads the food, stocks the shelves, and distributes the food to the clients. It is a very rewarding experience, with most of the volunteers saying they receive far more than they give. Elizabeth often brings her children to the pantry to help out. "It is important that they learn close up that people in need have faces and that they are real people who happen to be struggling at the moment. My hope is that when my children grow up that they take this experience with them and it will grow into a compassion for others."

Several years after the food pantry opened, the members of the church felt called to deal with the root causes of poverty. The idea for COMPASS came from Reverend Gerry Gregg, a former associate pastor in the church. Like so many inner-city churches, Broad Street Presbyterian always provided emergency funds to people who needed help paying their rent and utilities, typically twenty or twenty-five dollars to each person seeking help. However, because people's bills were usually much higher than that, they would stop at several churches, gathering a few dollars at each one but never having the root problem of their need addressed. Thus, COMPASS (Church Outreach Ministries Program Assistance and Social Services) was started in 1983.

The church hired Margaret A. Watson as COMPASS's full-time director and provided space in the church to carry on the ministry, which has two primary goals: to help provide funds to take care of the immediate need and to get to the root causes through counseling. Rather than individual churches parceling out small donations, COMPASS called on local congregations to pool their resources and refer all cases of need to COMPASS.

"Right from the start," Margaret A. reports, "we decided we didn't want any government funding because they would dictate how the program would run and who would qualify. We felt very strongly that nobody had the right to decide who qualified and who did not. Instead we do an assessment of need for everyone who walks in our door. If their rent is too high, a lower-cost apartment may be the answer; if their job isn't paying them enough, then they are provided with options for training programs that will increase their skill level; if they need work they are referred to the local job bank; and if they need help budgeting their money, they work with their counselor on a plan."

In addition to Margaret A., COMPASS's staff includes a part-time secretary and almost a hundred volunteers. Broad Street Presbyterian Church pays the director's salary, provides the office space, and also contributes to the funds for direct assistance. Twenty-three area churches also provide funding, which goes directly for aiding the clients. Over one thousand people a month are helped through the COMPASS program. "We are doing God's work," Margaret A. says, "by lending a helping hand. Our job is to share God's love and help people to help themselves. Often we bridge the gap between people receiving government assistance and seeing people living on the street because they have lost their apartments. We feel that there is no greater love than the love given and received when we help others." ∎

Broad Street Presbyterian Church, in downtown Columbus, Ohio, has a long history of reaching out to those in need.

"Then the LORD said, 'I have observed the misery of my people . . . I have heard their cry . . ." (Exodus 3:7)

ILLUMINATING THE COMMUNITY

The Kingsessing neighborhood of southwest Philadelphia is a struggling urban area.

Suburban church partners with an urban neighborhood.

Carey Davis remembers listening to a talk by a former drug dealer just out of prison. When asked who his role models were while growing up, the former addict said that he had chosen to hang out with the wrong crowd—the glitzy people in the drug trade, the ones everybody looked up to. Only later did he learn about the good people in the community—the "invisible" people who took their kids to school, had steady jobs, and lived faithful lives. He often wondered if his life would have turned out differently if he had spent his time with the people who were living as productive citizens, the community's real heroes.

This is what the CityLights coalition is all about: shining spotlights on those who are doing positive things within the community so others can see their contributions and follow. The name CityLights comes from Jesus' Sermon on the Mount: "You are the light of the world. A city built on a hill cannot be hid. . . . Let your light shine before others, so that they may see your good works and give glory to your Father in heaven." (Matthew 5:14-16)

CityLights, focused on the inner-city Philadelphia neighborhood of Kingsessing, is a mission project of the Wayne Presbyterian Church, an upscale suburban congregation. The ministry was begun by Carey Davis, a member of the church, who explains, "Kingsessing is a neighborhood that is struggling. About a square mile in size, it is a community of about sixty thousand that is primarily residential, has no remaining industry, few high-quality stores, and is mostly run-down. But Kingsessing also has many great assets, especially good people who are often overshadowed by the negative stories that are the focus of the media."

Through CityLights, Wayne Presbyterian Church partners with other organizations and churches within the community to celebrate and support people and programs that are making a positive difference in people's lives. From the start, CityLights was clear about its mission. Even though Wayne Presbyterian Church is affluent, they did not want the ministry to be driven by money. According to Carey, "Our church is used to supporting mission with dollars; this is a chance for us to use our bodies and spirits as well."

"When CityLights first began," Carey explains, "members of our church fanned out into the community to learn all we could, to find which people and organizations were involved in the community and what they did. Our approach was quite simple, we would visit sites in the neighborhood and introduce ourselves by saying something like, 'We're from Wayne Presbyterian Church, we care about what you are doing in the community, and thank you for your efforts. If you can think of any way our church might be helpful, we'd be glad to try.' This allowed us to both show our appreciation for what they did and learn how we could assist them."

According to volunteer Pat Leidy, "Early on we realized since we were not living in the area, we needed to establish hubs from which to work." These included two neighborhood Presbyterian churches, two city-run recreation centers, a small Christian school, and a health center run by the University of Pennsylvania's School of Nursing. "Once the hubs were identified," Pat continues, "we got to know the people who worked there and what services they offered. Then we assigned a liaison from CityLights to be our contact with the people and organizations in or near each hub."

One of the main roles of CityLights is assisting the various community organizations in Kingsessing to gain the much-needed attention of city officials, who often are unaware of the true needs of the community regarding city services.

Neighborhood mosaic depicts neighbors in the community.

Carey Davis and son, Graham, relax on the porch of their home in the Kingsessing neighborhood.

city lights

Students gather from Cornerstone Christian Academy, one of over twenty CityLights partners.

According to Bob Wilkinson, a volunteer from Wayne Presbyterian Church who teaches a computer literacy class in the basement of a local school, "There is a vitality in Kingsessing that is almost indescribable. People are very motivated to make their community a better place to live. Our job is simply to lend our support and let others know what is happening here."

A congregation in the Kingsessing neighborhood, Woodland Avenue Presbyterian Church, provides a lending closet for young mothers to borrow cribs, playpens, high chairs, toys, and other items for the care of their babies. CityLights helps this ministry by communicating the needs of the lending closet, thus encouraging members of the Wayne congregation to donate baby supplies for these mothers in need. According to Bill Yeats, pastor of the Woodland Avenue church, "It seems that every time Carey or one of the other CityLights volunteers comes down here they have a trunkful of baby furniture and supplies to donate. This is just one of the positive aspects of CityLights."

To demonstrate a personal commitment to the community, Carey, along with her husband, Gerry, and their son, Graham, moved out of their suburban home in Wayne and purchased a home in Kingsessing. According to Carey, "I've always liked living in an urban setting. I'm a real neighbor kind of person. I love block parties, talking over the back fence, and visiting on the front porch. In the suburbs you don't have the same type of relationships." CityLights has been a life-changing ministry for the people of Wayne Presbyterian Church by offering an opportunity to deepen their own faith while experiencing firsthand the closeness that can come when meaningful connections are made with others. ■

"There is a vitality in Kingsessing that is almost indescribable. . . . Our job is simply to lend our support and let others know what's happening here."

". . . let your light shine before others . . ."
(Matthew 5:16)

FORGING PARTNERSHIPS

Front Porch Alliance builds trust between a suburban church and a city neighborhood.

The inspiration for the Front Porch Alliance came when a task force of Village Presbyterian Church, a congregation with over six thousand members in suburban Kansas City, was dreaming about how to celebrate the church's fiftieth anniversary. Task force member Carol Cowden recalls that the task force kept coming back to one theme: mission. "We've always been known as the mission church on Mission Road. So, rather than pat ourselves on the back, it seemed better to look forward and mark the occasion by launching a new mission."

Pastor Robert Bohl gave the task force a creative suggestion: why not form a partnership between Village Church and a one-block-square area in the inner city? To his surprise, Robert later learned that the task force had decided not only to adopt his idea but also to greatly expand it. Instead of a partnership with one-square block, the task force had set its sights on a forty-block area!

As a next step, the task force decided to call a meeting of community leaders from the forty-block, inner-city area. At the meeting, one of the local leaders shocked the task force by saying, "You people from the suburbs have been coming down here for decades telling us what is wrong with our community. We're tired of that mentality; you don't live here, we do. The only way we would be interested is if it were a true partnership." A lively, sometimes heated, exchange followed between task force members and community leaders. Finally Robert addressed the group: "If we come down there, will you be there to fulfill your end of the partnership?" John Modest Miles, pastor of the inner-city Morningstar Baptist Church, responded, "We'll be there."

From the beginning, then, the Front Porch Alliance has made trust-building with the people of the community a top priority. "The easiest thing to do is write checks," states Carol, now co-chair of the Alliance. "The most difficult thing is to get volunteers to take time out of their busy schedules to go into an area that they are not comfortable in and to work hand-in-hand with people who come from a different perspective."

Village Church decided from the outset that they would place the emphasis on sending people rather than on providing funding. Moreover, to maintain the integrity of the partnership, it was important that there be an equal number of volunteers from the inner-city community. According to co-chair Betty Crooker, "The first person from the community to catch the vision of what our partnership could accomplish was Betty Brown. She mobilized her entire neighborhood and found people willing to help. Betty is a gift from heaven, and through her efforts instant miracles are happening and people are beginning to talk with us."

Although the Front Porch Alliance is still in its infancy, positive results can already be seen. Volunteers from the church and the community have worked together on such projects as cleaning up vacant lots and street corners, and they are beginning to get to know each other on a first-name basis. Volunteers for the Alliance have served as tutors and mentors for students from three neighborhood elementary schools; gardens have been planted; homes have been fixed up. "At first," Carol observes, "we thought that our involvement would be strictly a mission project for the church. What we have discovered is that we are the ones who are benefiting. We are making new friends in a neighborhood that we never would have gone into on our own, and they are teaching us many things." ∎

". . . constantly praying with joy . . . because of your sharing in the gospel . . ." (Philippians 1:3)

**Midtown Manhattan church
is learning to see the city
"through God's eyes."**

A BEACON IN THE CITY

One cold December evening in 1998, several elders and trustees were exiting the Fifth Avenue Presbyterian Church in midtown Manhattan after a budget meeting. They were startled to see two police officers telling the homeless people sleeping beside the church to leave the area. A NYPD van stood ready to carry the homeless away. Church members Ena Malone and Cress Darwin and staff members Oscar McCloud and Margaret Shafer immediately leapt into action, challenging the officers' activity. After a heated discussion, the police allowed the homeless to stay and the police moved on.

The night after that confrontation, Margaret Shafer, Associate for Outreach for the church, talked with some of the homeless on the steps. "There was a Jamaican woman reading her Bible by flashlight. I asked her what she was reading, and she quietly replied, 'Job.' That really touched me. Here was this woman who lived in a cardboard box and had nothing but a shopping cart reading about a man who had more troubles than anyone else, who had lost everything and yet refused to give up his faith in God."

Earlier an ad hoc committee on "The Homeless on Our Steps" had been formed to speak with the homeless, learn what services were available to assist them, and come up with recommendations for how the church could help. In their report issued in early 1999, the committee urged the congregation to include the homeless in the spiritual life of the church through prayer and worship, to assist Habitat for Humanity and other groups building permanent residences with funding and hands-on labor, to increase the number of temporary shelter beds available in area churches and synagogues, and to encourage members to befriend and mentor a homeless person.

The members of the Fifth Avenue Presbyterian Church have a special place in their hearts for the homeless and disenfranchised who are barely surviving in the city. In January 1998, Dr. Thomas Tewell challenged the church to reaffirm its commitment to those less fortunate by launching "Church in the City," a ten-year effort leading up to the two hundredth anniversary of the church. Dr. Tewell spoke with passion, "We're here in the wealthiest neighborhood in the country just a few subway stops south of the poorest neighborhood in the country. We need to reach out to our neighbors and learn to both give to and receive gifts from them."

"We've found that what the homeless need more than anything else is friendship."

Fifth Avenue Presbyterian Church pastor Dr. Thomas Tewell (left) leads area clergy and members in the Builders March for decent housing for the poor.

"Through Church in the City," Margaret says, "we are learning to see the city with God's eyes. If fundamental changes are to be made, a totally different way of viewing the world is required. We've found that what the homeless need more than anything else is friendship. Someone they can turn to at anytime, someone who will be there for them. While our hearts may be in the right place, it is important how we approach people. We must always treat people with respect."

In two short years, Church in the City has challenged the perceptions and attitudes of participants by taking tours into all five of the city's boroughs to speak with people and explore needs. Members have been asked to commit their time and talents resulting in a large pool of volunteers. Discussions have been held with other congregations throughout the city in order to look into ways of expanding the ministry, and a major commitment was made to partner with Habitat for Humanity to build homes throughout the city.

Like all initiatives, Church in the City is dependent on the passion and determination of the congregation, people willing to do the work that God commands of all people of faith. No effort is seen as either too large or too small because a transformation of spirit happens one heart at a time. Margaret tells of one such transformation: "A lot of people come to our chapel for meditation and prayer during their noon hour. One woman had recently experienced a difficult divorce and was in a lot of agony. As time went on and as she gradually began to feel stronger she became aware of the others in the chapel. Quietly she began to pray for them. Then one day she noticed a woman who was sitting alone crying. She went over and sat beside her. Then in a transforming moment, she asked if she could pray for the woman. When they finished, the woman asked, 'Will you continue to pray for me?' This was the beginning of a ministry, and the prayer list continues to grow. It's a wonderful example of one person finding a way to help others. It is how God is working in people's lives." ∎

The Builders March begins its journey on the steps of Fifth Avenue Presbyterian Church. The march was held in midtown Manhattan and, along the way, stopped for worship in several area churches and synagogues.

"You shall also love the stranger, for you were strangers . . ." (Deuteronomy 10:19)

Ecumenical youth program is a positive force in community.

Before becoming pastor of the Mediapolis Presbyterian Church in Iowa, Dick Reynolds was a youth pastor at the Clarendon Hills Presbyterian Church in Illinois. "Because the Clarendon Hills church is large," Dick observes, "I knew how to run a large youth program. Mediapolis has only two hundred members, and now I had to learn how to start a small youth program." Reynolds decided that the best strategy was to join forces with other area churches in an ecumenical youth program, and the opportunity presented itself when the pastor of the local Methodist church stopped by one day and said, "If you start a community-wide youth program, we will give you our children."

"After talking with the Methodist pastor," Dick recalls, "I stopped by the other churches in town and said, 'I'm thinking of starting a youth program at our church. Are you interested in doing it together? If you are, we will make sure it is an ecumenical partnership.'" In 1989, all four churches of Mediapolis—Presbyterian, Methodist, Lutheran, and Catholic—combined their youth programs into one. The youth group built its own youth center in the basement of the Presbyterian church, and a director was eventually hired.

The result has been a tremendous success. In a town with 450 students in its junior and senior high schools combined, over 150 youth are now active in the ecumenical youth program. The result is a higher level of spirituality among the students, a host of available youth activities, and a student-run youth center for fellowship, programs, and meetings. Youth Director Nancy Hitchcock explains, "The youth center is theirs. They have their own keys and can come in anytime, as long as an adult leader has been notified." Inside the youth center is a game area with a ping pong table, a pool table, a big screen television, a VCR, a stereo system, a computer with Internet access, couches and other seating for discussion groups, a microwave oven, and even a soda machine.

Youth meetings are held each Sunday evening followed by a meal and a contemporary worship service featuring praise music, scripture, and prayer. Bible study is conducted on Wednesday nights. The positive effects on the lives of the young people of the community are astounding and can be heard in the faith stories of its members.

Heather McLatchie is a sophomore in high school who grew up in a Christian family and can remember always going to church. While in junior high, Heather joined the youth group and found it helpful to talk about her faith with others her age. At a church camp one summer, the youth were given an opportunity to come forward during worship and recommit their lives to Christ. "It was something I wasn't comfortable doing a few years before," Heather reports, "but this time I felt moved by the Holy Spirit and went forward. It was awesome."

Anne Reynolds and Carrie Carruthers are talented singers who formed a Christian praise band. The group leads the contemporary worship for the youth group and has recently recorded a CD. Anne is the daughter of the pastor, Dick Reynolds, and has been active in church for as long as she can remember. "When I was six, our family moved to Mediapolis from the Chicago suburbs. Around that time, I started to pray on a daily basis. I always pray for God to come into my heart, because when I do, I know God will always be there." However Anne's faith really took hold while on a mission trip to Germany as part of the senior high youth group. "It was such a spiritual experience. We were surrounded by hundreds of other Christians. Just listening to their faith stories challenged me to want to learn more and to live a Christian life."

Carrie Carruthers, Heather McLatchie, and Anne Reynolds are members of the Ecumenical Youth Program in Mediapolis, Iowa.

While in junior high, Carrie didn't want to join the youth group and instead got involved with the wrong crowd in school. "I was starting to get in trouble and had experimented with alcohol," Carrie remembers. "My parents were concerned so they called our pastor, John Gaulke, at the Methodist church." As an ecumenical partner in the youth group John was aware of the mission trip to Germany that summer. "Reverend Gaulke knew I liked to sing," Carrie reports, "so he encouraged me to go on the mission trip to Germany and sing in the praise band with Anne. So I started practicing with the praise band and the chemistry was great, the way our voices blended was like magic."

The youth group left for Germany and Carrie was transformed by the experience. The way Carrie remembers it, "Words can't describe what happened to me, it took me until that trip to realize that God had blessed me with a voice and that I could use it to spread God's word to others. I could actually feel the presence of the Holy Spirit during those two weeks in Germany." When she returned from Germany, Carrie was concerned that she would fall in with her old crowd and start doing the wrong things again. "I prayed that God would give me the strength to resist the things that had been destructive in my life," Carrie recalls. "My prayers were answered and I didn't get involved with them again. God had transformed me, and Anne and I continued with our praise music."

"Positive things can happen when churches unite."

"The reason this program is so successful," notes Nancy, "is that we get a high percentage of participants from the students in school and the community is behind us. It is a real tribute to the positive things that can happen when churches unite ecumenically for the good of the entire area." ■

". . . your sons and daughters shall prophesy . . ."
(Joel 2:28)

RESPECTING ALL CULTURES

Congregation uses its location to blend Eastern and Western cultures.

A group of twelve street kids showed up one day on the rooftop basketball court at the Donaldina Cameron House, a community outreach mission of the Presbyterian Church (U.S.A.) in the Chinatown district of San Francisco. The young men were making a disturbance, so Laurene Chan, who at the time was working with the youth program at Cameron House, was sent to find out what they wanted. "What's up," Laurene said as she approached them. "How come you're not in school?" They said they just wanted to hang out and shoot hoops. Laurene gradually began to draw them into a conversation, and since it was nearly Thanksgiving, she decided to invite them to Cameron House to celebrate the holiday. "Hey guys, do you celebrate Thanksgiving?" she asked. "No, what's that?" they replied. "It's like potluck," Laurene responded. "My partner and I roast a turkey, and you bring the rest of the food. Anything is fine—rice, noodles, dessert, soft drinks. Bring what you like to eat." "What about our girlfriends?" they asked. "Bring them, too, and afterward we'll drive you home."

That Thanksgiving, they all came together in the main hall of Cameron House. Over dinner, Laurene asked each of them to share with the rest of the group what they were thankful for. At first nobody wanted to speak. However, after some prodding from Laurene, all of them named things for which they were thankful. Then Laurene spoke: "Do you know where I am on Sunday morning? I'm at church. I know some of you are Buddhist or Taoist and that you may even have altars in your homes. That's totally cool. What I want to share with you is that I'm most thankful for someone named Jesus. That's all

The rooftop basketball court at Cameron House provides a space for recreation and fellowship.

The Tai Chi class at the Presbyterian Church in Chinatown provides physical exercise and internal energy development.

The Reverend Calvin Chinn and Laurene Chan are developing ministries of wholeness and healing.

"If they end up on our doorstep, or even on our basketball court, it is our chance to share our love for God with others."

I'm going to say. I wanted you to know that I just like what he did and that because of what he taught me, I got to know all of you. I'm thankful for that and want you to know that you really are good people and even if you've been in trouble before, it doesn't matter." After that Thanksgiving, most of the young men kept in touch with Cameron House, and when they graduated from high school, they got together with Laurene to celebrate their achievement. "We need to understand," Laurene states, "that they are gifts from God. We can't afford to turn away people. If they end up on our doorstep, or even on our basketball court, it is our chance to share our love for God with others."

Cameron House is one block away from the Presbyterian church in Chinatown, and Laurene is now a staff associate at the church and works closely with the pastor, the Reverend Calvin Chinn. Currently they are striving to develop ministries that blend Eastern and Western styles of wholeness and healing. "Since I was in high school," Laurene recalls, "I've been interested in traditional Chinese medicine. My youth group advisor taught us how to relieve our headaches with acupressure rather than taking a pill. He also taught us how ginger could help us with motion sickness."

According to Calvin, in order to create holistic health programs in the Chinatown community, there were a number of significant issues to be faced. "We started with the broader issues first, such as what it means to be a church here in Chinatown on one of the busiest and noisiest streets in the country. Then we focused on the needs of our three congregations: English speaking, Mandarin, and Cantonese. We found that there was a great interest from some in our congregation for recapturing our traditions in order to grow spiritually and improve our health and happiness. However we also found that some of our members had a great distrust of the traditional ways and felt the Western methods were better."

Laurene and Calvin looked at ways to build bridges between the Eastern and Western ways. According to Laurene, "We called in some good people, like Dr. Benjamin Tong, a psychotherapist and college professor, who was interested in Eastern and Western thought, and Chris Jeong, my high school youth advisor and now a licensed acupuncturist. We looked at what our Eastern culture had to offer in terms of healing and wholeness and how we could make it available to people who were interested." Soon discussions and seminars were held and programs began to be developed. One well-attended program was "Chinese Herbs for Daily Living," which explored the relationship between Chinese herbs and Western medicine. Eyes lit up as people found that it was acceptable to be Christian while holding on to Eastern traditions.

Tai Chi, a traditional martial art form, is also taught in the church. "I have a history of high cholesterol," reports Calvin, who has been practicing Tai Chi for the past year. "A few months ago, I had a full medical examination, and my cholesterol level was not only lower but it was very low for a person in my age group. The doctor asked what I was doing differently as far as my diet and life-style were concerned. The only change I'd made was Tai Chi. What we are attempting to do in our church is to look at and investigate Christianity from the perspective of our Asian heritage and culture, which includes an emphasis on healing and wholeness."

Benjamin is a long-time community activist who left the church when he was young. "To me Christianity was imperialistic," he recalls. "Instead, I became interested in Buddhism and Taoism. One day, I was visiting a local temple and noticed that among the many Asian images on the altar were statues of Abraham, Moses, and Jesus. That had a considerable impact on me and showed me a side of ecumenism that I'd never thought about. After the birth of my son a few years ago I found myself, to my surprise, church shopping. When I came to this church, I heard a sermon that Cal gave. In it he talked about diversity, inclusion, and social justice. I felt at home and have been a member here ever since. This is a place were I can affirm my Asian American heritage while also feeling the presence of a God whose manifestations are infinite and most certainly *not* restricted to the phenomenon of the person of Jesus." ∎

The Donaldina Cameron House

The Donaldina Cameron House, located one block away from the Presbyterian church in Chinatown, is a mission of the Presbyterian Church (U.S.A.) started in 1874 as a refuge for Asian females who had been smuggled into the country. These women, many of whom were younger than ten, were bought and sold as property in a system known as the "yellow slave trade." Many of the young women were forced to become domestic servants or prostitutes. Miss Donaldina Cameron devoted her life to sheltering and educating these women and fighting for their rights. Cameron House continues to be a faith-based organization that helps low-income, mostly Asian, immigrants and families deal with a variety of issues. These include domestic violence assistance, legal help, family support, financial assistance, youth mentoring, and academic tutoring.

"Many nations shall join themselves to the LORD . . ." (Zechariah 2:11)

CALLED TO MISSION

Open for business! "Clothes Closet"
volunteer Jane Hueston is ready to
provide apparel for clients in need.

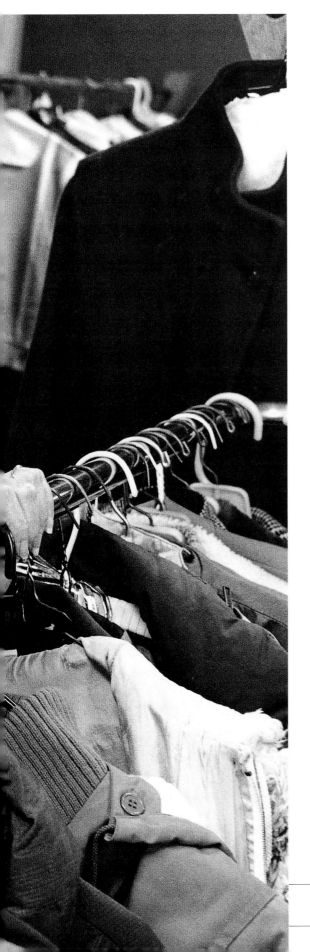

House churches provide members with hands-on mission experiences.

It's 6:30 P.M. on Wednesday night, and the doors to the Clothes Closet are about to open. Some fifty families stand patiently in line while volunteers make final preparations, ensuring that the clothes are properly displayed and arranged by size. When the doors open, the clients stream in, and for the next hour the Clothes Closet is a beehive of activity. "How may I help you tonight?" one volunteer asks. A young mother accompanied by her infant daughter and toddler son says she could use night clothes for her baby, a pair of pants and a shirt for her son, and a blouse for herself. "I was just going through our infant clothes and noticed a really nice sleep outfit for an infant. Let's check it out and see if it fits and if you like it," the volunteer offers. Soon, when all the family's clothing needs are met, the volunteer places the clothes in a shopping bag and then the mother and kids leave. "Thank you for coming," the volunteer adds, "we look forward to seeing you again." By 7:30 P.M., the doors to the Clothes Closet close for the week, and the volunteers gather for worship.

This is a typical Wednesday night for the Kara house church, which is one of the house churches of Trinity Presbyterian Church in Harrisonburg, Virginia. Since it was organized in 1962, Trinity Church has chosen to provide an unusual church experience. Beginning with the organizing pastor, Don Allen, and continuing today under the pastoral leadership of Ann Reed Held, Trinity Church has organized much of its life and mission around house churches modeled on the experience of early Christians of the first three centuries who worshiped in homes.

Each year a call for house churches is made from the pulpit, and members are urged to sign up for the house church of their choice, covenanting to stay with that house church for a full year. Each house church must have a clearly defined mission and a minimum of five members in order to be chartered. Kara house church runs the Clothes Closet; Sojourners house church works with the homeless and maintains an apartment that provides temporary housing; Restoring God's Creation is active in Environmental issues; Friendship house church works with a local senior center; and the AIDS Awareness house church provides support to people affected by AIDS.

Pastor Ann Reed Held and retired Pastor Don Allen spend an evening at the Clothes Closet.

Every house church meets weekly and offers worship, mission, fellowship, and spiritual nurturing. Leadership roles, which are spread among the members, include a pastoral leader, who moderates the meetings; a mission leader, who is responsible for coordinating the mission of the house church; a worship leader, who plans the worship; a fellowship leader, who organizes time for fellowship; and a nurture leader, who plans various study activities.

While most of the house churches rotate among the homes of members, some meet at their place of mission, such as the homeless shelter or a local retirement community. According to Emily, a member of the Kara house church, "This is what church is all about. It's about community and being part of God's family. We discuss our faith, we reach out to others, we come together in worship, and in the process we become close to each other, like an extended family." Amy, also active in the Kara house church, has been a member of the church for only two years. While raised in a Presbyterian church, she lost touch with the church during her college years and didn't attend for several years. After moving to Harrisonburg, she felt something was missing in her life. "It was difficult coming to church for the first time after being gone so long," she recalls, "but it was something I needed in my life." Being a member of Trinity Presbyterian Church has provided Amy with two things that she missed during her years away from the church: worship and the opportunity to serve the people of the community in mission.

"Because our house churches are centered around mission, we attract people with a great diversity of age, background, theological perspective, and economic situation. God brought us together for a reason."

According to pastor Ann Reed Held, "Because our house churches are centered around mission, we attract people with a great diversity of age, background, theological perspective, and economic situation. God brought us together for a reason. We may not agree politically or enjoy the same style of worship, but God has chosen us to be here, so we really need to work together and continually ask, What is God calling us to do?" ■

*"Greet . . . the church in their house."
(Romans 16:5)*

Unexpected change leads family to house church ministry.

Sally and Phil Boucher moved to the Harrisonburg, Virginia, area from a Washington, D.C., suburb when Phil's job as the chief financial officer for a nationally known magazine publisher was lost in a downsizing.

As Phil remembers, "I was totally immersed in my job and often worked seven days a week. The only time I saw our two kids was when they were in their night clothes. When I lost my job it was an incredible adjustment. Just trying to keep busy was a major challenge, and I was overcome by feelings of not being productive. My spirits were extremely low."

The family felt that they needed a change. "Phil was always so busy," Sally remembers, "so it was up to me to raise our children and keep the household together. I was exhausted both physically and spiritually." For over a year after Phil lost his job, he couldn't find work. During that time their faith began to grow as the family pulled together. The family decided that the sudden loss of Phil's job could be an opportunity for a change in lifestyle.

They decided to move to a smaller community in a less stressful area and chose Harrisonburg because of its location in the Shenandoah Valley. Phil opened a golf driving range,

and Sally took a job in public relations with a not-for-profit corporation.

According to Sally, "When we arrived here in 1993 we made a decision to join a church to nurture our spirituality. So we started looking at different churches. The first time we came to Trinity we knew it was different. The people were friendly, the congregation was just the right size, and it was informal. That first Sunday, which was around Christmas time, Trinity Church announced that it would be gathering that evening for caroling. The boys wanted to go so we came back that night and we walked around the community singing Christmas carols. We got to meet a lot of people that night, and soon we joined the church." The family especially enjoyed the opportunity for involvement in a house church, and a couple years later, Sally called the Sojourners house church to work with a local homeless shelter.

Sally has a passion for the homeless. "People don't understand that the homeless are everywhere," she notes, "even in small towns. Many people live one paycheck away from living on the street. Many of the government agencies who, at one time, were acting as safety nets have either had their programs cut or eliminated. What we in the church

do to help is becoming much more important."

Children are a part of many of the house churches at Trinity Church, and Sally and Phil decided that their children would also be part of Sojourners. According to Phil, "It is important to have the kids see people who are living out their faith. Being able to pray in a small group has a lot of impact, especially on the kids because they feel part of a community of faith. They also get to see faith in action as we minister to each other while helping the homeless."

As part of the ministry of the Sojourners house church, their members maintain an apartment called Harbor Room, which Trinity built in the upper level of the church to provide temporary housing for people who find themselves in need. As an ongoing ministry, Sojourners house church members help to maintain the apartment and donate items for people who occupy an apartment at Mercy House, a community-run homeless shelter. According to Sally, "Trinity Presbyterian Church stretches you to get involved in ways that you would never have imagined. In the process your spiritual life grows and your faith gets stronger. We really feel blessed to have found such an incredible church home." ■

John Tracy, Bob Smith, Lloyd Riffe, and Walter Trippe are just a few of the volunteers who work tirelessly to outfit computers for Christian missionaries and other worthy organizations.

SPREADING TECHNOLOGY

Ministry ships thousands of computers worldwide.

Something special is happening in the basement of the First Presbyterian Church of Orlando, Florida. Each morning a dedicated group of volunteers arrives for work, and soon the halls are buzzing with computerese. "Anybody see a motherboard like this before?" "Can we add another sixty-four megs of memory to this?" "Someone just called from Colombia. Are those fifty units ready to go yet?"

In the midst of this constant chaos stands Walter Trippe. In 1989, after retiring from a position with a major defense contractor, Trippe and a friend, George Wilson, decided to donate their time developing software for overseas missionaries. Within a year, they had added a team of volunteers and had branched out into hardware, adapting computers to run on batteries so they could be used in third-world countries lacking reliable electric power. Soon, the hearty band of workers expanded their work even farther, outfitting new and used computers for Christian organizations in the United States and abroad.

Gradually, they realized that shipping computers was not enough. Many missionaries did not have computer skills and, therefore, could not use the equipment they were receiving. So the computer volunteers began offering intensive training in their own lab, often to people who had never used a computer before.

Since 1990, the Computer Ministry of First Presbyterian Church has shipped over five thousand computers. A dedicated core group of over twenty volunteers works during the day, and another dozen volunteers with expertise in specific areas are available during the evenings. Some of the team are Presbyterian, but others are drawn from a variety of churches. Almost all the members of the team are retired, many from technical and engineering positions at a local military contractor. As one volunteer puts it, "In the corporate world we never had the time to do something for others. We spent our careers building advanced weapons systems for the military and are proud to say that these weapons helped maintain peace during difficult times. Now we can help people working in mission along with other Christian organizations to spread the word of peace in a different way."

Walter, who puts in up to sixty hours of week as a volunteer, knows that the computer world is constantly changing. "When we first started," he says, "we worked primarily with missionaries who in many cases had never used a computer before. So we had to teach them how to use a computer before we could give them one." Now most missionaries are computer literate, so the greater need is to provide computers for the schools and churches where the missionaries teach.

The Computer Ministry relies totally on volunteers to provide the labor and expertise. The facility, utilities, telephones, and bookkeeping are provided free of charge by First Presbyterian. Used computers are donated by area companies and are completely refurbished by the volunteers. Those who receive the computers are asked to pay only for parts and shipping costs.

Why do these volunteers give so generously of their time? Some joke that after they retired their spouses wanted them out of the house. Others, more seriously, say that the ministry is about fellowship as well as mission. But, to the many hundreds of missionaries, schools, and Christian groups that have received computers from this ministry, these volunteers are using modern technology to help spread the word of Christ in a fast-paced world. ∎

Volunteers unload yet another shipment of donated computers.

Computer Ministry volunteers give of their time so others can benefit from the gift of technology.

"Go . . . and make disciples of all nations."
(Matthew 28:19)

Declining urban church opens its doors to a new congregation.

One night in 1995, Alika Galloway had a disturbing dream. She was living in Atlanta at the time with her husband, Ralph, and their children. "In the dream, Ralph and I were walking in this dark, dark place. We were holding hands, and things were falling out of the sky. It was a very strange dream." Suddenly Alika woke up and couldn't get back to sleep. She got up to get a glass of water. "While I was standing at the sink, I heard a voice, which to this day I'm convinced was the voice of God. The voice said 'Go back to sleep, you didn't understand that dream.' The voice scared me, but I got back in bed, and soon I was asleep. The dream returned; however this time I let go of Ralph's hand and stuck my hand out. It was snow that was falling from the sky. I started screaming." Alika woke again, and this time she felt she understood the meaning of the dream. She shook Ralph awake and announced, "We're moving to Minnesota." He turned to me and said, "No we're not." I said, "We're moving."

The next morning the phone rang. It was Peter Carlson of Hospitality House, a social service agency in Minnesota. He was calling to offer Ralph the opportunity of applying for the position of executive director. Ralph eventually got the job, unaware at the time that this move to Minnesota would also involve the Galloways in a bold new congregational ministry.

Alika is a third-generation Presbyterian from San Bernadino, California. She married Ralph, a Baptist minister, in 1976, and the couple settled in Ralph's hometown of Minneapolis. After the birth of their first daughter, Iesha, the family moved to Atlanta so Ralph could work on his doctor of ministry degree.

While in Atlanta, Ralph participated in a program called "Urban Training," which was housed in a Presbyterian church. He got to see firsthand the results of Presbyterian support in oppressed and depressed neighborhoods. Impressed by the Presbyterian belief in social justice, Ralph decided to become a Presbyterian minister. In the meantime, Alika herself had felt the call to ministry and started attending Johnson C. Smith seminary. "We loved Atlanta," Alika recalls. "There are seven African American Presbyterian churches there. We learned what it was to be both African American and Presbyterian, which is something we would have never experienced in Minneapolis, because it doesn't have any predominately African American Presbyterian churches.

Around the same time that the Galloways moved back to Minneapolis, Highland Park Presbyterian Church, a century-old urban congregation with a dwindling, mostly white congregation, was prayerfully looking at ways to continue its ministry. According to elder John Ivers, a lifelong member, the church had fallen on hard times. "Growing up, this was my neighborhood. I can remember during the fifties we had over five hundred members, mostly due to the post-war baby boom. But then during the sixties, when housing prices in the suburbs became attractive and highways made it possible to live on the outskirts of town, the membership gradually began to fall. By the mid-seventies, we had only around 250 members, and those people were older. Their kids had moved away and no longer wanted to attend a church located in a run-down urban setting."

"We were a dying church. In the past we had tried to open our doors to the neighborhood, but nobody came."

By the mid-nineties, only seventy-two members remained, and it was feared that the church was critically ill. The presbytery funded a probe to determine what would be in the best interest of the neighborhood, which was racially mixed. After prayer and reflection, a recommendation was made to preserve the Highland Park Church but also to start a new congregation in the same building. The new church, named Kwanzaa Community Presbyterian Church, would concentrate on attracting the people of the neighborhood, who were mostly African American. "Something needed to be done," John says. "We were a dying church. In the past we had tried to open our doors to the neighborhood, but nobody came. Now we know that our approach was wrong. We were inviting them to worship like us instead of asking people to come and worship in the manner in which they were most comfortable."

A dream led Alika and Ralph Galloway from Atlanta to Minneapolis.

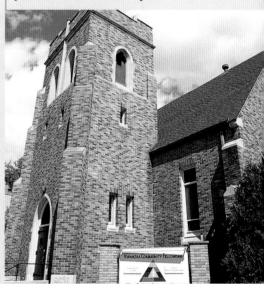

Kwanzaa Community Presbyterian Church is located in the former Highland Presbyterian Church in an urban neighborhood of Minneapolis.

Alika Galloway watches while John Ivers mounts a plaque commemorating the Highland Park Presbyterian Church.

Kwanzaa co-pastors, Ralph and Alika Galloway, stand in front of the former Highland Park church.

In January 1998, the first worship services were held in the Kwanzaa church. Ralph and Alika were called as co-pastors, with Ralph working part-time at the church while still handling his full-time responsibilities at Hospitality House. Alika remembers, "At first we had trouble getting people to attend. Now we are gradually growing with almost eighty at worship on Sunday."

At the end of May 1999 as a testimony to their faith, the members of Highland Park Presbyterian Church ended their ministry after 115 years and gave their church and all its contents to the Kwanzaa church. "Our members are thrilled to see that this church will stay in the neighborhood," John says. "We feel our legacy will be that the church existed to serve the community. This allows the church to continue. After all, we're not in charge here, God is. The timing of this exciting new ministry couldn't be better."

Alika adds, "This is truly a gift from God, that people would actually open their hearts and give this church to the community. That's what the congregation of Highland Park is saying to us, that God's love for the community is consistent and persistent. They understood the needs of the neighborhood and had the courage to make this new church happen, even at the expense of their own ministry."

The members of Kwanzaa feel they are being called to rebuild the spirituality of the community. Many encouraging things are happening. Through community organizing, people are starting to take more pride in their neighborhood: Lawns are starting to be cared for, litter in the streets is disappearing, and affordable housing is being planned. Ralph talks about the need for recovery. "For years there was a loss of faith, self-esteem, and pride. We are in a transition area. People are starting to come back to the church and a lot of good things are happening. There is still plenty of work ahead of us, but a new energy is emerging and we look forward to a bright future." ∎

"I the LORD . . . speak to them in dreams." (Numbers 12:6)

THE **HEALING** TOUCH

Healing ministry transforms the spiritual life of congregation.

A healing ministry? For many people, the very idea conjures up images of tent revivals and televangelists dramatically curing the afflicted on cue.

The Gospels, however, make numerous references to the healing ministry of Jesus. Jesus healed not only those with diseases of the body but also those with mental and spiritual illnesses. Moreover, he commissioned the apostles to provide healing in his name, and consequently, healing became an essential part of the ministry of the church. As modern medical science became more sophisticated, though, healing as part of the spiritual journey was increasingly neglected, even looked upon with disfavor.

However, spiritual healing is alive and well at All Souls Parish in Port Chester, New York, a small bedroom community just north of New York City. According to pastor Deborah Rundlett, "Our belief is that Christ desires

Pastor Deborah Rundlett, shown with daughter Elizabeth Greenwood, has seen her spiritual life touched by the healing ministry.

A Testament to God's Healing Power

Ellen, a long-time member of All Souls Parish, was diagnosed with cancer. Her healing journey inspired the congregation, as she continued to sing every week with the choir. Even though her body was dying, her spirit stayed strong. Ellen was especially touched by the choir's chanted prayers for healing, and her favorite included the affirmation, "My soul is at rest in God alone, my salvation comes from God."

"Ellen was an incredible testament to faith and living in the moment" Pastor Deborah Rundlett remembers. "Toward the end, when she could no longer stand on her own, the other choir members would help her up so she could sing with them. She touched everyone's heart. Physical healing was not in God's plan, but spiritual healing certainly was, and she lived life to the fullest right until the end."

wholeness for all people, and healing is an integral part of that ministry. We also recognize that a physical cure is not always part of the journey. It is God who ultimately determines the terms and pace of the healing."

The healing ministry at All Souls was begun in 1997 when a task force was formed to study the role of healing in the life of the church today. Through discussion and prayer, the task force sought to discern God's will for this kind of ministry and to explore the possibility that God is calling people in our time to the work of healing. Several people in the congregation responded to that call and, after extensive training, were commissioned as healing ministers. Now, each Sunday after worship, the healing ministry team is available for prayer, for laying on of hands, and to offer love and support to all who have a need or concern.

"Our church has been transformed by the healing ministry," Debbie explains. "We were an aging church that had to make a decision whether to live or die. Many of our older members were suffering from a host of diseases and other ailments. There were cancer patients, heart surgery survivors, and people who had recently experienced the loss of a spouse. The healing ministry seemed well-suited for both our established members and the younger people we were hoping to reach." While the healing ministry is important, it is not meant as a replacement for traditional medicine, which Christians see as a gift from God. Spiritual healing goes hand-in-hand with traditional medicine.

"Our healing ministry allows us . . . to be channels for God's love."

Not all suffering, however, is physical. Sometimes people struggle with loneliness, a breakdown in relationships, or a loss of faith, and the church's healing ministry addresses these needs also. As one member puts it, "Our healing ministry allows us to reach out and touch people who are struggling and to be channels for God's love."

The healing ministry is central to the worship at All Souls. The choir sings healing chants from the Taizé chant book, and the congregation is invited to join in open prayer requests and personal testimony. Healing ministers are available at the conclusion of worship for personal prayer and the laying on of hands. In addition to regular Sunday worship, periodic healing services are offered several times a year, featuring powerful testimony from those whose lives have been touched by the healing ministry.

As one of the healing ministers shares, "This has been a wonderful experience for each of us. People of many faiths have been drawn to our ministry with some traveling great distances to join us. It is very gratifying to see people who are looking for a personal relationship with the Lord finding our worship and ministries helpful." ■

". . . pray for one another, so that you may be healed." (James 5:16)

WARM SMILES AND HOT COFFEE

Burger King ministry in Opelika, Alabama, brings the church to the people.

Sitting in the corner of the Burger King in Opelika, Alabama, is a large man with an athletic build, sipping on a cup of coffee. In front of him are the tools of his trade: a note pad, a stack of papers, and a Bible. A young woman approaches. Obviously distraught, she sits down and begins to talk. Her face is wet with tears that are streaming down her face. Several minutes pass and finally a hint of a smile appears. Before she gets up to leave they bow their heads in prayer. It is a typical morning in the life of the Burger King ministry of Opelika's First Presbyterian Church.

It all started about twenty-one years ago when Jim Bankhead accepted the call to this eastern Alabama town of thirty thousand. Unable to find the time to prepare his sermons amid the constant disruptions in the church, Jim sought a place close by where he could be anonymous and work on his weekly message. After trying several restaurants he settled on the local Burger King, not knowing that his place of refuge would soon be transformed into a ministry.

All through his life, Jim has been pursuing a different type of ministry. A ministry not confined to the four walls of the church building but one that extends into the community. His faith journey started during high school when, probably to the shock of his classmates, he arose from his seat at a Billy Graham

crusade in Charlotte, North Carolina, and approached the stage. Later in the parking lot he felt, to quote John Wesley, "strangely warmed." Today he sees it as God's grace. In college, Jim was a three-sport, lettered athlete on a full scholarship at Presbyterian College in Clinton, South Carolina. He never considered the ministry and, instead, saw himself as an athlete. But Jim was troubled about what profession to choose after graduation. At a friend's wedding, he met a pastor who had recently returned from the Peace Corp. The pastor confided that he had gone to seminary to "get his head straight." "It was a steering moment for me," Jim recalls, "those words kept coming back to me. I had never considered the seminary and always felt it was a place for people who had an understanding of their faith and not a place to sort things out."

Upon graduation Jim received a full scholarship to attend Columbia Theological Seminary in Decatur, Georgia. In seminary, he spent his time playing touch football and basketball instead of concentrating on his studies. All this time he struggled with the question, what is a Christian? The more he read, the more confused he became. Then one day Jim read about what it was to be a disciple or learner. "I immediately was touched by the meaning of the word 'disciple' and felt it fit me personally."

When summer recess came, Jim took a job with Young Life working with troubled inner-city youth in a ranching program in Colorado. The rugged, outdoor atmosphere appealed to him. "It wasn't church-like," Jim remembers. "I saw hardened street kids coming to Christ. It was a great experience." However, he also saw a problem with the short-term nature of the program. "The tragedy of this type of program is that after these kids get home and back on the street, much of what they've learned is wiped away and they return to their previous behavior. As a society the challenge is how to help these kids to live their faith when the conditions in which they live their lives is militantly opposed to the teachings of the Bible."

After his experience with Young Life, Jim decided to take a year off from seminary to research the questions he had about Christianity, the Holy Spirit, and his own life's direction. During that year he studied scripture and married his wife, Cissy, who "Listened to my heart and helped me to understand my call." The next year when Jim returned to seminary it was with a renewed sense of purpose. "I crammed three years of seminary into my last year." Upon graduation from seminary he served as a solo pastor in two country churches in South Carolina, as an associate in Atlanta, and as an associate in Dallas, Texas, before being called to Opelika.

Once in Opelika, Jim discovered that he could combine the work he did in Young Life with his daily pastoral duties. As the pastor of a local church he could create an environment for nurturing both adults and children as they grow in their faith. The Burger King ministry allows that nurturing to extend into the heart of the community.

Jim's table at Burger King is a gathering place for those desiring a spiritual connection.

Over the years the Burger King ministry has provided a terrific opportunity for those who are uncomfortable with church buildings to sit down and have a meaningful conversation about their lives and their faith. "I remember when I first started coming here," Jim recalls. "There was an employee who was suspicious of me. She thought I was a spy from Burger King who was checking up on them. She actually went through the garbage and checked out my discarded papers. Once she discovered that the papers were actually drafts of sermons she sat down and talked with me. Now she's an active member of our church."

"Another time a woman came in and told me that she was carrying a gun and was going to threaten her abusive husband with it. I asked her if it was loaded and she said it wasn't. She was just going to scare him with it. I told her that if she waved that gun at him and he found out it wasn't loaded, he would probably kill her. I also told her, on another occasion, that if she ever loaded it and shot someone, I wouldn't visit her in jail. Today this wonderful woman has turned her life around, moved out of subsidized housing, and teaches Sunday school in the church. She has also extended her ministry beyond the church and reaches out to others, many of whom live in the projects." Events that touch Jim's heart in Burger King often find their way into his Sunday sermons. This allows the ministry to touch the lives of the members of Opelika's First Presbyterian Church. The ministry is a very important outreach for the church, and members often refer to Burger King as "the home office." Jim puts it another way, "We use our church building for worship and preparing ourselves for ministry. What happens at Burger King is simply putting those words into action." ∎

"Go . . . into the main streets, and invite everyone you find . . ." (Matthew 22:9)

Mark Epperson accompanies the
Bridges class in singing praise songs.

MAKING A CONNECTION

Bridges class unites young single adults through scripture, praise music, and fellowship.

One by one they enter. Some hold cups filled with espresso, others are carrying boxes of bagels. At first there is a time of fellowship as people catch up on the happenings in their lives. Then, as the conversations continue, Mark Woody, the praise music leader, picks up his guitar and begins the first praise song. The talk turns to song as people begin to join in, and soon everyone is singing. After a few songs, Mark Epperson, the director of young adult ministries, steps to the front and leads the group in prayer. Reading of scripture follows and, then, either a discussion of what the scripture says to each participant or a talk on scripture aided by overheads, videos, or other visual aids. The hour ends with prayer and more praise music.

This is a typical meeting of the Bridges class, a ministry for young adults in their twenties who live in and around the Colorado Springs area. With a database of over three hundred people, Bridges attracts nearly ninety people on Sunday mornings and another sixty for Bible study on Monday nights.

But Bridges is more than just a class; it is also an opportunity for fellowship and mission trips. According to Mark, "This is a connection to the Church, a church that often misses this generation in a transitional time in their lives between college and marriage. This can be a difficult time. Thoughts like 'What am I going to do with the rest of my life' and 'I feel a need to be connected

"The goal of Bridges is to have fun while serving the Lord and living a Christian life. We really have a good time."

Class members Greg Lazor, Ben Hall, and David Stotts enjoy the fellowship and spiritual community Bridges provides.

with others who understand where I'm coming from' can be foremost in their minds. In Bridges we have a great time getting to know each other while exploring what it means to walk with Jesus in today's world."

Besides the Sunday and Monday classes, Bridges offers a chance to get involved in mission trips, many of which involve travel to other countries. One trip was to Mexico to help build a house. Another was to Cairo to build relationships with Christians in Egypt. Mark describes the goal of mission as "an opportunity to see another country, meet new people, see how God's church is functioning, and begin to think about what it is to serve the Lord. It's also fun." Social events are often organized around a theme, such as a ski outing or a murder mystery night with people dressing up in costume. Mark says, "Our goal is to have fun while serving the Lord and living a Christian life. We really have a good time."

Bridges also offers an opportunity to do community mission work in Colorado Springs. These opportunities include anything from working at a local soup kitchen to helping in a battered women's shelter. Local mission projects help people get involved without their having to make a major commitment in time. "Our greatest hope is that the people who come to Bridges eventually get involved in the larger life of the church," observes Mark, "that they participate in worship and connect to God in deep ways." ■

The sanctuary of First Presbyterian Church of Colorado Springs is filled to capacity for three identical worship services that blend both traditional and contemporary styles of worship.

"Worship the LORD with gladness . . ." (Psalm 100:2)

Presbyterian-Jewish alliance lifts up the hopes of area young people.

It all began in early 1990, when Chris Hexster, a Jewish lawyer, met with Bill Gillespie, a Presbyterian minister. Gillespie was the minister at the Cote Brilliante Presbyterian Church in St. Louis, and Hexster was a member of Central Reformed Synagogue in the same neighborhood, an area scarred by poverty, crime, loss of self-respect, and a lack of educational opportunities. In the 1960s, both of these men had been involved in the civil rights movement, marching with Martin Luther King in Selma.

As the two talked, they remembered how the civil rights movement involved people of all races working together for a better society. Gradually, an idea began to take shape. Wouldn't it be great to recapture some of the dedication and passion of the movement today in order to make a difference in their own troubled neighborhood?

In 1956, Bill Gillespie was a young minister, and he used his energies to help open Cote Brilliante Presbyterian Church, a nonsegregated congregation in St. Louis's central city. Its membership, mostly African American, was dedicated both to increasing their faith and to improving their educational and economic conditions. The church's ministry was effective, and the membership flourished. Now, however, many of the original members have left the neighborhood and commute to the church from other areas. Their former homes, which are mostly owned by absentee landlords, have become run-down, and the new tenants struggle with similar challenges to those the former residents faced years before.

Growing out of the meeting between Gillespie and Hexster, an alliance was formed between the two congregations—Presbyterian and Jewish. The dream was to create programs that would lift up the hopes of the neighborhood and make a difference in people's lives, and a decision was made to concentrate on the future of the neighborhood, the young people. A joint oversight committee was established, and volunteers were recruited from both congregations who immediately began donating time tutoring and mentoring students, running after-school programs, and leading scouting groups. Their approach to community development has become so successful that over one hundred other churches in the St. Louis area are adopting this model for outreach into their communities.

Cote Brilliante Presbyterian Church and Central Reformed Synagogue have further strengthened their relationship by building habitat houses together, assisting victims of burned-out homes, establishing food banks, and helping people with special physical challenges. According to Gillespie, "traditionally the Jewish and African American communities have had much in common. Both have suffered greatly at the hands of others and still face discrimination. But during all the suffering, they found that others could take their rights away but they couldn't take away their faith. This has created a natural bond between the two groups." ■

"God . . . has given us the ministry of reconciliation . . . ." (2 Corinthians 5:18)

Melissa Williams receives help with her school work from Marilyn Smith.

Being A Mentor

Marilyn Smith is a volunteer in the mentoring program. She initially got involved to demonstrate that African Americans were interested in working together to make a difference in their communities. During her eight years as a mentor she has worked with several children. According to Marilyn, "Being a mentor is very rewarding. The happy looks on their faces and hugs of appreciation along with the opportunity to do new and exciting things has made the mentoring program invaluable to the mentors and the children alike. It's a way to make a significant difference in a child's life."

Arts and crafts summer program participants enjoy their time together after returning from a field trip.

The Reverend William Gillespie spends time with summer day camp students.

BEING THERE FOR **EACH OTHER**

To this day, Anita Gayette can't remember exactly what happened. She recalls that she was driving with her husband, Andy, back to Lemmon, South Dakota, from a trip downstate. The next thing she knew she was lying in the hospital emergency room being told that her husband had died at the scene of the accident. "Andy and I did everything together," Anita says. "He was only forty-two when he died, and I remember telling my sister when she first arrived at the hospital that Andy and I were supposed to grow old together and that I had never imagined living my life without him."

At first, family, friends, and the members of her church were there for Anita, but after the funeral, her mother and one of her sisters had to return to Sioux Falls, South Dakota, four hundred miles away, and later her other sister returned to Arizona and her son, Michael, returned to school. "Pretty soon," Anita recalls, "I was at home alone with the cat, trying to let time and prayers help me recover." One day, the phone rang. It was a woman named Chris Block, who had lost her husband to a heart attack the previous year, inviting Anita to meet her for coffee. "Getting that call from Chris was a godsend," Anita remembers. "Over coffee we were able to talk about our common bond. She knew exactly what I was going through, since her husband had passed away just over a year earlier. I needed someone who would just sit with me and listen. Talking with her made an impossible situation more bearable. She understood my pain, my frustration, and my anger."

The Widowed Persons Services is a support group that provides one-on-one counseling by volunteers who have also lost a spouse. Developed by the American Association of Retired Persons and provided as an ecumenical ministry of the Spencer Memorial Presbyterian Church of Lemmon, South Dakota, the Widowed Persons Services was brought to the area by Reverend Kenneth Meunier, the church's pastor, and one of the first volunteers was Alice Ashmore, who had lost her husband several years earlier. Volunteers contact people who are newly widowed and provide support and friendship for at least the first year after the loss. As Chris explains, "We become involved after the family and friends have gone on with their lives, thinking the widowed person is doing better. We know from experience that this is not true. Widowed people are experiencing a variety of emotions and need support for at least a year after their loss. We understand that because we have all faced the same thing."

When Gene Block, Chris's husband, died, it was a shock, even though he had experienced chest pains once about two weeks before. As a nurse, Chris knew the importance of early medical attention. "When Gene felt chest pains, I rushed him to the hospital, and after several tests, he was released, because they couldn't find any problems," Chris remembers. Two weeks later, Gene had

after the loss of a spouse.

a massive heart attack while at work. "When I arrived at the hospital," Chris recalls, "my three children and I were taken to a private room. A few minutes later a doctor called me into the hallway to tell me that Gene was getting CPR. Then, awhile later, he met with me in the hallway again and told me Gene was dead and that I needed to tell my children. I remember looking at him and saying, 'How can I tell my children that their father is dead?' I was angry at the health system, which had just told us a couple of weeks before that Gene was going to be fine. He was only forty years old. This couldn't be happening to us."

A few months after Gene died, Chris received a letter from Alice. She remembers thinking, "I didn't even know that Widowed Persons Services existed. When I received that letter from Alice and then met with her, I understood the common bond we had." For the next year, Alice and Chris met or talked by phone on a regular basis. "Only Alice understood what I was going through," Chris remembers. "When a special holiday or date came along, like Valentine's Day, Christmas holidays, Gene's birthday, or our anniversary, I'd either get a phone call or a letter from Alice. Words can't describe how much she helped me."

A year later, Chris became involved in the Widowed Persons Services as a volunteer, because she appreciated what they had done for her. Anita was her first referral. Both Chris and Anita have come a long way since the loss of their husbands. However, at times things can still be difficult. According to Anita, "I still have a lot of anger, mostly directed at myself because I was driving the car when it crashed. My memory of the accident still is missing. Part of that could be shock, the other may be because it might be too painful to remember. Three years later I still have my good days and my bad days. But as time passes, things are getting better."

"I don't think closure ever happens," Chris says. "There are still times of the year and moments of each day when I think of Gene. Even little things can affect me, like seeing couples together at a restaurant or going to a family event. But you somehow get through it. You just hang on and things gradually get better. It's all you can do."

Anita has some advice for people who are wondering how to deal with a person who has just lost a partner. "Don't ask them how they are doing. The pain is so intense and they hurt so much, there is nothing you can do to help relieve their suffering. Instead, just ask if you can help in any way and be specific. For example, I'm going to bring a meal over tomorrow or I'll take care of your kids so you can go shopping. Another thing that helped me was when people came up to me and gave me a hug or said they were praying for me. That was very comforting." ■

Chris Block and Anita Gayette are volunteers for Widowed Persons Services, an ecumenical support group that reaches out to people who have recently experienced the loss of a spouse.

"Religion that is pure . . . is this: to care for orphans and widows in their distress . . ." (James 1:27)

AN ISLAND OF HOPE

The Stewpot serves hot meals along with offering services to the homeless of Dallas.

One day in the mid-1970s, a homeless man came into First Presbyterian Church of Dallas and asked for food. The pastor at the time, Jack Moore, went to the food pantry and was surprised to see that only a single can of beans was on the shelf. He gave it to the man who promptly left. A few minutes later, Pastor Moore looked out of his office window and was shocked to see the man sitting on the church steps trying to open the can with his pocket knife. He made a promise to himself that never again would a person needing food be treated with such indignity.

The idea for the Stewpot was born that day, and soon, through the gift of a donor, the church was serving hot food to the homeless in the church basement. As word got out on the street and more homeless found out about the Stewpot, additional room was needed. So it was moved from the church basement to the gymnasium, then to the church parking garage and finally to its current location in its own building across from the church.

Providing food is still the primary function of the Stewpot, but over the years many other services have been added. One of the most successful is the dental clinic, a fully outfitted dental facility, with x-ray and other modern equipment, staffed by a local group of dentists. So far, over seventeen thousand patients have been served. The Stewpot operates under the direction of the Reverend Bruce Buchanan, an associate pastor of First Presbyterian Church, who has served in this capacity since 1987 and who describes the ministry by saying, "We are part of the community safety net. One of our specialties is providing roots for rootless people."

The Stewpot includes a postal station for the homeless clients, a job referral agency, and a photo identification service. Client pictures are taken and a photo identification card is produced. Each card is then added to a database of over fifteen thousand cards and used to provide the documentation needed for employment and next-of-kin information in case of death, illness, or inquiries from families around the country.

Originally Stewpot meals were served in a room filled with long tables, but this arrangement reminded the guests of the impersonal treatment they

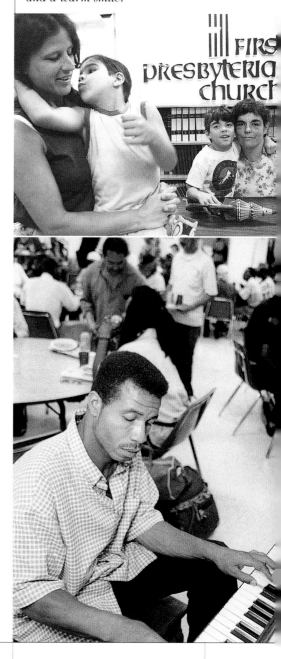

Below:
The face of homelessness is often young families.

Mealtime at the Stewpot is a time for fellowship, a hot meal, and a warm smile.

Volunteers often comment that it is they who get the most out of the ministry of the Stewpot.

Below:
Among the services provided by the Stewpot are arts and crafts along with a fully staffed dental clinic.

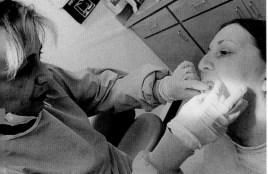

received in prison or in some other institutions, and frequently fights would occur. "I remember one day," recalls Bruce, "when a police officer dragged a guest who was fighting into the street in order to quiet him down and, when that didn't work, put his service revolver against his head. I knew we had to do something to change things." So, the Stewpot moved into a new facility and changed the atmosphere. They replaced the long tables with smaller round tables, which created a sense of community and invited more conversation. Salads and desserts were added to most of the meals, to make them more home-like. Now fights are very rare.

Volunteers from many Dallas churches, businesses, and schools do the bulk of the work at the Stewpot, and each is trained to follow the Golden Rule, treating other people the way they themselves would want to be treated. Guests are greeted with a smile, served their meals cafeteria style, and have their beverages refilled at the tables by volunteers. Meals are accompanied by live piano music, played by talented musicians who also are homeless. Each person is thanked for coming to the Stewpot and wished a good day.

Many of the volunteers have served at the Stewpot for several years, and when asked why they volunteer they say that they get more out of it then they give. Theirs is a testament to what giving is all about—the more we give, the more we receive. The Stewpot is a place where people can practice their faith. ■

"For the LORD your God . . . loves the strangers, providing them food and clothing."
(Deuteronomy 10:17-18)

A Lost Lamb

The Reverend Bruce Buchanan, Director of the Stewpot in Dallas, Texas, does more than just feed the hungry—he cares deeply about them.

"His name is Richard," states Bruce Buchanan, recalling one Stewpot client who really touched his heart. "He stands six feet, six inches tall, and his problem is his temper. We were unsure how to best work with him since he had been the cause of numerous fights. One day I took him into my office and began to explain what we were trying to do at the Stewpot and what we needed from him. As I spoke, Richard began to weep. It was as if it was one of the first times in his life that someone had reached out to him."

It was after that pivotal conversation that the Stewpot offered Richard a second chance—true to its motto: "We serve second chances." Since the Stewpot has sought to be creative and appropriately responsive to the great variety of human needs, Bruce had an idea. A local three-on-three basketball tournament was planned, so Bruce invited Richard to put together a team. But on the day of the tournament, only Richard showed up to play. The next year, Bruce tried again. However, this time Richard quickly got into an angry argument with an official, and his team was abruptly disqualified.

Over the years the Stewpot offered some incentive in exchange for a step forward from Richard. Favors were exchanged for psychiatric exams, completed job applications, and other rehabilitative steps. While some advances were made, Richard's temper was never successfully capped or channeled. After getting caught in a street fight with a broken bottle as his weapon, Richard landed back in jail.

Years passed and on a cold winter's day not long ago, Richard showed up at the Stewpot, a free man, coatless and shivering. Bruce found him a warm coat, and they sat down and talked about his future. The conversation was filled with quick promises and repeated pledges from the past. When Bruce thinks of Richard, he says, "I am reminded of the parable of the lost lamb and how the shepherd left his flock to find the one that was lost. Richard is my lost lamb. He is in a downward cycle, and we'll try to be there for him and keep him in our prayers. We'll continue to hope that our Good Shepherd rescues him before he becomes a fatality of the street." ■

HIGH PLAINS OASIS

Isolated community church serves people of all denominations

Most people will never venture to Whitlash, Montana. Getting there requires hours of travel through the northern Montana plains, culminating in a forty-mile rough-and-tumble ride over gravel roads. Once there, one finds that Whitlash consists of a few buildings and a corral surrounded by rolling prairie and three nearby mountains. In the middle of this isolated setting is the Whitlash Community Presbyterian Church, which serves people of all denominations who live both in northern Montana and over the border in Canada, about six miles away. According to longtime member Jeanette Brown, "This is our community church, and many who come are not Presbyterian. We don't care about a person's denomination. We care about the person. When I taught Sunday school we had more Catholic kids than Presbyterians." At the Whitlash church, community is at the core, and people travel for miles to attend. One family has been coming for three generations and drives to church more than twenty-five miles along dirt roads. The faith community comes alive as people come to worship together and then gather to catch up on local news, many times over a potluck dinner.

Ranching life today is difficult. The price that ranchers receive for their cattle is lower now than it was a few decades ago. To make ends meet means investing in expensive equipment and working more acreage. It is not uncommon

The Whitlash Community Presbyterian Church has welcomed people of all faiths for years.

living on both sides of the border.

for one person to work ten thousand acres—over half the size of Manhattan—with a single piece of equipment. One rancher lamented that today's consumers have no idea where their food comes from. "They think milk comes from a carton, potatoes come from a bag, and a hamburger comes from a drive-thru window of a fast food restaurant." Yet for all its hardships, nothing can compare to life on a ranch, with its open spaces, traditional values, and an understanding of what it means to help a neighbor. However as ranches continue to get bigger, there are fewer people to support local businesses and schools. "Our population is falling," notes one resident, "which means no farm implement dealers, hardware stores, or supermarkets." In fact the closest food store is over forty miles away, and traveling to a department store means making a several-hour trip.

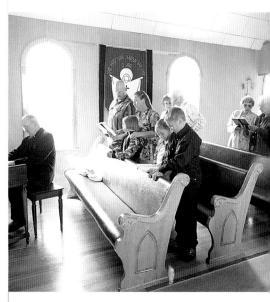

A community of believers comes together to praise God, care for each other, and enjoy fellowship.

Retired rancher Irvin Brown remembers his years growing up: "In my day we worked a fraction of the land that my son works today. Back then, we hired lots of people to help, especially during harvest. Now my son works over ten thousand acres and supports two families, ours and his. However, our ranch provides enough food to feed hundreds of people."

The Suttons, Jim and Gayle, are examples of the survival spirit that still lives in the West in the younger families. "My husband's grandparents came here in the late 1800s as homesteaders. Our ranch is small by today's standards, only twenty-seven hundred acres, and is owned by Jim's father, Robert Sutton. We don't ranch it; instead Robert leases the land to our neighbor who raises cattle on it." The Suttons make their living as wood brokers in a business they own in Wisconsin. In their spare time, the Suttons raise a few horses. Church is important to them. "We love our church," says Gayle. It's our place to give thanks, praise the Lord, and then catch up on what's happening."

An occasional visitor to Whitlash Community Church, Michael Eayrs, a brother of Gayle's from Kalispell, Montana, speaks of his experience growing up. "I was acquainted with those who went from being part of the counterculture of the late sixties and early seventies to being the yuppies of the late eighties. They always did what felt good at the time, and nothing worked. Finding real value in life was hard. Finally, I think many of these people are coming around to understand that the only thing of value in life is eternal. Life is not about self. It is about glorifying God. It has taken a lot of years to understand this, and unfortunately many of our generation never will. I think when you live in the open spaces of Montana, like the generations of people in Whitlash have, you are more likely to understand things that are spiritual. ■

"The wilderness . . . shall be glad . . ." (Isaiah 35:1)

John and Jeannie Fauerbach and
sons, Michael and Johnny, pose on
the Montana-Canada border.

Young couple moves from Broadway to Paradise.

Many of the people who live in the plains of Montana have lived there for generations. Jeannie and John Fauerbach are exceptions. Both were raised in a working-class neighborhood in Philadelphia and were friends while growing up. After school, they each went their separate ways, but several years ago Jeannie and John were reunited, their friendship grew, and they married. The couple shared a dream—to get away from the hectic lifestyle and congestion of the East Coast for a new life in an isolated area.

After much research and travel, they decided to move to the plains of Montana, which offered a slower pace and open spaces. After John found work in the Whitlash area, the couple moved west. "We'll never forget that first white-knuckle trip, fishtailing down the dirt roads leading to Whitlash," John remembers. "But once we arrived we felt like we were finally home. However, because we were used to big city living, it took time to slow down and adjust to our new lifestyle. The mentality of independent Montana ranchers is not the same as networking city types. But gradually our attitudes changed and soon we felt like we belonged."

When they moved west, matters of faith were not a high priority for the Fauerbachs, but the cold, hard Montana winters afforded them time for spiritual reflection. John began to read his Bible regularly, and Jeannie began to ask questions of faith. Then one night over dinner their lives changed when Jeannie asked, "John, what does it mean to be saved?" That night Jeannie turned her life over to Christ, and John recommitted himself to the Lord. What followed was a time of spiritual discovery. They made calls to the Billy Graham Crusade, and John completed a Salvation Army correspondence course on the Bible.

Miles from the nearest paved road, Main Street, Whitlash, is often used for cattle drives.

They had been attending the Whitlash Community Presbyterian Church. John récalls his feelings about going to the Whitlash church. "I once visited a Presbyterian church in Iowa. All the men seemed to be dressed in the same dark suits and white shirts. The place seemed very proper and cold. I left thinking that I'd never be a Presbyterian. But in Whitlash there was no choice, so Jeannie and I studied what it meant to be Presbyterian and learned about some of the struggles in the denomination in regard to some controversial issues. We felt that joining the Presbyterian Church would run counter to our beliefs." Jeannie and John continued to be involved in the life of the church. Then one day, after much prayer and contemplation, it occurred to them that the Holy Spirit was alive and at work in the Whitlash Community Presbyterian Church and they were being called to join.

Since that time, Jeannie and John have become active members, with John serving as elder and clerk of session, attending Glacier Presbytery meetings, and teaching Bible study. Jeannie, who also serves on session, felt called to teach children's church and act as director of Christian education. They were also blessed with two sons. John says, "God has performed many wonders in our lives. Our faith has been strengthened through study, prayer, worship, and Christian fellowship. We have been led to open our home to missionaries to Russia and Scotland, representatives from Mongolia, and people of various denominations."

Each year Jeannie and John host a Christmas party. It follows the prairie Christmas caroling, which according to John, "consists of a caravan of 4 x 4s sometimes covering over sixty miles of dirt and gravel roads to bring the news of our savior's birth and the love of our Lord into the homes of our neighbors."

The ecumenical life of the Whitlash church can be best summarized by a recent ceremony where Jeannie and John restated their wedding vows on their tenth anniversary. As John recalls, "The opening and closing prayers were offered by a Salvation Army Captain, the Moravian ceremony was performed by the church's former pastor who is Anglican, and the sermon was given by their current pastor who is Evangelical. Sitting in the pews were a host of friends and neighbors of several denominations and backgrounds, including Baptist, Four Square, Mennonite, Catholic, and Presbyterian, and it all took place in our little Presbyterian church." ■

BRINGING HOPE

Storefront ministry is a sanctuary to the residents of a run-down urban neighborhood.

The Peoples Ministry in Christ is a storefront ministry in a decrepit, crime-infested neighborhood of Rochester, New York. In 1989, the only Presbyterian church in the neighborhood closed its doors, but not wanting to abandon the neighborhood, the presbytery in the Rochester area, Genesee Valley, decided to investigate other possibilities. In 1993 the Reverend Fritz Longabaugh was called to move into the neighborhood and start a street ministry.

At first, Fritz walked the streets with his guitar in hand and his dog by his side. He met the people of the neighborhood, learned of their challenges, and offered them counsel. A couple years later, a storefront was rented in order to hold Sunday worship, conduct Bible study, and provide an island of hope and refuge.

Often Fritz was asked to speak at area churches, and one Sunday he preached at the Third Presbyterian Church of Rochester. During the service, a check for the storefront ministry was presented to him, and he became indignant. "Our ministry is not a charity," he protested. "I am looking for a real partnership and want volunteers who are willing to become missionaries in the inner city. A check does not make a partnership, so I can't take it." With that, Fritz placed the check on the pulpit and left the church. Many of the members were angered by Fritz's words, but a few were energized, and a committee was formed to decide how to respond to Fritz's request for a partnership. After much thought and prayer, the church decided to support the ministry with volunteers and funding.

Bob Graham, a member of Third Presbyterian Church who now works as a volunteer in the storefront ministry, states, "The Peoples Ministry in Christ provides hope and support to residents of the area, many of whom suffer from a loss of self-esteem due to poverty, drug or alcohol abuse, infirmity, or other circumstances. The vision was to call a pastor who would live and work on the streets. At first many of us were complacent, but when Fritz challenged us to come down and volunteer, many of us responded. After going there a couple of times I was hooked."

Carmen is a testament to the ministry. A recovering drug and alcohol abuser, she says the ministry has meant much to her. "The reason

Steven Behnke worships at the Peoples Ministry in Christ.

Gladys Draper, who works in a laundromat, is an active member of Peoples Ministry in Christ of Rochester, New York.

Members of Peoples Ministry in Christ gather outside the nearby laundromat.

Dr. Val Fowler is stated clerk of the presbytery of Genesee Valley and pastor of the First Presbyterian Church of Chili, New York. The presbytery along with area churches help provide funding for the Peoples Ministry in Christ.

I came in here was because I was scared. I felt abandoned, abused, and ashamed. There was no purpose to my life. I remember saying, 'Get me straight, get me clean, get me happy.' This is where my life started, right here. I'm going for a new life, and it helps to be able to come here and pray, because I can't do it by myself. I work at a laundromat, and everyone who comes in there knows I come to this church because I talk to everybody. They tell me about their problems and after they finish, I say, 'You've got to pray because when you do, God hears you.' I owe my recovery to this church and the people here. Now when I cry it's because I'm happy. Nobody knows how happy I am right now. That's what church is all about. God says the kingdom is within you. Knowing that gives me peace."

Another member, Sharon, recalls her experience. "I met Fritz while I was walking down the street. He was playing his guitar one night, and he had his dog with him. He was just singing away. So I went up and talked to him. I was going through a divorce at the time and he really helped me. He was there for me and continues to help me. Right now I have cancer and face an operation next week. I know the people in this church will be there for me and help in my recovery."

When Fritz talks about the ministry, he speaks with passion and intensity. "We've come a long way in the last few years, but there is still an incredible amount of work that needs to be done." Since the ministry moved into the storefront, weekly worship is held along with a weekday Bible study, and after worship a potluck lunch is available for all to share. "We are a mission church. The primary needs in the inner city are spiritual in nature. People are isolated and need positive relationships with each other and with our Lord. In this neighborhood, most people exist with just enough money to buy drugs and alcohol. Sometimes our message gets through and other times it doesn't. This is not a ministry for someone who wants to see wide-scale improvements in a short time; it takes a long time to see large-scale improvement. We can help only one heart at a time."

Fritz recalls a young man who was in the recovery group at the church. "After the meeting he stood up and exclaimed, 'I've found my church.' A few days later, he was shot on the street and killed for a small drug debt. I think he found God before he died. It's how I can make sense of it."

In 1999, after six years of living in the neighborhood and successfully starting the ministry, Fritz and his family left the area for a pastoral call in Maryland. Since his departure, the Peoples Ministry in Christ has continued to reach out into the community through God's grace. With the support of the presbytery, individual Presbyterian churches, and individuals, missionary volunteers have continued to come to provide outreach, Bible study, and recovery groups along with conducting weekly worship services. ■

"In the day of my trouble I seek the Lord . . . ."
(Psalm 77:2)

The Reverend George Pasek stands beside the Shell Community Presbyterian Church in northern Wyoming.

PLEASE DON'T TIE HORSES HERE

GROUNDED IN FAITH

The Holy Spirit is alive in two small Wyoming churches.

One Sunday, as the Reverend George Pasek was preaching the sermon at the Shell Community Presbyterian Church, he glanced out the window and was surprised to see a four-point buck. Another week, a squirrel dashed into the sanctuary through the open front door, ran down the center aisle, and scampered past the pulpit and through the rear door before anyone could react. Such is church life in the small ranching towns of Greybull and Shell, Wyoming, where the unexpected is expected and anything can happen on any given Sunday.

"I was first called to the Greybull church in 1983 as a part-time pastor," George recalls. "By the mid-eighties, as membership grew, it became a full-time position." After moving on to serve another congregation, George retired to Cody, Wyoming, in 1995. "When I retired, I agreed to serve the Greybull and Shell churches as an interim pastor part-time because they couldn't find a pastor willing to take the call." After a couple of years has passed and no pastor has been found, the temporary position became permanent and George is still at the two churches.

"This area of the country is unique," George says, "and powerful things happen here. But the prosperity of the late 1990s simply passed us by, and the growth that the rest of the country had simply didn't happen here." The Greybull community, offering spectacular panoramic mountain views,

nevertheless continues to decline in population. People make their living working for the railroad, working at the local refinery, or ranching. Since the climate is naturally dry, water is diverted to the fields by a series of canals that channel the snow melt from the mountains. Sixteen miles away is Shell, which is largely an agricultural settlement.

"These are far from dying churches. We have an active youth group, and worship attendance is growing."

"In an area like this, there is no population growth," George observes. "As soon as they are able, young people leave for better-paying jobs elsewhere. The church in Greybull has fifty-five members, and the Shell church has only ten. Our dream is to attract a full-time pastor, but to do that we will need more members. However, these are far from dying churches. We have a very active youth group, and Sunday worship attendance is growing. So by the grace of God, a full-time pastor will be possible within the next five years."

To understand the importance of the church in rural Wyoming, one has to look only as far as Kathleen and Walt Howe, who have been active members of the Greybull church for decades. Thirty years ago, as a young family, they experienced a loss that no parent should have to face. Their seven-year-old son was accidentally struck on the head during a baseball game and, tragically, died. As Kathleen remembers, "I don't know what we would have done without the help of the church. The genuine caring and the support we received were very important. While you never get over the loss of a child, just knowing that our church family was there for us helped keep us going." The Howes raised three other children, and as is typical of rural families across the country, all three have left the area in search of better jobs.

Worship at the Greybull and Shell churches is filled with the unpredictable. One week, the congregation sings hymns accompanied by a piano or organ, while other weeks the glorious sounds of a marimba and xylophone can be heard. On still other occasions, praise music will be played by a guitarist or fiddler. "There is a lot of talent in the area," George maintains, "and our people love variety. One week, one of our young people was going to do a reading. Since he's always got a skateboard tucked under his arm, I told him to ride it down the aisle and jump off when he got to the front and do his reading then. People just loved it."

"Our spiritual roots run deep around here," George says. "Even though things can get a little tough at times, we never waiver in our faith." ■

". . . Christ may dwell in your hearts through faith, as you are being rooted and grounded in love."
(Ephesians 3:17)

The Reverend George Pasek and longtime Greybull Presbyterian Church members Walt and Kathleen Howe understand the importance of church in rural Wyoming.

The Shell Community Presbyterian Church is located sixteen miles east of Greybull at the foot of the Bighorn Mountains.

SHARING THE BURDEN

Dynamic suburban church owes its spiritual growth to a lay-led ministry.

By most accounts, Glenn McDonald's ministry was successful. As organizing pastor of Zionsville Presbyterian Church, he had seen the membership of the church grow from a handful of people to over two hundred in four short years.

But to Glenn and his family, his ministry was tearing them apart. As he remembers, "One day in 1987, I was heading out the door with a pile of papers in hand, and my wife, Mary Sue, was standing over a pile of laundry. We were yelling at each other, and our four young children were listening from another room. Finally I said, 'What happened to the beautiful woman I married?' Her response was, 'Oh, she died, and you never noticed. You were too busy doing church.' That was a horrible moment in a terrible day, and I thought, 'God is blessing me on the outside, but on the inside there is emptiness.'"

Since its organization in 1983, the Zionsville Presbyterian Church has grown from a group of thirty meeting in a local school cafeteria to a sprawling campus with over sixteen hundred members. Located northwest of Indianapolis, the church attracts mostly younger families who live in suburban neighborhoods within a twenty-mile radius. "When I first arrived in the spring of 1983," Glenn recalls, "I was twenty-nine years old, married with four kids, and had been the youth pastor of Northminster Presbyterian Church in Indianapolis for five years." When the presbytery approached him about being the organizing pastor of the Zionsville church, they told him that with a little hard work, the church would grow. "They told me it wasn't 'rocket science,'" Glenn says. "If I followed the plan, around 2 percent of the local population that lived within eight miles of the church would at least check it out. After all, that's the Presbyterian 'slice' of the population, and just knowing that a church was being organized in their area, they would surely want to come."

But what Glenn did not expect were the emptiness and feelings of guilt this new ministry would generate. "When I was at home with my family," he remembers, "I thought, 'What kind of pastor am I? My responsibility is to be visiting church members and building programs.' When I was with the members of the church, I was thinking, 'What kind of husband and father am I? My responsibility is to spend time with them.' After the argument with Mary Sue, I knew something had to change."

Glenn called a meeting with the officers of the church and told them that he just couldn't keep the same schedule anymore without jeopardizing his relationship with his family. The endless night and weekend meetings had finally taken their toll, and he needed to spend more time at home. To his surprise, the officers said, "Fine. Stay home with your family; we don't need you at those meetings anyway."

Once a month the CHEFS small group meets in the church to create gourmet meals. Some of the food is taken home to their families and some is left in the church freezer to be distributed to a family in need.

Reaching New Generations

The average age of members at the Zionsville Presbyterian Church is thirty-eight years old, far younger than in the typical church. Over 60 percent of the members came with no immediate church background and haven't been to church for at least seven years prior to joining Zionsville.

Because so many people weren't raised in the church, few initially have religious knowledge. For example, "we can't tell people to turn to a particular verse in Luke without giving out page numbers to guide them. It is very different than the experience our parents had where being active in church was the norm," minister Glenn McDonald says. "We live in a consumer-oriented society. It is not uncommon to have a family arrive at church in three separate vehicles, and all at different times. People today live very hectic lives, and often their spiritual life has taken a back seat. But there is a great thirst for meaning in life. "

Recently the church decided to start a Bible study called "God for Dummies" and thought few would attend. It was surprised, however, when the course quickly became fully booked. Older approaches to Bible study simply assumed that the participants accepted the Bible as a truthful authority, but the "God for Dummies" course recognized that, in a consumer society, people are accustomed to being given choices. Therefore, the course presented the claims of the Bible as if they were being heard for the first time. When the participants were able to discuss and debate those claims, the Bible came alive and their faith emerged.

"Our primary job," Glenn states, "is to teach people the gospel so that the Christian story is told in a compelling way. Our mission is clear: to make disciples who are growing in Christ and who become lifelong followers of Jesus Christ. This is accomplished through worship, study, and mission. Our small groups provide a connection to the church and allow the mission to be fulfilled."

"At first, I was a little disturbed with their enthusiasm," Glenn recalls, "but as I started to disconnect from the meeting schedule, it turned out to be a very positive thing for both my family and the church. I didn't realize it at the time but the members of the church were also tired of the time the meetings had taken from their families. Every year we re-started ten or more committees, and a dozen people would sign up to work on each committee. The committees would each start with great enthusiasm and high attendance, but by the end of the year each committee was down to two or three in attendance."

Glenn began to contact the people who had dropped out of committees and found each had a similar story: "I joined the worship committee to be involved in worship, and all we did was meet once a month and decide on the worship schedule. If I'd known that, I never would have signed up." Glenn began encouraging the church to move away from being a pastor-centered, committee-driven church. Almost all the existing committees were changed into ministries, lay-led teams with specific tasks. The result was that the work of the church was still being done, but instead of spending time and energy in meetings, the teams would get together and actually perform the work.

"Our church is run by teams, or in other words, small groups," Glenn explains. "Many churches today have small groups, but it's almost like church membership is a restaurant entrée and then the server asks, 'And would you like small groups with that?' Instead of being a church with small groups, we are a small group church. When someone joins the church they are encouraged to either start or join a small group, not as a requirement for membership but as a way to participate in the work of the church."

One of the benefits of the small group approach has been an empowering of the ministry of the laity. "This is truly a decentralized ministry," Glenn observes. "The pastor's desk is no longer the place where everything needs to be touched or supervised. Many days I am startled to know how many of the small groups exist without my knowledge. Our session is aware of the groups and the work they do; however, it does not provide any direct oversight. This has freed up our session meetings to come together in worship, do the business of the church, and take the time to brainstorm and plan."

One small group is named "CHEFS," which stands for Creating Heavenly Edibles From Scratch. It was an idea brought to action by Stacey Wong, who is a young mother with a gift for gourmet cooking. Once a month up to twenty people gather in the church kitchen to cook several meals for their families and to give away. The week before, each person in the group gets a shopping list of the items that need to be purchased. Then, under the direction of Stacey, the group gathers for an evening of learning a new recipe, preparing the meal, and enjoying each other's fellowship and prayer requests. Each participant takes home seven meals and leaves seven meals in the church freezer to be distributed to people in need.

Another ministry began early one Sunday morning several years ago when Ruth Hicks, a member of the church, felt a special calling to pray before worship for the ministries of the church. At first Ruth did this on her own. Arriving before dawn on Sunday mornings, she walked the perimeter of the church property praying as she went, claiming the property as holy ground and praying for the safety of all who would come. Next she entered the building and prayed in every classroom for the teachers and students to have open hearts and minds and do God's will. Ruth then entered the sanctuary and prayed that the Holy Spirit be present in worship. Finally just before worship, she prayed with the pastor, asking the Lord to provide strength and guidance.

"It was just something I felt called to do," Ruth states. "However, because I was praying alone in the pre-dawn hours, I was a little concerned about my safety. I prayed that others would join me and knew in my heart that God would provide the people." A few weeks later, Pam Ferree, another member, joined Ruth in prayer. Since that time, even in the rain or snow, a dedicated group of three or four meets just past seven each Sunday morning and follows the same route that Ruth first established.

"When Ruth first started what we refer to as the Sunday morning prayer team, I thought she was nuts," recalls Glenn. "I'm not a morning person, and so when I drove in on Sunday mornings and saw this group of people, I wondered if they had taken leave of their senses. Now if they weren't there, I would truly miss their presence. I can't quantify this, but since the prayer team started, something changed in this church, both spiritually and emotionally. They pray for the spiritual safety of those who will worship here, they pray in every classroom and stand in the spot where the teachers will teach and pray for the kids and the teachers, then they pray with me just before worship. Words can't describe how that makes me feel." ■

Early Sunday mornings, prior to worship, the prayer team prays along the perimeter of the property, claiming it as holy ground. Then they pray in each classroom, in the church, and with the pastors.

". . . to equip the saints for the work of ministry . . ."
(Ephesians 4:12)

TRANSFORMING
A COMMUNITY

Church mortgages property to build affordable housing.

Helping Those in Need

Jay Rustoven's life is a testament to serving those who are less fortunate. When Jay was in high school and serving as a volunteer in a city rescue mission in Chicago, a homeless man was dropped off by the authorities. "He told me he was from Indiana and wanted to return there. The man was in bad shape. He had just been released from the hospital, his clothes were tattered, and he was in need of a bath. So I took him to my parents' home, where I was instructed to get him cleaned up while my parents searched for clothes. He was so filthy that it took two baths to get him clean."

The only spare clothes his parents could find that would fit the man were work clothes. The day was Sunday, and Jay wanted to take the man to church with him, but knowing that the man would feel uncomfortable at his family's very formal church, Jay decided that he and the man would attend a local storefront church. "I'll never forget that day," Jay remembers. "I introduced the man to the pastor, who shook his hand and said, 'Bring your friend to the front pew.' Then during worship the pastor introduced the man to the congregation and asked them to welcome him. Everyone came forward and introduced themselves, shook his hand, and gave him a hug. They really new what Christian hospitality was all about. That experience had a profound influence on me."

In the midst of the social turmoil of the late 1960s, with the war in Vietnam dividing the country, civil unrest experienced in every major city, and schemes of urban renewal displacing the inner-city poor, Dayton Avenue Presbyterian Church in St. Paul, Minnesota, had a vision. Affordable inner-city housing could be built on recently cleared land near the church. At the time, the only affordable housing available in the area consisted of older, run-down houses that had been divided into apartments.

To make the Dayton Avenue church's dream a reality required money. In order to raise the funding, it was decided to seek partnerships with other area churches. So, Dayton Avenue's minister at the time, the Reverend Harry Maghakian, assembled the leaders of several neighborhood congregations and was shocked to discover that there was no interest. Undaunted, Harry approached several national and regional organizations for support, but again he found no one wanted to get involved. "Since nobody was interested in joining us in this ministry," comments Arthur Sternberg, an active member of the church, "and since we were committed as a church to proceed, we decided to go it alone. The problem was that we had no money. So we agreed to do it without any money and use the church as collateral. It was a great leap of faith."

The church borrowed the money from a bank and guaranteed a forty-year mortgage on the development. Jim Vellenga, another active member, adds, "We are not a large church. In fact our membership is under two hundred. But we have always been driven by a strong sense of social action, and we often do things that larger churches may never attempt. So taking a leap of faith is not uncommon in our church."

In November 1967, ground was broken on what was to become Liberty Plaza, a 172-unit, affordable housing complex consisting of townhouses, apartments, and a community center. By late 1968, the first residents moved in to

May Tho Ly and May Cha Ly, mother and daughter, have been residents of Liberty Plaza for twenty-one years.

the complex. The first few years, however, were rocky. An inexperienced manager, a board that had never run a housing complex, and other problems combined to make Liberty Plaza a money-losing project.

Enter Jay Rustoven, a Presbyterian pastor who left his position as director of a Presbyterian camp and conference program for the synod to become the administrator of Liberty Plaza in 1969. Jay recalls his early days with Liberty Plaza: "I'd be walking the grounds and residents would be yelling at me from their windows, 'My plumbing is backed up,' 'the roof leaks,' 'my refrigerator won't work.' It seemed overwhelming."

To make matters worse, there were domestic problems among the residents. Jay recalls one such incident: "A woman came to the office and said, 'I just shot my boyfriend and his body is still in my apartment.' I remember following her to the apartment and finding things just as she said. The man's body was sprawled on the floor and blood was everywhere. It was in those early days that I wondered if I was in the wrong place." Gradually things began to improve as new rules were put into effect, repairs were made, and trouble-makers were evicted. Within a few years, the complex began to pay its own way, and crime in the area decreased.

Today, Liberty Plaza is a success with all units occupied. The development has encouraged a revitalization of the entire area, with people again taking pride in their neighborhood. The area has become a very desirable place to live, and many of the older homes have been restored and returned to single family status. The area around Liberty Plaza is a meeting place for cultures and classes, a neighborhood where diversity is welcomed and celebrated.

According to Arthur, "I think Liberty Plaza is God's idea of how a group of believers can transform a community and make the world a better place to live." ∎

". . . there is hope for your future, says the LORD."
(Jeremiah 31:17)

Harry's Journey

Harry Maghakian was well suited for the ministry of the Liberty Plaza development. When Harry was eighteen, his father died, suddenly leaving him as the head of the household and needing to earn enough money to support his mother and his two younger sisters. Harry took a job in real estate and did quite well financially. However, he also wanted to serve the church. One day he met with the executive of his presbytery and asked what he could do for the church. "Go into the ministry," the executive bluntly said, and although Harry had some misgivings, he enrolled at San Francisco Theological Seminary.

During his time in seminary, Harry was given the assignment of going into the most run-down area of San Francisco and surveying the people he met. "That opened my eyes to the other America," Harry remembers. After graduation, Bryant George, head of National Missions for the Presbyterian Church, challenged Harry to engage in inner-city ministry. Harry was amused by Bryant's efforts to recruit and said, "The last person who recruited me was Uncle Sam, and I ended up in Europe fighting and getting wounded during the Second World War."

"Harry, God brought you this far by faith," Bryant boomed in reply. "God will see you through." And that is how Harry found himself called to the Dayton Avenue Presbyterian Church, an inner-city ministry that would last for twelve years and result in the construction of Liberty Plaza.

Dynamic Brooklyn church is home to over thirty different nationalities.

When the Reverend Victor Aloyo first arrived at Presbyterian Church of the Redeemer in the Cyprus Hill neighborhood of Brooklyn, the building was a mess. Beams were protruding through the roof, plaster was falling from the ceiling, and birds were flying around the sanctuary. The odor of bird droppings and mildew permeated the air. Vandals had broken many of the windows and covered parts of the building with graffiti. To put it mildly, Victor was faced with a challenge.

Things were not always this way. When the church was built in 1898, Cyprus Hill was filled with young families who had immigrated from Poland, Italy, and Germany. The church flourished and soon had over four hundred members. But after World War II, the neighborhood changed as people moved out to the new suburbs of New Jersey and Long Island. By the mid-1980s, the congregation had dwindled to only a dozen members.

In the nearby Bushwick neighborhood, a new Presbyterian church had just been commissioned to serve the recently arrived immigrants from Cuba, Puerto Rico, and the Caribbean. This mostly Hispanic congregation was meeting in a storefront and growing very rapidly. More space was needed, and when the storefront congregation asked the Church of the Redeemer if it could help, the answer was yes. The two congregations agreed to occupy the same building, with the host congregation worshiping on Sunday mornings and the Hispanic church conducting worship on Sunday afternoons.

As the members of these congregations grew to know each other, they began to discuss the possibility of merging. A true merger would require that worship be conducted in both Spanish and English, and to make this possible, the congregation would need to call a bilingual pastor. Thus, in 1989, Reverend Victor Aloyo accepted the call to be the first pastor of the newly joined church.

The two congregations combined their financial resources and, with some help from the presbytery and the denomination, started renovations on the building. "It was a huge challenge," Victor observes, "but our members rose to the occasion, doing much of the work themselves. When specialized work was required, they called in friends who were bricklayers and roofers. It was incredible what we were able to accomplish with the limited resources we had. In addition to updating and rehabilitating the building, the experience had another effect: The two congregations worked together on the building, and by the time the construction was completed, we had united as one."

Classrooms were built in the basement of the church, a children's nursery was constructed where the balcony had once been, and the sanctuary was repaired and updated. Outside, the grounds were cleaned up, the graffiti-scarred walls were painted, and the broken windows were replaced. The once-dilapidated church was restored to its former glory.

"An amazing transformation began to take place once the people in the community realized that we had fixed up the building and were here to stay," Victor recalls. "People started to return, attracted by the bilingual worship service, which celebrated our multicultural worship."

Included in those who streamed to the Church of the Redeemer were many young families and others who had previously felt alienated from the church. The congregation also began receiving inquiries from people from India, Africa, Korea, and other Asian nations who had recently moved into the neighborhood. Within a few years, worship services in Hindi, Pujovi, and Korean were added to the bilingual Spanish and English service. "We worship together as one congregation the first Sunday of every month for Communion," Victor explains. "It shows that the love of God transcends language and culture." The congregation also gets together for special events, such as Agape meals, their version of the traditional potluck. *Agape* is a biblical word meaning 'self-giving love.' "Everyone loves the Agape meal," Victor says. "On one table are foods from Hispanic, African American, German, Polish, Hindi, and Korean cultures. The food covers the entire taste palate from spicy to bland and everything in between."

"Our goal," Victor states, "is to be as open as possible to the creativity of the spirit of God." This has led the church into many new ministries, including the House of Praise Coffee House, which features music from a variety of reggae and rap praise groups. The congregation of the Presbyterian Church of the Redeemer reflects all the colors of God's children, with over thirty different nationalities represented in the two-hundred-member church. Even though much has been accomplished there is so much more to do. The Cypress Hill neighborhood is still one of the roughest areas in the city. The neighborhood has the lowest percentage of kids graduating from high school in the city and one of the highest homicide rates in the country. Crime is all around, with drugs being sold everywhere from the school yard to the street corner.

Because of its active worship and programs that benefit the community, the Church of the Redeemer is now seen as a place of opportunity, and very little crime is reported in and around the church. "The God we serve is a God of second chances," Victor explains. "What we have done here in this church is appreciated by the people of the community. It is a place where they can exercise their second chances in the name of our Lord." ■

Above:
Members of Presbyterian Church of the Redeemer in Brooklyn assemble on the steps of the church.

The flags of many nations line the sanctuary.

". . . like living stones, let yourselves be built into a spiritual house . . ." (1 Peter 2:5)

FOR THE GOOD OF THE VILLAGE

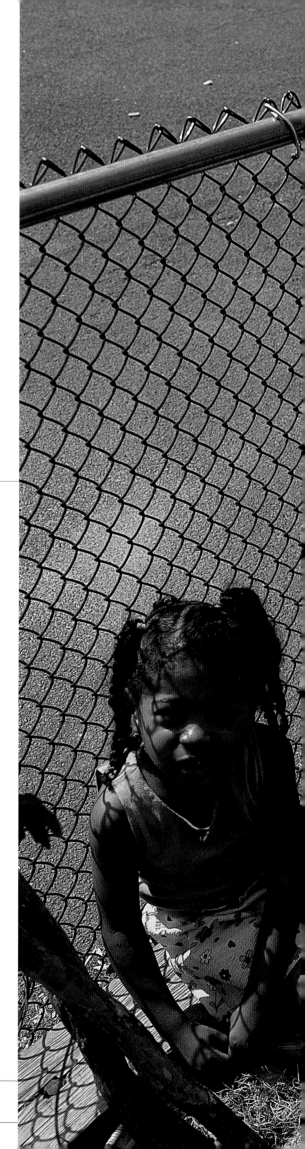

Church finds space to fill needs of community.

"Harambee" is a Swahili term signifying the bringing together of a village's resources for the good of all who live there. "This church has always had a great love for community ministry," explains the Reverend Robert N. Burkins, Sr., pastor of Elmwood United Presbyterian Church of East Orange, New Jersey. "We fully embrace the spirit of Harambee in serving the needs of the people of our community." It was that passion for combining the resources of the greater community that led the congregation to form the Harambee Community Development Initiative, a not-for-profit organization that serves the people of its village, East Orange, New Jersey.

The road that led the congregation to Harambee was one of growth, both spiritual and numerical. Located in an older residential neighborhood, Elmwood Church was growing in membership and mission. More space was needed, but the church was landlocked, and property was not available for expansion. So the church looked for other sites in the community. Vacant land

Harambee Center day care kids gather in the outdoor play area.

The Harambee Center is an important part of the support system of East Orange, New Jersey.

Below: Harambee Center director, Renee Hooks, tends to the needs of some of her younger clients.

was at a premium, though, and few suitable building sites were available. When a multistory office structure across town became available, the congregation decided to purchase it.

As they studied the possible uses of the site, they realized that they had two options for their property: Tear down the office building and build a new church or renovate the building and use it for community ministry. "We looked at what we could provide the community from that location and determined that the needs of our village were great, so our congregation decided to remodel," Reverend Burkins notes. "Our community had a shortage of quality day care, so that became our first ministry. Once the Harambee Family Academy day care was up and running, we added a summer day camp and a youth mentoring program. In the future we plan to explore programs such as an after-school care program, a fitness center, food service, job training, and a computer training lab."

The Harambee Center has almost twenty-five-thousand square feet of space on three floors and includes a commercial kitchen, numerous meeting rooms, office space, and ample storage. Much of the renovation has been completed, and the staff and director are now in place. Just walking through the Harambee Center provides a sense of loving care and great joy. It is an example of how people of faith can come together in the Spirit and, with vision, build a resource that can be shared with the entire community. ∎

"All who believed were together and had all things in common . . ." (Acts 2:44)

STRONG BACKS AND HELPING HANDS

Prior to beginning construction, the volunteers and staff of Hosanna Industries take a moment for prayer.

Building and repairing homes for those in need is the mission of Hosanna Industries.

Donn Ed's life changed forever on Christmas Eve 1987. As the associate pastor of Bakerstown Presbyterian Church, Donn always experienced the Christmas season as busy, but this year was particularly hectic. Traditionally the ministers of the church personally delivered holiday gift packages filled with groceries and turkeys to needy families of the area. In between the two Christmas Eve services, Donn realized he still had one package to deliver, so he hurriedly jumped into his car and made his way to the last family on his list.

When he arrived, he found a dilapidated concrete block home that had no insulation, a roof that was barely attached, and a pathway made of discarded wooden pallets. Donn was greeted at the door by a single mother and her five children. "I handed her the package," Donn remembers. "She thanked me, and I promised I'd keep her in my prayers." As he made his way back to his car, Donn looked back at the house and was touched by the beauty of the evening. The snow was gently falling, his footprints were neatly imprinted on the pathway, and the moon was in its glory. A picture-postcard Christmas Eve . . . except for the house. "My heart hung heavy," Donn recalls. "The words I had just conveyed to her and the mother's 'thank you' meant nothing, because it wasn't going to change the situation. Tomorrow they would still be needy."

Hosanna Industries' work crew
construct a new home on a rural
site near Pittsburgh.

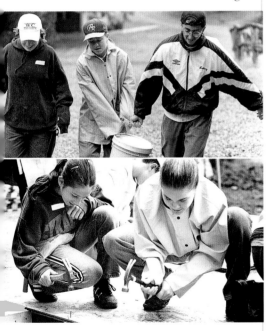

The Reverend Donn Ed and wife, Amy,
work in the office of Hosanna Industries.

As he reflected on their situation, something mystical happened.
"As I got into my car and glanced back at the house, it was almost as if I saw
the image of Jesus Christ going into that home to relieve their pain and to love
them," Donn said. "My life changed that night. I suddenly realized that even
though I was an ordained minister, I wasn't doing what Jesus would have done.
The Spirit started to work within me, and I began a two-year long search, asking,
'What shall I do, Lord?' I thought the answer was to become an overseas missionary, building homes for the poor. However, my dear wife, Amy, took me
aside and urged me to help the people around here, because I didn't have to
look beyond our own area to find people in need."

Months later, unable to get this Christmas experience out of his mind,
Donn was reading the Bible and came to the story about how the crowds shouted
"Hosanna!" as Jesus entered the city of Jerusalem. "Having been raised in a
Christian home, I always considered the word *hosanna* as meaning 'praise and
celebration.' But my studious side wondered about the real meaning of the word.
I looked it up in my Hebrew dictionary, and nothing has really been the same
since. The definition of the ancient word *hosanna* was 'rescue me now Lord.'
Jesus went to the cross because he heard people crying out for help. That's where
salvation begins."

On Easter Sunday 1990, Hosanna Industries was commissioned during worship at Bakerstown Presbyterian Church. The name was selected to reflect the importance of the word *hosanna*, the mission to rescue people in need through the efforts of dedicated Christians. During worship, Donn shared his vision of building and renovating homes, churches, and other buildings in the hope that lives would change for the better. It was an ambitious dream, but the Bakerstown congregation was up to the challenge.

Hosanna Industries was an immediate success, and during the first year one new home was constructed and thirteen renovation projects were completed. However, the need far outweighed the availability of workers, funding, and equipment. "We had no idea that there was so much suffering," Donn states, "so we made the decision to allow the ministry to grow by involving more organizations." Today funding is provided not only by Bakerstown Presbyterian Church but also by nearly one hundred partner churches, many individuals and businesses, and several foundations. In a typical year, Hosanna Industries completes six or more new home construction projects along with approximately 150 renovation projects.

A visit to Hosanna Industries is a humbling experience. Dotting the landscape is a fleet of bright green trucks with the name Hosanna Industries blazed in yellow, all donated by local businesses. The pace of activity is feverish as volunteers and staff move at breakneck speed to get ready for the next project. It is not uncommon for a new home construction project to be completed in three to five days and a major renovation to take a day or less. Most projects are regional, but Hosanna has provided hurricane relief in Florida, helped out during the floods in Missouri, and rebuilt a church in Arkansas torched by a racially motivated arsonist.

Many of the staff members have been with Hosanna almost from the beginning, and their faith stories are inspiring. Scott, for example, sacrificed a large salary with a computer firm in Washington, D.C., to join the ministry. Mark, Mike, Brian, Jeff, and Becky came originally as mission volunteers and stayed because of their passion for working with the needy. Herb originally served on the board of directors, but he was moved to join the ministry as a mission worker.

Once a building project is complete, Hosanna Industries continues to stay involved through a client care program, which helps to provide furniture, draperies, linens, and appliances. When clients move in to their new homes, they are given a "welcome home" packet, which includes training on how to take care of the home, and a framed poster of Jesus as a reminder that Jesus is alive in the home and lives in the hearts of the family, volunteers, and staff who worked on the construction. ■

A Wonderful Child of God

Donn Ed was once invited to make a presentation about Hosanna Industries to the Women's Missionary Society of the First Presbyterian Church of Pittsburgh. After he made his speech, the group's treasurer approached him with a question: "How much does one of those yellow bulldozer machines cost that we saw in your presentation?" Donn responded that they were very expensive, so expensive—over fifty thousand dollars in fact—that Hosanna Industries could not afford to buy one and had to rent instead. That Christmas, the Women's Missionary Society invited Donn back to speak, and at the conclusion of his address they presented him with the keys to a brand new bulldozer. The treasurer told Donn that the money came from the estate of a woman who had attended one of their meetings years ago. She was ragged in appearance and did not even have a winter coat. The group welcomed her, gave her food, and provided her with a warm coat. They never saw her again. A few years later, however, the society unexpectedly received a large gift of money from the estate of this woman. The woman they had cared for long before had become wealthy in her last years. She had willed this money to the group that had been kind to her in her need, with the request only that the money go to help the poor. "When the bulldozer arrived," Donn explains, "we had a plaque inscribed with the woman's name and installed it on the dashboard. Now every time anybody uses the bulldozer, they are reminded of that wonderful child of God."

"Hosanna! . . . Blessed is the one who comes in the name of the Lord!" (Matthew 21:9)

A PROUD CULTURE

The Reverend Enright Bighorn
with church members Joyce and
Jack Tootoosis stand in front of
the historic Red Eagle Church,
named after Joyce's father.

The churches of the Dakota Presbytery blend tribal spirituality with the gospel.

When Enright Bighorn began his ministry in 1972, he was assigned to two churches on the Sisseton-Wahpeton Sioux Reservation in northeast South Dakota. The problem was that Enright didn't own a car. Soon, however, he discovered the ingenuity of the people of the congregations. "One of the church families approached me," Enright remembers. "They knew about a car I could get from a man named Leo Greycloud. It was a 1962 Chevy that was sitting up on blocks." The car was missing the engine, transmission, and tires, which a member assured him could probably be found. The people of the church were happy to put the car together if the missing parts could be located. Soon the parts started arriving from others on the reservation and, as promised, members tried to get the car in working order. According to Enright, "I drove that car for several years and it served me well."

The former Mnisda Presbyterian Church just west of Poplar, Montana, stands as a tribute to the role of the church in the spiritual life of the reservation.

This is the way of life on many Indian reservations. The people make do with very little in terms of material wealth and instead use their gifts of creativity and spirituality to make things happen. The Fort Peck Indian Reservation, where Enright is originally from, is located in the northeast corner of Montana and has a population of about twelve thousand people spread over land bordering the Missouri River and covering an area roughly the size of Connecticut. Home of people of Sioux and Assiniboin descent, the reservation was initially settled by tribes who either fought in the Battle of the Little Big Horn or were displaced after the Minnesota Uprising in the late 1800s.

The tribes were very spiritual people, and they welcomed the Christian missionaries who came to them in the mid- to late-1800s. While the sharing of the gospel was welcomed, some of the other ideas of the missionaries had a negative impact that is still evident today. The missionaries taught that the Indian ways were wrong and that tribal customs and languages should be abandoned. In the past several decades, however, the church has realized that many of these missionary injunctions were misguided, and now many of the tribal customs are being recovered. Moreover, the Bible is now readily available in several of the tribal languages.

As Irma Reddoor, a member of Lindsey Memorial Presbyterian Dakota Church in Poplar, Montana, recalls, "When my mother was in grade school, she was punished if she ever used the Indian language. So when I was growing up, she refused to teach me our Indian language for fear of my being punished the way she was. The only way I was exposed to our language was through our Indian Bible and our songs. Later when I traveled to Oglala on the Pine Ridge Indian Reservation in South Dakota with my

*Joyce Tootoosis takes a moment
for reflection on the porch of
Redlightning Hall at the Red
Eagle Presbyterian Church.*

*Enright Bighorn leads
Native Americans in worship at the Lindsey
Memorial Presbyterian Dakota Church.*

father, who was a Presbyterian missionary, I was exposed to Lakota while attending school. Within a couple of months, I was speaking it too." Several months later, her mother was trying to have a private conversation with her father one evening so they were speaking in the Dakota language, which is similar to Lakota. When Irma all of a sudden started to join in, her mother knew that her attempts to keep the language from her daughter had failed.

Enright tells a story that illustrates the ways in which the gospel interacts with ancient Indian views. "One of the most well known of the Indian leaders was named Norman Hollow," Enright remembers. "He served on the tribal council for forty-nine years, twelve of which were as tribal chairman. I sat down with him one day years ago and he told me about a dream his father, Harry, once had." The dream takes place in the early morning during the summer. The sky is red as the sun begins to reveal itself and the sound of birds singing can be heard in the distance. A person appears carrying a colored cloth and just stands there, not saying a thing. After a while, the person turns and leaves. He asked his son Norman what he thought of the dream and his son didn't know what to think. The dream returned two more times, the only difference was that each time the person in the dream is carrying a cloth of a different color. After the third dream, his father told Norman that he thought he knew what the dreams meant. Each of the men who appeared in the dreams had sung with him around the drum during powwows years before and they had all since passed on. Since they were appearing before him, it meant they were coming for him and that soon it would be his time to die.

Harry became sick just after the dreams occurred and asked to be placed in an old log house on his property. The family took turns watching him. Early one morning, just as he had dreamed, as the sky turned red and the birds were singing, Harry died. After sharing his father's dream, Norman turned to Enright and said, "What do you think of that?" When Enright didn't respond right away, Norman said, "I can look at these dreams in the Indian way and say that they had come after my father or I can look at it as a Christian and say, it was his time to go and God came after him." Enright and Norman offered prayers for understanding.

About three years later, Enright again visited with Norman and they talked about his father's dream. "I asked him if he had made up his mind about the meaning of his father's dream," Enright remembers. "Norman said he had dealt with that, and in his mind it was his father's time and God had come after him." According to Enright, "Here was this man who had served on the tribal council for forty-nine years and was known throughout the Indian world, and he was Christian. So there is room for both the Indian ways and Christianity to be practiced without excluding one for the other. It is important for us as Indian people to celebrate our heritage without sacrificing our Christian beliefs."

heritage without sacrificing our Christian beliefs."

Unlike most other presbyteries in the Presbyterian Church, the Dakota Presbytery is not contained in a small geographic location. It serves twenty-three Native American churches located in South Dakota, North Dakota, Montana, and Minnesota. While the total official membership for the presbytery is just over one thousand people, the church serves over five thousand, who refer to the Presbyterian Church as their own.

According to Enright, "A great many people identify with the Presbyterian Church, yet they may attend only once or twice a year and never actually join. However, when a death occurs or they need pastoral counseling, they call our church. The same is true of the other denominations on the reservations."

A local Catholic priest tells the story of a young intern who was assigned to his care. This young man was given an assignment to conduct worship at a small church over an hour's drive away. He was so excited that he bounded out the door early that Sunday. When he returned it was time for the noon meal, so the priest called for the associate to join him. A few minutes later when the young man didn't respond, the priest went up to his room to find him. There, sprawled out on the bed was the young intern, weeping. The priest asked what was wrong, and the young man told him that no one had shown up for worship. The young man, so eager earlier that morning, was now devastated. But that is often the way with the small rural churches on the reservation; few people attend except during special occasions.

Nevertheless, Enright is hopeful. "We are very encouraged by our younger people who seem to be open to spirituality, and many now are coming back to the church. They want to keep their Indian customs and often want to continue their tribal customs."

A constant challenge for Native American Christians is determining which Indian spiritual traditions are compatible with the church. According to Enright, "The medicine man is important to Indian thought, and people go to him for a variety of medical, spiritual, and personal reasons. However, the medicine man can also be asked to perform bad medicine on someone for reasons of revenge; but not all medicine men will do ceremonies for bad medicine. God through Jesus Christ teaches love and commands us to reconcile with our fellow humans. I have a problem with any religion that allows the asking of bad medicine. At the same time, however, I am proud of who we are as people and want to keep as many traditions as possible."

"The gospel was brought to our people by the early missionaries," Enright states, "many of whom were from the Presbyterian Church. The churches of our Dakota Presbytery continue this work by bringing the good news to our people. We are still mission churches, and the challenges can be difficult at times, but we are faithful in our devotion to our Lord and are excited that our people are increasingly looking to the church for guidance and support." ∎

> ". . . all the families of the earth shall be blessed."
> (Genesis 12:3)

3 | Connectional Bodies

The Presbyterian Church has its roots in the theological vision of a sixteenth-century French-Swiss lawyer by the name of John Calvin. Influenced by Martin Luther, a German priest and professor who started the Protestant Reformation in Wittenburg, Germany, in 1517, Calvin further developed Reformation ideas by emphasizing the goodness of God and God's supremacy over all life. Becoming a pastor of Protestant congregations in Geneva and Strassburg, Calvin taught  that the ultimate purpose of human life was the joyful glorification of God through worship, obedience to God's Word, seeking justice in society, and caring for creation. Calvin's thought, which eventually became known as Reformed theology, spread throughout the world. John Knox, who studied with Calvin in Geneva, took Calvin's teachings to Scotland, and from there they traveled to England and to America in the form of the Presbyterian Church. Calvin gave Presbyterians not only Reformed theology but also a distinctive style of church government. In Presbyterian churches, most key decisions are made by elders, laypersons who are elected to serve by congregational vote. Indeed, the word "Presbyterian" comes from the Greek word *presbyteros*, meaning "elder." There are many denominations around the world that bear the name Presbyterian. The Presbyterian Church (U.S.A.), the largest Presbyterian group in the United States, still seeks, in its life and mission and in its cooperative work with Christians of many denominations around the world, to carry out the Reformation goals of joyful worship and faithful obedience to God's Word. The stories that follow show how Presbyterians are making a difference in the world today.

Allison Ash is the worship leader of the contemporary service at First Presbyterian Church in Grand Haven, Michigan.

WORLD–CHANGING FAITH

Faith and witness in the Presbyterian tradition continues to thrive.

When Robert Bohl, pastor of Village Presbyterian Church in Prairie Village, Kansas, is asked about the influence of the Presbyterian Church, he responds by holding his hands out and saying, "It is a joy to be part of a church on which the sun never sets. We are truly global, and somewhere the light of day is shining on the Presbyterian Church."

To illustrate his point, he recalls something that the late Dr. Frank Harrington of Peachtree Presbyterian Church in Atlanta once told him. One day, when Frank was riding in the car of the pastor of the largest Presbyterian church in Korea, a church with over forty thousand members, they passed by an old man on the road. It was a cold and rainy day, and the man was soaking wet. Even though they were running late for an appointment, the pastor stopped and took the man into the car. They drove the man to the church and gave him some dry clothes. After they had done this, the pastor turned to Frank and said, "Jesus invited us to do that." It is just one quiet example of what Presbyterians are doing in the world every minute of every day.

Marj Carpenter, an elder who has served the church as moderator of the General Assembly and has spoken in over five thousand churches worldwide, became famous for the phrase "mission, mission, mission," which she uses to describe the presence of the Presbyterian Church in the world. She says, "We Presbyterians have constantly brought the gospel into new places and to different people in the world. This makes me sinfully proud to be Presbyterian. Even in this country, as we grew west of the Mississippi, not only did the Presbyterian Church build churches, it also built hospitals and schools. It was a different approach than many others took, but I am convinced it was part of God's plan."

Silhouetted by the John Hancock Building, Fourth Presbyterian Church is located in the heart of Chicago's busy northside.

Vernon S. Broyles, III, associate director for Social Justice Ministries of the National Ministries Division of the Presbyterian Church (U.S.A.) adds, "We are also a denomination committed to social justice in the world. Our Presbyterian tradition is one where people feel comfortable wrestling with controversial issues of faith. We have squabbled and fought and divided on some of society's major issues. Yet through it all, we have a system of accountabilities. The genius of Presbyterianism is that through our connectional system of governance, no one person or ruling body has control over any church, and no church is completely individual. We are one body in Christ gathered together as members, congregations, presbyteries, synods, and the General Assembly."

According to Laird Stuart, pastor of Calvary Presbyterian Church in San Francisco, the Presbyterian system of governance is striking a chord with many in today's world. "People have a hunger for spiritual growth. We can offer them spiritual guides that are reliable and tested. We have doctrines, traditions, and creeds that are reliable. They are not perfect, but they are remarkably powerful and viable when used and shared in a faith community." While growing up in a Presbyterian church in New Jersey, Laird experienced a deepening of faith when he was exposed to the church's commitment to the civil rights movement of the 1960s. "I was very proud that a Presbyterian leader, Eugene Carson Blake, was an outspoken advocate for civil rights. I was also learning from sermons and classes in my home church that faith could have intellectual credibility. Being Presbyterian meant that you could use your heart and mind in the service of our Lord."

Parker Williamson is the executive editor of *The Presbyterian Layman*, an independent journal that is committed to the authority of scripture within the Presbyterian Church and that has often taken issue with the views of national church officials. He, too, was strongly influenced by the civil rights movement. "I marched with Dr. Martin Luther King from Selma to Montgomery. It is impossible to describe the emotion of those times and the way my faith grew through them. Faith is a lifelong adventure that grows and deepens as we reflect on our experiences in the light of God's Word. I believe with all my heart that scripture is God's Word, the place where we meet Jesus Christ. It is also a lens through which we interpret the events of our lives. I love the Presbyterian Church, for this is the church that introduced me to Jesus. Even though we sometimes disagree with other members, we remain committed to the Presbyterian Church."

Dr. John Buchanan, pastor of Fourth Presbyterian Church in Chicago, reflects on the diversity of opinion that has been a hallmark in the Presbyterian Church. "You will find Presbyterians on all sides of political and social debates.

Right:
The Reverend Robert N. Burkins, Sr., preaches at Elmwood United Presbyterian Church in East Orange, New Jersey.

"It is important for all cultures to meet and understand each other, but not at the expense of our individual experiences."

We have never stayed away from controversy. Our church was deeply involved in the civil rights movement and has historically been opposed to any government coercion of conscience. We are for the dignity and rights of individuals to determine their own destiny. Because we believe so passionately in the sovereignty of God and the human conscience, we believe the question of truth is an open one and that we are called to seek the truth with our minds and hearts and spirits. We believe that science and academic inquiry are holy pursuits, never the enemy of religion."

Diversity in worship is also a valued part of the Presbyterian Church, as expressed by Jim Baird, conference planner at the Plaza Resolana national conference center in Santa Fe, New Mexico. "I was a '60s activist growing up. At one time I wondered why all cultures couldn't mix and be one. After all we love the same, have the same basic human needs, and share the same creator. I've since changed my stance and realize we are not all the same and that there is beauty in the uniqueness of different cultures. This is also true in worship. We show our diversity in worship through Asian, Afro-centric, Hispanic, native-culture, charismatic, traditional, contemporary, suburban, urban, and other worship traditions. These worship styles should be celebrated and not simply watered down and mixed together. It is important for all cultures to meet and understand each other, but not at the expense of our individual experiences."

As the church moves forward into a new and exciting century, it is important to look at the faith challenges that lie ahead. Harry Eberts, retired pastor of Westminster Presbyterian Church in Akron, Ohio, has thought about issues Presbyterians will face in the future. "During this new century, we're going to have to make decisions that are tremendously complex in nature. Our faith needs to be prepared to address bioethical, political, and gender issues. For guidance I feel we should look to the Bible for answers. For example, the prophet Micah in the Old Testament was asked, 'What does the LORD require of you?' He responded by saying, 'to do justice, and to love kindness, and to walk humbly with your God.'" (Micah 6:8)

As for the future of the Presbyterian Church, Reverend Eberts says, "I am very optimistic about what the future holds and excited by the energizing Spirit of God in Christ. The Presbyterian Church provides the resources for all these faith journeys. When we say that the church is 'reformed and always reforming,' we are really talking about reforming our lives around the center, which is Jesus Christ." ∎

Clergy couple in Utah celebrates diversity of thought.

Bobbie and John McGarey, a clergy couple, are co-pastors of the First Presbyterian Church in Logan, Utah. According to Bobbie, "In our community, 84 percent of the population are members of The Church of Jesus Christ of Latter-day Saints, otherwise known as the Mormon Church. Because we are in such a minority in our state, we have a true understanding of the need for diversity of thought. In Utah, diversity isn't something we can ever take for granted; it's something we long for. That's why when the Presbyterian Church (U.S.A.) is locked in a heated debate concerning a controversial issue and people in the church are yearning for unity, we tend to experience the debate as a reason for celebration."

"In Utah, diversity isn't something we can ever take for granted; it's something we long for."

While attending a regional gathering of Presbyterian Women, Bobbie overheard two women having a spirited discussion on the issue of abortion. One woman was pro-choice, while the other saw abortion as murder. Suddenly one of the women asked how they could both be in the same church when they disagreed so passionately. Hearing this question, Bobbie imagined the Presbyterian Church as a wagon wheel. "I think a wagon wheel best illustrates how we can have such varied opinions and still remain in one church. We look at each other as spokes within the same wheel joined at the hub, which is Jesus Christ. Holding us together is the outer rim, which is the Holy Spirit. The movement of the wheel shows God's grace never favoring one side over another. This is the image of the church that I so cherish."

Reflecting on life in Utah, Bobbie says, "One of our challenges here is to continually remind people who have lived for years in a non-Christian cultural system what it means to be Christian—to believe in Jesus Christ, not merely as a man who did good deeds but as the one true son of God. As Christians we believe in the Trinity, in God incarnate as Jesus Christ who died and arose again so that we could have everlasting life, and in the Holy Spirit who makes us one with God in our daily lives." ∎

". . . with everlasting love I will have compassion on you, says the LORD." (Isaiah 54:8)

Mother of two brings the first fruits of the harvest to the Lord.

Judye Hartman's faith journey started as a simple matter of convenience. "When we moved to Houston I was a young mother rearing two boys. I desperately needed some relief from the daily stress of parenthood, and I heard that this church had a wonderful program called 'Mother's Day Out.' However to get higher on the waiting list we had to be members of the church. So we joined."

Little did Judye know that it would be a life-changing experience. "Both my husband, John, and I were reared Methodist, however my parents seldom attended church so it was never a big part of my life." Once the

"We once thought that giving was an expense. Now we realize it is about trust . . ."

Hartmans were members they gradually began to get more active in the life of the church. "We started by getting the boys into Sunday school, soon I was a Sunday school teacher, then I took Bible study courses, and finally I was on a capital campaign committee." It wasn't long before Judye became an elder and John a deacon.

"When you become an elder you are asked to select which committee you prefer to serve on. I selected the new members committee and said I would serve on any committee except stewardship. I didn't want to ask people for money." A month later Judye was standing in her kitchen when the telephone rang. It was Tom Tewell, then pastor at Memorial Drive Church, and he said, "Have I got a deal for you." He wanted her to serve on the stewardship committee. "I agreed, and when I told my husband he laughed and said he would keep me in his prayers. God knew where I was headed. I had no earthly idea."

The first time Judye attended a stewardship committee, she was exposed to a Bible study based on stewardship. "I had no idea that the Bible is filled with examples of stewardship. I learned that giving has nothing to do with money. It is about trusting God with our most valued possessions, and when you do, he will provide." Judye and her husband decided to try tithing as an experiment for one month and then to continue only if they felt the spirit of God working in their lives. They have been tithing ever since. "It transformed our lives. We once thought that giving was an expense. Now we realize that it is about trust and that worrying over money is one of the most difficult things to let go of when we learn to trust. It is also about wealth and how wealth does not cure emptiness."

When Judye talks about stewardship, she relates a story that touched her life. "When my youngest son was two we took him to the park. He wanted to go down the slide. So we held his hands while he climbed the stairs. Once at the top, he froze in fear and began to scream. We helped him back down the stairs. From that day on whenever we went to the park the scene was repeated. He'd beg to go down the slide and then his fear would consume him and we'd help him back down the stairs. This went on for over a month. Then one day without warning we helped him to the top and he let go and slid all the way down. Once at the bottom he yelled, 'Wow, that was fun!' This is what tithing is all about. It's God saying, 'Come on, let go. I'll protect you and transform your life.' Once you do and learn to trust God you'll wish you had done it sooner." ∎

"O Lord . . . in you I put my trust."
(Psalm 143:7-8)

Let God Take Control

When the Hartman's oldest son was three, the doctors told them that he was either autistic or mentally challenged. Later, they discovered he was actually extremely bright and that the diagnosis was incorrect. However, growing up, he was withdrawn and had difficulties relating to the other kids at school. After he graduated from high school, he was accepted at Texas A&M University. While there he got into alcohol and drugs and withdrew from his parents. "He began to hate us," Judye says, "and no matter what we did, it was wrong." His grades started to suffer, he was caught possessing drugs and alcohol, and finally he was suspended, pending treatment. "It was a blessing." Judye recalls. "We got him into treatment and he turned his life around. He was readmitted to school and later graduated with honors. It was a miracle."

After receiving his degree, he was hired as a CPA with a major firm but then lost his job six months later due to a reorganization. "My son lost all his confidence," Judye remembers. "One evening he came over to the house to tell us how he felt. This was amazing because he was always a loner and kept things to himself. Even as a child he never wanted us to hold him or touch him. After he told us the news that evening, like a typical mother I wanted to take away his pain, try to motivate him, and build up his confidence. But I held back, and instead I just let go and said that he must be devastated, angry, and terrified. For the first time ever he let me hold him and he started to sob. He had never allowed us to see him get emotional before. In that one moment our relationship changed. I learned that by letting God take control miracles can happen and that we sometimes need to listen instead of trying to make things better by ourselves."

ANSWERING

Presbyterian Seminaries

"All ministry in the Church is a gift from Jesus Christ. Members and officers alike serve mutually under the mandate of Christ who is the chief minister of all. His ministry is the basis of all ministries; the standard for all offices is the pattern of the one who came 'not to be served but to serve.' (Matthew 20:28)" *Book of Order* (G-6.0100), Presbyterian Church (U.S.A.)

The ten seminaries of the PC (USA), along with those related to the church through a covenant relationship, help ministerial candidates to discern their call and provide these candidates the theological training needed to equip them for ministry.

Former prosecutor finds second career in the ministry.

Chris Harrison, the chief prosecutor in the district attorney's office of Fort Worth, Texas, received an urgent page. He was scheduled to be in court that day but had adjusted his schedule so that he could take some long-needed handgun practice on the police firing range. Answering the page, he learned there was an emergency at the courthouse and he was needed immediately. He raced to the scene to discover that an unbalanced man had burst into the courtroom with a gun and had opened fire. Two people lay dead, and three others, including the judge, were injured. One of the dead was Chris Harrison's associate, a man also named Chris.

"The shooting was all over the news, and the news reports had leaked the information that one of the victims was named Chris. I knew my wife would assume it was me." At the time, Chris's wife and children were living across the state in Tyler. After an hour of trying, he was finally able to reach his wife on the phone. He recalls, "As I suspected, she had heard the news and thought I was the one who had been killed."

Because of this traumatic experience, Chris decided it was time to realign his priorities. "It was crazy, commuting to Fort Worth while the family lived in Tyler. Sure it was a great promotion, but in that instant, as I talked to my wife, I realized that everything I had done had been to further my career, many times at the expense of my family." It wasn't long before Chris resigned from the district attorney's office and opened a private law practice in Tyler. When he talks about the legal profession, Chris's eyes light up. "I loved being a lawyer, especially a trial lawyer. However, I also knew there were other challenges in life."

Growing up in Dallas, Chris and his family were active in an Episcopal church. After college, he considered seminary but decided instead to go to law school. When the family moved to Tyler, they joined a Presbyterian church because it was very active in the community. "After I opened my law practice in Tyler, I found myself acting restless one summer while on vacation. My wife said, 'You've always talked about seminary, why don't you try it?' It occurred to me that if I ever wanted to go, I should do it now. After all, the kids were growing up, and after twenty-two years in the practice of law, we were doing well."

Chris contacted an old friend who had left the practice of law to become a Methodist minister. "Being a typical lawyer, I needed facts, so I asked him about the positives and negatives of being a pastor. He said the most difficult part was providing for a family. Since our kids were in high school and the funds were there to provide for them, I asked him what else was a negative, and he said, there are no other negatives. He told me that he loved the work. 'It's difficult,' he said, 'but your faith carries you through."

"It was like an awakening for me," Chris remembers. "Within a couple of weeks I enrolled in Austin Seminary." Chris says he chose to become a Presbyterian minister because of the system of government. "Being a lawyer, I love having the *Book of Order* as a means for conflict resolution and governance. I also like the Presbyterian style of open debate. It reminds me of some of my arguments in the practice of law."

> "The more you learn, the more you realize you have more to learn. Because it's my second career, I'm very focused and my work ethic is well developed."

Above:
Chris Harrison's faith journey took him from the practice of law to the ministry.

Below:
Chris enrolled at Austin Presbyterian Theological Seminary.

The family made the move from Tyler to Austin, where his wife found a job teaching school and the kids enrolled in a local high school. "I love being in seminary," Chris explains. "The more you learn, the more you realize you have more to learn. Because it's my second career, I'm very focused and my work ethic is well developed."

During his second year of seminary, on a visit to his home church in Tyler, Chris was asked if seminary had changed his faith. "Not really," he replied. "I think of my experience in seminary like the old sports car I've been trying to rebuild. When I started, the first thing I had to do was disassemble it and then gradually rebuild it. In seminary they totally disassemble your understanding of your faith and then tell you that you've got three years to put it back together again. When you leave seminary, it's still the same faith you always had, only now you know more about what makes it work inside of you." ■

". . . a life worthy of the calling to which you have been called . . ." (Ephesians 4:1)

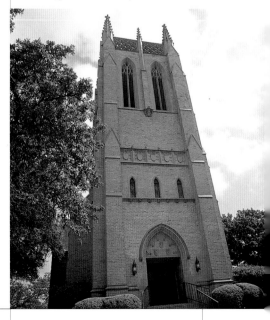

A strong sense of call leads student from college graduation to seminary.

When Christina Parker was a freshman at Converse College in Spartanburg, South Carolina, faith was the farthest thing from her mind. "I grew up in a Catholic home," Christina says. "However when I was in junior high, my family stopped attending. For a while I was in a Baptist youth group and then went with some friends to a Methodist church. Finally I lost interest and stopped going all together. Church just wasn't giving me what I needed. At that time, the whole idea of church seemed almost cult-like because they had the same routine week after week."

One day during that first year in college, Christina met the director of the Presbyterian Student Association. "She was so excited about her ministry," Christina recalls. "I remember her saying that we just had to go to the Presbyterian Student Association meeting because it was so much fun. My roommate said if I'd go, she'd go with me. So we went and had the most amazing time. Here were kids our own age learning what Christ wanted us to do and how to put the Bible into action in our community." Christina joined the group and became very active. She also started attending Covenant Presbyterian Church in Spartanburg, becoming active in the youth program.

Through her involvement with Presbyterian Student Association and her serving as an assistant youth director at Covenant Presbyterian Church, Christina's faith began to deepen. When the summer break came, she became the camp nurse at Camp Buc, a Presbyterian summer camp. All through her college years, her pastor at Covenant Church, Amos Workman, took a special interest in her. "I remember being upset with someone at camp and writing a letter of frustration to Amos," Christina recalls. "He wrote back saying that as bad as things get, God is always there for us. Here I was spiraling down, and his letter brought me back up and lifted my spirits."

Christina Parker's faith deepened through her involvement with the Presbyterian Student Association and her serving as an assistant youth director at Covenant Presbyterian Church in Spartanburg, South Carolina.

"It was an intense feeling that God was calling me to serve, and it was something I just couldn't deny."

As she progressed through her college years, Christina began to think about the possibility of attending seminary, maybe later in life as a second career. She attended a weekend seminary inquirers' conference, which allows students the chance to explore attending seminary. While at the conference, she experienced a sense of God speaking to her. "It was an intense feeling that God was calling me to serve, and it was something I just couldn't deny," Christina remembers. "So, I decided right then that seminary was something I couldn't put off."

That fall, Christina enrolled at Austin Presbyterian Theological Seminary. "My experience has been both challenging and thought-provoking," according to Christina. "The people here are so supportive. Everybody is really pulling for you." On Sundays Christina attends First Presbyterian Church in Austin and has made many new friends both on campus and in the church. Asked what others can do to support students in seminary, Christina replies, "The prayers, letters, and gifts from congregations are so important. Just knowing that people of faith are behind you makes a huge difference. I'm so thankful that others have taken the effort to care." ■

"I am the vine, you are the branches." (John 15:5)

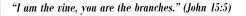

Auto parts dealer gives up the security of a family business to accept God's call.

C. F. Hoffman's experience at Pittsburgh Theological Seminary is "like a spiritual awakening."

In 1976 after C. F. Hoffman graduated from college, he joined his father and brother in the family auto parts business in Butler, Pennsylvania. Since childhood, C. F. had been active in the local Presbyterian church. "I remember staying out late one Saturday night," he recalls. "I told the friends who were with me that I had to get to bed because otherwise it would be difficult to get up in time for church. One of my friends said, 'God wouldn't mind if you missed church one Sunday,' to which I replied, 'God may not mind, but my father sure would.' That shows how important church was to my family."

In the mid-1980s, after he and his brother took over the family business, C. F. began attending a Bible study class at the church. "I remember it as a time when my spiritual switch was turned back on. So I talked with a pastor when I was at a weekend conference about the possibilities of going into the ministry. He told me that it was certainly an option; however, it was important for me to know that God also needed people in the auto parts business." So, C. F. felt a renewed commitment to his business along with a thirst to explore his spiritual calling.

Another decade passed, and C. F. was still feeling called to the ministry. "I was working by day in our family business but my heart just wasn't in it anymore," he recalls. C. F. had been involved teaching Bible studies and in prison ministry and found the experiences rewarding. "I was energized by the visits I had with inmates. They were so appreciative. Soon I was more interested in my work with the church than in my own business. I felt God was pulling me closer to the ministry and that my spiritual life was growing in leaps and bounds." Finally C. F. shared his feelings with his brother and was comforted to discover that his brother fully understood his feelings and would support whatever decision he made. "That opened the door to explore the possibilities of going into the ministry," C. F. remembers.

In March of 1998, C. F. left the family business and started attending classes full time at Pittsburgh Theological Seminary. All of a sudden what was once a comfortable lifestyle changed. C. F.'s wife, Colleen, who manages a local jewelry store, became the couple's sole source of income, and paying for seminary while also maintaining a household became a challenge. "My home church in Butler has been a godsend," C. F. says. "They are helping me with tuition and have started a fund to help support us. Still, we now live financially on the edge. But it's incredible; every time our backs are against the wall, someone is there to help us get through."

C. F. has no doubts about his decision to go to seminary. "It is like a spiritual awakening," he states. "Every day there is a new challenge. The atmosphere is wonderful, and everyone is so supportive. I feel a true sense of call. The rewards are well worth the sacrifices." ∎

". . . be strong in the grace that is in Christ Jesus." (2 Timothy 2:1)

Successful lawyer finds fulfillment in seminary.

For fifteen years, Lant Davis was a successful lawyer in Birmingham, Alabama. Raised as a Baptist, Lant became a Presbyterian when he married a woman who was a member of the Independent Presbyterian Church in Birmingham.

"From the time I was a child I was always involved in the church," Lant says. "But after we joined the Presbyterian Church, I realized that it was more suited to my needs. It offered a theology that went beyond the conversion experience, dealing also with the practices through which faith is deepened in the Christian's life."

At a critical point in his law career, Lant began to feel a sense of restlessness in his professional life and powerful spiritual stirrings to do something else. He decided to take a leave of absence from his law firm in order to explore whether or not he was being called into the ministry. "The first person I spoke to was my pastor, Dr. Scott McClure. I asked him to describe his own call to ministry. The emotion and intensity of his call were dramatic and specific. I realized that my own feelings were different, and I wrongly concluded that I had not experienced a call. So instead I volunteered to help the local symphony orchestra to draft a new business plan. After that, I went back to the law firm, thinking that the time spent away would energize my practice."

A couple years later, Lant again began to experience the same restlessness. Dr. McClure had since retired so he met with the interim pastor, Morgan Roberts. "Instead of asking about his call, I explained my own feelings. Morgan acted like I had already made my decision and offered to introduce me to Dr. John M. Mulder, president of Louisville Seminary, who happened to be coming to town." After the meeting with Dr. Mulder, during which they discussed the theology of call in the Reformed tradition, Lant decided to visit the seminary and soon made up his mind to enroll.

"The course work in the seminary is as difficult as law school," according to Lant. "One of the first things I learned was that you don't go to seminary because you have the answers, you go to build your faith through study. What attracted me to the Presbyterian Church in the first place was the tradition of an educated clergy—an openness to new ideas in the theology, the church reformed yet always reforming.

The decision to go to seminary required the Davis family to make many adjustments. They sold their dream house in Birmingham, and Lant's wife, who had previously been a high school teacher, took a teaching position in an elementary school. Money, which had been plentiful, became a resource to be both conserved and appreciated. Lant sums up his feelings, "Seminary required sacrifices for our family. But we learned that it is very satisfying to be receptive to whatever God may be calling each of us to do. God is truly working in our lives." ■

"Of this gospel I have become a servant according to the gift of God's grace . . ." (Ephesians 3:7)

Lant Davis enjoys a quiet moment at Louisville Presbyterian Theological Seminary.

Lionel Dhrenoncourt and Kathlene Ockles hold two of their children, Jabril and Jasmine. Kathlene is studying for her masters of divinity at Louisville Seminary.

Majid Abel and his wife, Hina David, are from Lahore, Pakistan. Majid is a doctoral candidate at Louisville Seminary.

SEALED IN
CHRIST

Carrying Out the Work of the Larger Church

"All power in heaven and earth is given to Jesus Christ by Almighty God, who raised Christ from the dead and set him above all rule and authority, all power and dominion, and every name that is named, not only in this age but also in that which is to come. God has put all things under the Lordship of Jesus Christ and has made Christ Head of the church, which is his body." *Book of Order* (G-1.0100), Presbyterian Church (U.S.A.)

Presbyterians and other Christians are at work in ministries all around the globe, carrying out the mission of the larger church. The staff of the Presbyterian Center in Louisville, Kentucky, is in service for this larger mission, both in the United States and throughout the world.

Presbyterian Frontier Fellowship reaches unreached people.

In 1966, Harold Kurtz and his family were on furlough in the United States after ten years of missionary work in Ethiopia. At a missions training course at Fuller Theological Seminary in California, the professor advanced the view that the traditional methods used by many missionaries were culturally insensitive and needed to be changed. Harold went to the leader and said despairingly, "I'm thinking of getting out of missionary work. I've just wasted the last ten years of my life doing things the wrong way." The leader looked at Harold and said, "How do you think I feel? I wasted the last thirty years of my life before I realized that we had to change our approach."

Little did Harold realize at the time that it wasn't the end of his ministry; it was just the beginning. Harold was raised on a farm in eastern Oregon in a community that had no church. A Presbyterian mission church was organized, however, and Harold began to attend. "I went from chasing jack rabbits on the rim rocks to an involvement in the church," Harold remembers. While serving as a pilot in World War II, he was assigned to transport survivors of the holocaust. "My spiritual journey began in earnest when I saw what human beings were capable of doing to others."

After the war, Harold attended Monmouth College in Illinois, graduating with a degree in chemistry. However, Harold soon felt the call to ministry and attended Pittsburgh Theological Seminary. Upon graduation, Harold was called to be pastor of a small Presbyterian church in Portland, where he served for three years. During that time a young missionary from Egypt visited his church, met Harold, and, without Harold's knowledge, submitted his name as a possible missionary candidate to the Mission Board. One day Glen Reed from the Mission Board called to offer Harold a post in Ethiopia.

"I was awestruck," Harold states. By this time, he was married to his wife, Polly, and had a family. "We had three young daughters and our hands were full," Harold says, noting that Polly was firmly against moving to Ethiopia. However one day when she was outside, the sun broke through the clouds during a rain and the beauty and warmth she experienced was

Harold Kurtz enjoys a
moment of reflection in a
local coffeehouse in Portland,
Oregon.

*Harold and Polly Kurtz
are partners in mission.*

like a sign from God, and at that moment her heart changed. Polly came into the house and said, "The God that makes the sun shine here will also allow the sun to shine wherever we are, even in Ethiopia."

Just after the family arrived in Ethiopia, Polly gave birth to a son. Four months later, the child died suddenly from what was then referred to as "crib death." That day, women from the village arrived with pots of hot coffee. They came with their husbands into the Kurtz's living room and sat quietly in a circle. The next day and the day after that, they came again. It was then that the Kurtz family learned that in Ethiopia, when a member of a community dies, the people go and sit with the grieving family, returning each day until they are sure the healing process has begun. As Harold remembers, "It was a ministry to us that we never forgot. They brought us into their community through their actions. The women didn't see our skin color or our nationality, they saw us simply as parents who had lost a child."

During their first ten years in Ethiopia, the Kurtz family lived atop a mountain, isolated from the developed world. The closest link to the outside world was a dusty airfield with infrequent service, thirty miles away. For most local travel they had to rely on pack mules for transportation. They lived in a one room, thatch-roofed hut connected to another hut by a metal roof. Except for rain water, their water had to be hauled up from a well a half-mile away. There was no electricity; they used kerosene lamps for lighting, and a wood stove for heating and cooking. Harold's eastern Oregon farm upbringing came in handy: he grew crops for eating, built a water-powered mill to provide flour for the community, and found a way to build a water-powered pump to bring water up to the village.

As an experienced pilot, Harold helped build airstrips in remote areas so supplies could be brought into places where the only previous access was by pack mule. As Polly remembers, "Before the airstrips were built, Harold would be gone for days without any communication. The girls and I would watch for his return and then all of a sudden, we'd see him coming over the hill riding a pack mule and our wait would be over."

In the late 1960s, the new view of missionary work that Harold had learned about at the Fuller training took hold, and dramatic changes took place in mission methods. They were asked to move to Addis Ababa so Harold could help facilitate a rapid expansion of the mission into even more remote areas of Ethiopia. He also went back to flying and piloted a small mission plane for six years to coordinate that expansion. Instead of trying to impose the gospel on people and their culture, missionaries became more culturally sensitive, alert to the ways of the people they were sent to serve. According to Harold, "We became more aware of how God had prepared people in other cultures to receive the Word. We began to approach people through the community in order to be more respectful of their social and political structure."

When revolution came to Ethiopia in 1974 and the communists took over, the church and missions were gradually closed down or tightly controlled because they were believed to pose a threat to the new government. Because the safety of the missionaries was no longer assured, Harold was called upon in 1977 to help get people out of the country. "It was a horrendous time; over a million people were killed. Churches were being closed down and the missionaries had to be evacuated. We got our people out, but the people in Ethiopia suffered terribly. It was a very dark time." The Kurtz family served in Ethiopia until 1977 when Harold was called to help reorganize a church in Portland, Oregon, which he served for ten years.

In 1983, Harold became aware of yet another new approach to mission, this one started by Ralph Winter, a former Guatemalan missionary who taught at Fuller Theological Seminary. Called the Presbyterian Frontier Fellowship, its mission was to bring the gospel to those peoples of the world untouched by Christian missions. While sitting at his kitchen table one day with Ralph, Harold was asked to be the director, and he has held this post as an unpaid volunteer ever since.

"We have gone back to the revolutionary roots of the church rather than the imperial or expansionist methods of the past."

The Presbyterian Frontier Fellowship was originally formed as a protest movement within the Presbyterian Church by people who felt the denomination was pulling away from its mission roots. In 1981, the Presbyterian General Assembly agreed and approved the Frontier Fellowship as a validated and fully accepted mission of the national church. The Frontier Fellowship has identified ten thousand groups of people around the world with a population of two billion, or a third of the world's population, who have never been told the gospel. The Presbyterian Frontier Fellowship has six coordinators across the United States who raise funds for mission and help develop partnerships with sister churches around the world. That way, the message of Jesus can be shared in a multicultural fashion with the world's unreached people. According to Harold, "what we do is a new way of mission. We have gone back to the revolutionary roots of the church rather than the imperial or expansionist methods of the past. The result is a dramatic de-westernization of the missionary message being shared in the context of people's local culture. People around the world want to worship and live out their faith in their own way, not ours, and that is revolutionary and exciting." ■

"Turn to me and be saved, all the ends of the earth!"
(Isaiah 45:22)

The Reverend Marian McClure is the director of the Worldwide Ministries Division, PC(USA).

Worldwide Ministries Division understands all cultures.

In 1980, Marian McClure was doing research in Haiti for her doctoral dissertation on the role of the Catholic Church in the life of that country. For several months she worked with a priest named Jean Marie who had helped to form a farmer-run co-op. The co-op gave local farmers, who previously had to sell their harvest to wealthy middlemen at below market prices, an alternate market for their crops, thus breaking the financial stranglehold of the middlemen.

On one occasion, Jean Marie could not attend a meeting of the co-op, and he asked Marian to take his place. The meeting involved the annual election for president of the co-op, and the current president, who had served for several years, did not want to serve another term. Even so, the other members of the co-op begged him to stay. "Each time the president tried to step down," Marian recalls, "the others would plead with him to accept another term. It went on and on. Finally I came forward and spoke to the president, saying, 'Sometimes you have to listen to what someone's trying to tell you and be willing to serve if they ask you to. That's what democracy is all about.' He was struck by what I said and finally agreed to serve another term."

Marian left that meeting proud of what she had done. That night, however, when she returned to her village, she was confronted by a spokesman for the farmers who said, "You stepped out of your role today." When Marian asked the man what he meant, he replied, "None of us wanted the president to accept another term. We were all asking him to stay on in order for him to save face. It is part of our culture, and you didn't understand. He agreed to stay because in his eyes, you were speaking for the priest. Since Father Jean Marie is so important to the co-op, he had to accept."

"Often when we look at the world it is through the prism of our own eyes. It is important to realize that prism is distracting and can get in the way of our understanding of what is really going on in mission.

"I felt awful," Marian remembers. "I thought I had an understanding of the people of Haiti. My mistake taught me that working in other cultures is like peeling an onion. You keep peeling off layers and, as you do, you're going deeper. I had just gotten several layers deeper by learning from a mistake."

In her role as director of the Worldwide Ministries Division, Marian understands that "often when we look at the world it is through the prism of our own eyes. It is important to realize that prism is distracting and can get in the way of our understanding of what is really going on in mission. Our job is to connect individuals and churches who have a passion for mission with reputable partners in other lands."

Worldwide Ministries is involved with more than 160 mission partners in over eighty countries around the world. Area coordinators, each responsible for a group of countries, act as the conduit between local churches and mission partners. According to Marian, "We view the process of mission involvement by a church as seriously as calling a pastor. A period of discernment, prayer, and study is needed before committing to any mission project. Once that commitment is made, it is important to stay with it and not walk away or lose interest in a few years. Often people feel pressured into making a hurried decision about a mission project, which many times results in disappointment. Remember, if the need is there today, it will also be there tomorrow." ∎

*"The earth is the LORD's . . . , the world,
and those who live in it." (Psalm 24:1)*

The Social Justice Program Area advocates for social justice, the environment, and health.

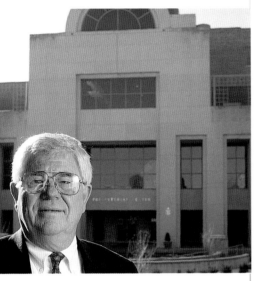

The Reverend Vernon Broyles is the associate director of the Social Justice Program Area.

Vernon Broyles' involvement in controversial issues goes back to his first experience in ministry, when he served as pastor of a small rural church in the south during the height of the civil rights movement. Both his faith and his leadership were challenged when the church session (the governing officers) voted that the congregation should remain segregated and deny membership to nonwhites. As Vernon remembers, "I cast the only dissenting vote. I argued, to no avail, that this was not our church but the church of Jesus Christ and that the vote was inconsistent with the gospel."

Several months later, the General Assembly of the Presbyterian Church passed a measure stating that the only requirement for church membership was simply "faith in Jesus Christ." Vernon decided to call a special meeting of the session to discuss the issue again. "I said that the previous action ran contrary to the constitution of the Presbyterian Church. Therefore we needed to reconsider." After a long, anguished meeting, another vote was taken, and this time the session opened the church to everyone. The motion passed without opposition.

"I learned a great deal from that vote," Vernon states. "The elders took their ordination very seriously and realized they were subject to both the Lord and the courts of the church, even though not a single person wanted to vote the way they did." The next Sunday when the decision was announced, several members of the congregation became angry, and some confronted the elders. But the elders never wavered, and after a couple of very rough years, the church was much stronger than ever before.

Today, as the associate director of the Social Justice Program Area, Vernon is still engaged in controversial issues. His staff is charged with carrying out the policies adopted by the General Assembly of the Presbyterian Church relating to economic justice, the environment, health, and human rights. Working closely with the Presbyterian Washington office, Vernon's office informs Presbyterians about the policies of the General Assembly and joins them in advocating those policies with public officials and social agencies.

"We are aware," Vernon says, "that individual Presbyterians may not agree with every decision that the General Assembly makes. The strength of the Presbyterian system allows each individual to look into his or her conscience and make a decision. Our job is to help Presbyterians think through how they are going to approach these issues and allow for a reasoned discussion. We are a very diverse church, and we never lose sight of that. We work very hard to keep all lines of communication open on all issues facing the church." ∎

". . . righteousness and peace will kiss each other." (Psalm 85:10)

Presbyterian Disaster Assistance helps survivors to rebuild their lives.

When a disaster occurs anywhere in the world, the people of Presbyterian Disaster Assistance spring into action. Working under the umbrella of the Worldwide Ministries Division, Presbyterian Disaster Assistance coordinates the church's response to catastrophes and emergencies worldwide.

"We have a team of forty disaster response volunteers based around the country," notes Stan Hankins, the staff member responsible for organizing disaster response in the United States. "When a disaster occurs, two or three members of the team are immediately dispatched to assess the situation, meet with those affected, and report back to this office. Together we decide how best to help."

One example of the help offered by Presbyterian Disaster Assistance occurred in early 1997, when the Red River in the upper midwest overflowed its banks, causing extensive damage, most dramatically in Grand Forks, North Dakota, and East Grand Forks, Minnesota. Thousands of people were displaced, hundreds of homes and businesses were heavily damaged, and two Presbyterian churches and the presbytery office were flooded. As Stan recalls, "Unlike most weather-related disasters, which typically have pockets of damage, the flooding in the Grand Forks area had immersed the entire region. No one was spared. It was terrible." Before the waters receded, three response team members from Presbyterian Disaster Assistance were onsite. While the team worked on the scene of the flood, churchwide appeals were made to assist those in need and to raise money to help the damaged churches rebuild. "This is the beauty of the Presbyterian connectional system," Stan observes. "We can connect churches and volunteers from across the country to local churches and survivors of a disaster."

Presbyterian Disaster Assistance is supported by a network of volunteers, countless prayers, and the financial support of many Presbyterians, including a portion of the annual denomination-wide offering called "The One Great Hour of Sharing." Stan has been profoundly inspired by the response his office receives: "Presbyterians care. We see it every day. They send money, they volunteer their time, and they help in other ways too numerous to mention. It makes me proud to be Presbyterian." ∎

Stan Hankins organizes disaster response in the United States for the Presbyterian Disaster Assistance.

"Our help is in the name of the LORD, who made heaven and earth." (Psalm 124:8)

WALKING
SIDE BY SIDE

Chaplains: Called to Serve

Over six hundred Presbyterians serve as chaplains in prisons, colleges, the armed forces, hospitals, and other settings around the world.

Chaplains lead worship, provide pastoral care, conduct religious and ethical education, and offer support to individuals and families. They are active in crisis intervention, community service, and projects of humanitarian aid.

Most Presbyterian chaplains serve in contents where they provide care and ministry to people of many denominations and faith traditions.

Retired death house chaplain ministered to prisoners on their final day.

The turning point for Carroll Pickett came in 1974, when three convicted murderers took several hostages at a maximum security unit in Huntsville, Texas. The siege lasted for eleven days, one of the longest prison takeovers in U.S. history. Although Carroll was the pastor of the local Presbyterian church, the prison director asked him to be the chaplain to the hostage families. Two of the hostages were women, members of his own congregation, who worked in the prison library. For the next eleven days, Carroll was stationed in a building across the street from the prison with the families of the hostages. He counseled the families of those held and relayed messages among the three hostage takers, the hostages, and prison officials.

On the eleventh day the prisoners tried to escape by handcuffing themselves to some of the hostages. Prison officials tried to stop the escape, and Texas Rangers and DPS troopers were placed in position. Just before the breakout, it was learned that the hostages handcuffed to the prisoners were, in fact, the two women who were members of Carroll's church. "I talked to both of the women by phone before the escape," Carroll remembers. "They both knew they were going to die, so we planned their funerals and got messages to their loved ones. It was very sad."

That evening the doors burst open and the ill-fated escape attempt began. When it was over, the prisoners had executed the two women before one killed himself and the other was killed by authorities. After this incident, Carroll vowed never to enter a prison again. But, as Carroll later said, "Don't ever tell God never because when you do, it may happen."

Six years passed, and one day the prison director called. He wanted Carroll to be the chaplain of a two thousand inmate unit of Huntsville prison. "I didn't want the job," Carroll says, "but, as I thought about it, being a prison chaplain would allow me to complete my ministry. As the Gospel of Matthew says, 'I was sick and you visited me, I was thirsty and you gave me drink, I was in prison and you came to me.' Well as a pastor I had visited the sick and given drink to the poor, but I had never been with prisoners."

The Reverend Carroll Picket has served as chaplain to ninety-five executed prisoners.

"An inmate's life is one of untruths—if inmates couldn't be honest with themselves, they couldn't be honest with God."

Although "Old Sparky" is no longer in commission, it stands as a reminder of a time when the electric chair was used to carry out executions in Texas.

Little did Carroll realize that he was to be assigned to the same unit where the deadly siege had occurred. "My office was in the chapel where the hostage takers worked, and I conducted Bible classes in the same library where the two slain women had worked. Every day I had to walk up the same ramp where the shootings occurred. So at first it was very traumatic. But I realized that the prisoners needed Christ more than anyone."

"Inmates," maintains Carroll, "are dealing with two primary issues: anger and truth." Chapel services, Bible study, and music help them to release their anger. Truth is more difficult. "I had a handwritten card in my desk drawer," Carroll states. "On it I wrote the word 'truth.' Whenever I felt an inmate was not telling me the truth, I simply held up the card and showed it to him. Sometimes the inmate would get so upset he would walk out. Other times he would smile and then tell the truth. It is important for a chaplain to know that an inmate's life is one of untruths. But Christ's ministry is one of truth, and without it you have nothing. If inmates couldn't be honest with themselves, they couldn't be honest with God."

In 1982 capital punishment was reinstated in Texas, and Carroll was assigned the position as chaplain to the death house. He was surprised to learn that the execution chamber was located just twenty yards from the chapel where he worked. The first execution by lethal injection was scheduled a few weeks later. Now Carroll had to determine what he was going to do. Would he stay and be the chaplain for a practice he considered inhumane or would he leave. "I knew the Presbyterian Church's position against capital punishment and supported it. But early in my ministry I had made a promise to one of my members who had a terminal disease and who was afraid of facing death alone that I would be with him when he died. I kept that promise. Now I felt that same way about the prisoners I was chaplain to, that I needed to be with them when they died."

"When I told the warden that I would accept the position," Carroll says, "he made it clear what he expected from me. 'Your job,' he said, 'is to make sure the prisoner walks quietly into the death chamber and doesn't fight getting onto the table. What you do spiritually with them is up to you and God.' However I saw my responsibility as one of friendship and honesty."

In 1995, after sixteen years and ninety-five executions, Carroll retired. "I have never favored capital punishment. The worst punishment a prisoner can receive is a life sentence with no possibility of parole. Taking a person's life just creates more victims." ∎

". . . I was in prison and you visited me."
(Matthew 25:36)

College chaplain helps others to enjoy a lifetime love of learning.

For Brenda Tapia, school integration during the sixties was not a positive experience. After years of being an exceptional student in a segregated school, she was suddenly the only African American in her college prep high school classes. "I felt like a fly in buttermilk," Brenda recalls. "I would be the first to raise my hand in class and the last to be called on. I'd turn in a paper that I was proud of only to get it back graded as a C, yet there were no negative comments from the teacher on it. When I'd ask what I did wrong, I was told to sit down and be quiet."

Brenda came from a home where her parents stressed it was their job to provide for the family and her responsibility to do well in school. "You didn't bring C's home to my mother's house; A's were expected." Brenda's family were fourth-generation Presbyterians, and faith was at the center of their life. "I can remember when I was four years old. I was helping my grandfather dry the dishes, and he began to tell me about God and Jesus Christ." For the next fourteen years her grandfather helped Brenda to understand the two most important keys to life: a strong relationship with God and the need for a sound education. "The first thing my grandfather did each morning and the last thing he did at night was to get on his knees and pray. Each day he lived the type of life Jesus did, loving everybody and helping those in need." Brenda can remember when her grandfather became sick, she would help him out of bed so that he could pray.

The strength and faith Brenda received from her family helped her to stay in school and to excel, even during the difficult times of school integration. As a senior, she received guidance from a group of volunteers from the local YMCA. One of the volunteers took a special interest in Brenda and suggested that she apply to prestigious Howard University. When she asked her high school guidance counselor about Howard, he said he never heard of it and then added, "I don't know why you people bother to go to college anyway. I've got a friend at Howard Johnsons, and I'll bet you could get a job in housekeeping there." She recalls quietly biting her lip, saying that she wasn't interested in the job, and then thanking him for his time.

Brenda applied to Howard University, was accepted, and graduated with a degree in psychology. During her college years her faith was tested. University life in the late sixties and early seventies were tumultuous. The Vietnam war was dividing the nation, civil rights was a burning issue, and some theologians had proclaimed that God was dead. Caught up in the spirit of the times, Brenda stayed as far away from church as possible.

Upon graduation, Brenda took a job as a counselor, met a man, and married him. But the marriage was not a happy one. "It took being married to an abusive husband to rediscover my faith roots," she recalls. "I was mentally

The Reverend Brenda Tapia works with Love of Learning students to prepare them for college and life beyond.

Love of Learning students are nurtured throughout their high school years resulting in over 90 percent going on to earn a college degree.

and physically abused. My back was to the wall, and I had nobody to turn to except God. That was the beginning of my return to spirituality. I rediscovered who God is, what her relationship to me is, and what my relationship to her is. I realized my problems were not psychological but instead spiritual."

After two-and-a-half years, the marriage ended. Brenda decided to return to school to get an advanced degree in psychology, with an emphasis on Christian education. She sought the advice of her uncle, a Presbyterian minister, and he suggested that she consider seminary. At first, Brenda resisted. "I didn't feel the call to ministry," Brenda remembers, "but my uncle asked me to at least visit a seminary before making a decision." She decided to interview with Dr. James Costen at Johnson C. Smith Seminary in Atlanta. "Dr. Costen made such a powerful impression on me." He suggested that she consider pursuing a master of divinity degree because, even though at the time she didn't feel the call to ministry, she could still work in Christian education. "As I got up to leave, Dr. Costen hugged me. It was an emotional experience. I felt the love of God, the presence of God, and the grace of God during that interview." Brenda enrolled at Johnson C. Smith seminary and earned her masters of divinity degree.

After graduating and spending a year as a hospital chaplain, she returned home to Davidson, North Carolina, and took a part-time position as assistant chaplain at Davidson College, a Presbyterian-related college. Davidson was developing programs to reach out to minority students, and Brenda soon had a full-time position in this area. Under Brenda's guidance, the program "Love of Learning" was developed. Based on Matthew 6:33, "Strive first for the kingdom of God and his righteousness, and all these things will be given to you as well." Love of Learning seeks to identify ninth grade students from area schools who otherwise would never have the chance to go to college and to prepare them for college and life beyond. The students are nurtured academically and spiritually all through their high school years through counseling, tutoring, training, and Christian education classes.

Astoundingly, over 90 percent of Love of Learning students go on to college. More important, the students discover that they are not just physical beings but persons created in God's image. Since the beginning, Love of Learning students have gone on to assume leadership roles in society. They have earned advanced degrees, and some have become teachers or corporate executives. Others have gone into fields such as engineering, finance, international banking, and marketing.

For Brenda, Love of Learning is a continuation of what her own grandfather taught her long ago: combine a strong relationship with God with a sound education. ■

"Strive first for the kingdom of God . . ."
(Matthew 6:33)

Military chaplain Reverend Lucy der
Garabedian has served in both active
Army units and military hospitals.

Army chaplain has a passion for the people in the military.

Lucy der Garabedian grew up in Lebanon. She remembers the pre-war country
of her childhood, a peaceful place where people flocked from all over the world
to enjoy the wonderful beaches and the stable society. But when Lucy was in high
school, that all changed. Her older brother, Mosig, who was serving in the military, was killed by a radical religious group who had taken over the barracks and
executed him along with all the other Christian soldiers who were housed there.

Amazingly, Lucy emerged from that devastating experience with a
deepened faith. After college, she was employed as a religion teacher at the
Armenian Evangelical College in Beirut, when civil war broke out. "It was
terrible," Lucy remembers. "Nobody was safe, particularly Americans and
people in the universities. I decided to leave the country and further my education in the United States."

Getting out of the country meant being driven to a coastal port since the
airports were closed. After a harrowing ride with gunfire and explosions along
the way, Lucy boarded a ship to Cypress with only one bag of luggage. "I came to
Richmond, Virginia, to study at the Presbyterian School of Christian Education

because I thought I had been promised a full scholarship. But when I arrived, they told me that there was no scholarship; it had been a miscommunication."

Without any money and with no scholarship, Lucy was in a desperate situation, but then she ran into Joan Gallagher with the Resource Center of the General Assembly of the Presbyterian Church. Upon hearing Lucy's story, Joan was able to secure an educational grant from the denomination along with additional money from the Grace Covenant Presbyterian Church of Richmond. "Joan had this huge smile on her face," Lucy says, "when she told me about the funding. It was God's faithfulness, and I was being trained to trust in God. Here I was a woman with an accent in this strange country so far from home. This act of kindness showed me that I was in a universal body of Christ."

After earning her masters degree, Lucy accepted a Christian education position at a Presbyterian church in Wooster, Ohio. It was not long before members of the congregation recognized that Lucy had many pastoral gifts and suggested that she might be called into ministry. So, Lucy enrolled a year later at Union Theological Seminary in Richmond, Virginia, with the financial help of the Wooster congregation.

After seminary, Lucy sensed that God was calling her into military chaplaincy, and she applied and was accepted into the Army. Lucy explains, "My whole life I've had a special place in my heart for the people in the military. The chaplaincy is a wonderful ministry because you are called to be with the soldiers wherever they are. Four days in a foxhole can leave a person with an extreme level of isolation. Soldiers begin to think about life issues more deeply. That is why we are there, to be with them and to help them sort things out."

Once, when Lucy's unit was deployed to Egypt, a newly married soldier was concerned about his young wife, who was left behind at Fort Stewart without any friends. Lucy was able to arrange emergency long distance phone calls so the soldier could keep in contact with his wife. As Lucy explains, "When a soldier has a personal problem, he or she is at high risk because it becomes difficult to concentrate on the mission at hand and the soldier will become a liability to the unit. As chaplains we are there to provide assurance of God's love and to do what we can to relieve their anxieties."

During the summer of 1999, Lucy was given a new assignment: hospital chaplain. She engaged in a year-long training program at the Walter Reed Army Medical Center in Washington and the National Naval Medical Center in Bethesda, Maryland. Before Lucy enters a patient's room she says a prayer for the soldier she is about to see and thanks God for allowing her to be there for that person in his or her pain. "People who are undergoing treatment in a hospital often are dealing with extreme feelings of anger," she says. "Some will say, 'Why me; what did I do to deserve this?' As chaplains, we become their sounding board. We listen, and hopefully we have an opportunity to say something that builds their faith. The important thing is that we're there for them." ■

Above:
"Lucy D.," as her soldiers and co-workers call her, serves as hospital chaplain at the Walter Reed Army Medical Center in Washington D. C.

Below:
Lucy visits with Ensign Daniel Johnson, the son of Presbyterian missionaries, who lost his legs rescuing a fellow sailor.

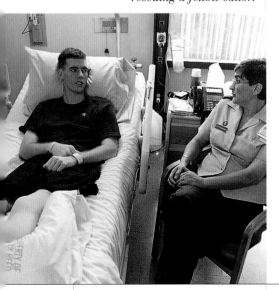

"Even though I walk through the darkest valley, I fear no evil . . ." (Psalm 23:4)

The Reverend Jeannette Sutton is a chaplain to victims of domestic abuse.

Chaplain mends the broken wings of women in abuse shelters.

When Jeannette Sutton first approached Colorado domestic violence shelters about the possibility of being a chaplain, they were not interested. After all, the officials at a not-for-profit corporation that runs shelters for battered women in the Denver area knew that many victims of domestic violence are abused in the name of religion. "They were afraid," Jeannette explains, "that a chaplain would come in and do what some religious groups have been doing to women for centuries: telling them that they need to pray more and to go home, be a servant, and submit, as if it is their cross to bear."

Jeannette grew up in southern California. While involved in the youth group of Trinity Presbyterian Church in the Orange County suburb of Santa Ana, she was influenced by her youth leader, Volet Weber, a native of the Philippines. Volet placed the pictures of each of her youth group members on the bulletin board in her home. Each evening before going to bed, she would pray individually for every member of the group. "When I found out that she did that," Jeannette remembers, "I was touched that someone would pray for me every day."

Jeannette received a scholarship in track and field at Seattle Pacific University and decided to pursue a degree in Christian education and sociology. While at the university she had an experience that would shape her faith and guide her future. "The father of my boyfriend at the time was dying. We all gathered around his hospital bed and sang songs and prayed for him. It was very emotional. At the moment of his death, I saw a white dove fly by the window, as if his soul were leaving his body and going on. I was suddenly overcome by a feeling of peace."

After graduation, Jeannette was still hungry for more education and wanted to attend a seminary, not to become a minister but to further her spiritual growth. She chose Princeton Theological Seminary in New Jersey, and while at Princeton she served as a student intern at Trenton Psychiatric Hospital. "When I first applied for an internship," Jeannette recalls, "I was asked what most frightened me. I told them that my biggest fears involved old people and bad smells. 'Well,' they told me, 'that is where you are going,' and they placed me in the geriatric infirmary of the hospital."

During her internship at the hospital, Jeannette learned what it was like to be with people outcast by society. Many of the patients spent their time in silence, withdrawn from the world. "They had very little human contact," Jeannette remembers. "At mealtime someone would put a tray of food in front of the patients and, when the patients finished, someone would wipe their faces. When I first arrived, the patients would just stare at me. So I would find an empty seat and sit next to one of them, talking quietly while we held hands. Sometimes when I sat with them, I would pray. This is when I realized that I wanted to be a minister, sitting with these people, doing what Jesus would do."

After graduation from seminary, Jeannette and her husband, David, also a seminarian, moved to Denver, Colorado, and became involved in Shepherd of the Hills Presbyterian Church. After a brief hospital internship, Jeannette talked with her pastor, Alan Landes, about where her gifts could best be used. He told her about the important work of one domestic violence organization and suggested, "I'll bet they could use a chaplain there." So, Jeannette approached them, only to be rejected at first. But Jeannette was persistent: "I told them what a chaplain does, that we are called to be with people in their pain and to use whatever resources we have to help them, not in order to indoctrinate them but to help them deal with their pain through their own theological perspective."

"The gathering place in a women's shelter is in the kitchen."

After several months, the agency decided to allow Jeannette to occupy a small office in the basement of one of the shelters. However, she was not to go to the women in the shelter; they had to come to her office. "I said I'd try it," Jeannette recalls, "but it was contrary to what a chaplain does, to be with people in their environment, working by their side." As Jeannette thought about how to get to meet the women in the shelter, she kept thinking about that image of the chaplain being with them in their environment. "Where is the gathering place in a woman's shelter?" she wondered. Then it occurred to her: "The gathering place in a woman's shelter is the kitchen. So I began to go to the kitchen before meals and help them cut up the vegetables. Then when it was nearly time to eat I'd help them set the table. After the meal, I'd play with the children."

Within a short time, she and the other women were talking and beginning to build relationships. Soon Jeannette was working with several shelters in the Denver area. "I decided to call my ministry 'Mending Wings' after listening to a song by Martina McBride called 'Broken Wings.' The song tells of a woman whose wings have been broken by a lover who keeps telling her that she has no worth. This woman can still sing, but, as the song laments, 'You should see her when she flies.' The women in the shelter have somehow managed to escape and, by mending their wings, someday they will fly again. That is our hope." ∎

". . . the Lord is faithful; he will strengthen you and guard you . . . (2 Thessalonians 3:3)

The Columbine Tragedy

In the spring of 1999, two heavily armed students forced their way into Columbine High School in the Denver suburb of Littleton. As a result of their terrifying violence, twelve students and one teacher lost their lives. Jeannette Sutton was hired by the Jefferson County Sheriff's Department to be the coordinator for the victim advocates who were brought in to help the victims' families.

"Nothing like this had ever happened before," Jeannette says. "The sheriff's office was so overwhelmed with offers of help from all over the nation. Nobody on staff knew how to handle something of this magnitude, so they decided to bring in additional people to help coordinate the efforts." In addition to her organizational responsibilities, Jeannette directly counseled two of the families who lost children. "I helped to make sure that the families had the information they needed, that they had someone to listen to them, and that they got the support they needed."

"Many positive things are coming out of this tragedy," Jeannette goes on to say. "The community is becoming tightly knit, and churches are more involved in the life of the people who live here. People across the nation have opened their hearts by sending thousands of letters of support and volunteering to help in any way they can. The families are extremely touched by the outreach and words of encouragement."

"I have a new respect for the law enforcement officers," Jeannette says. "As soon as the officers left the high school after the shooting, they had to respond to another tragedy. A little girl fell into a river. The same officers who were involved at Columbine had to search the river for the little girl's body and then retrieve it. Without even getting a chance to deal with their emotions from the shooting they had to go on to another terrible assignment. It is a dimension of public service that most people never realize."

0
0
ON CAMPUS

0
0
Colleges Affiliated with the Presbyterian Church

Presbyterians have a long heritage of supporting higher education. Today there are sixty-seven colleges affiliated with the Presbyterian Church (U.S.A.), and in addition to helping these colleges, the Presbyterian Church supports the work of campus ministries on nearly eight hundred college and university campuses.

The goal at Whitworth College is to foster a lifelong commitment to service.

Over fifteen hundred students attend Whitworth College, a private, liberal arts college affiliated with the Presbyterian Church (U.S.A.) and located in Spokane, Washington. Whitworth's mission "is to provide its diverse student body an education of the mind and the heart, equipping its graduates to honor God, follow Christ, and serve humanity."

Along with a full complement of academic programs in many fields, from business to education to the sciences, Whitworth also offers programs in religion and pre-ministry. According to Whitworth president, Bill Robinson, "Our school isn't just affiliated with the denomination, it is spiritually connected with the Presbyterian Church. We are very proud of that relationship. I love Whitworth, the campus environment, what we stand for in our mission, and our people. We have a strong Christian commitment coupled with a strong commitment to the free exchange of ideas. It's an important distinction. People here talk about our vitality of being Christian in our emphasis and our perspective while being very open and unrestrictive in our intellectual inquiry. I think that is a very accurate description of Whitworth."

Another aspect of Whitworth College is its commitment to community service. "It is one of the things that drew me to Whitworth," says recent grad Janise Matyas. "There are real opportunities for service in the community." According to vice president for Student Life, Kathy Storm, "It is part of our world view commitment that no matter where our students end up living after college, part of our mission is to foster a lifelong commitment to service."

Whitworth student Brenna Robinson talks about her life growing up in the midwest and northwest. "I've been a church kid all my life. Our family was first involved in a conservative Bible church in Illinois, then a liberal Brethren church in Indiana, and now a Presbyterian church right here on campus. The contrast among these three traditions gave me an incredible insight into three different approaches to Christianity."

0
0

In her spare time Whitworth College undergrad Brenna Robinson loves to climb trees.

Whitworth student Brenna Robinson, recent grad Janise Matyas, and vice president for Student Life, Kathy Storm, take time out of their busy schedules to chat.

Outdoor activities are a big part of life on the Whitworth campus.

Whitworth Chaplain Terry McGonigal is accessible for all the students on campus.

One of Brenna's first memories of church was in Illinois when all the young people were asked to give faith testimonies before being baptized. "The girl who spoke before me had the most amazing faith story. It was about how God had thundered into her life, a larger-than-life God who spoke to her in a loud, clear voice. It was so incredible that I went home and prayed for God to come into my heart in the same way. But nothing dramatic happened so I thought I was doing something wrong. I still felt that God loved me, but there just weren't any fireworks."

It wasn't until Brenna was in her mid-teens while attending youth camp that she realized that God can come to people in different ways. "We were sitting around a fire telling our faith stories when one girl said something that opened my eyes. She told how God hadn't come to her with big banging cymbals and loud trumpets, but instead had come into her heart with a whisper. It was so enlightening, because for the first time I realized that God doesn't have to come with great fanfare but can come quietly. My faith finally made sense to me."

After her family moved to Indiana, Brenna, who had just gotten her driver's permit, was involved in a minor traffic accident. She had backed the family's minivan into a parked flatbed truck, and she recalls being terrified to face her father. "I avoided him for almost a week. Finally, one day I was outside cutting the lawn when he came up to me and said to shut off the mower. My heart was beating fast, because I knew he wanted to talk about the accident. He asked me to tell him about it. And, as I did, my eyes began to well up with tears and I started to shake. That is when I learned about grace. He simply said that everyone has at least one small accident and I just had mine early in my life. My father never mentioned another word about it. He didn't make me the butt of any jokes, he didn't keep bringing it up, and he didn't assess blame. It was a pure act of grace, something I will never forget."

The Robinson family moved to Spokane while Brenna was in high school so her father could assume the presidency of Whitworth College. "I looked at a lot of colleges, but I felt led by God to stay here. It was a struggle at first because my father is president, but the classes here and the dedication of the professors and instructors are great. Whitworth is also a very spiritual school with a great religion department and a philosophy program."

Brenna, along with many other students, has developed a warm relationship with the school's chaplain, Terry McGonigal. "He is a very warm and nurturing man. Everyone feels they can stop in and talk with him. It's not uncommon to see Terry interrupt his walk across campus to stop and ask a student how things are going and to invite students to his office just to talk. He is one of the reasons this is such a friendly and dynamic school."

After graduation, Brenna is planning to go into the ministry, at first either working with youth or possibly in inner-city mission work. After getting some practical experience, she will decide whether she feels called into the ministry and be open to seminary. ■

"The fear of the LORD is the beginning of knowledge . . ." (Proverbs 1:7)

The Mary Holmes choir under the direction of Hugh Davis has performed in many locations across the country.

At Mary Holmes College, educational opportunities are provided to all.

Mary Holmes College, located in West Point, Mississippi, is a two-year college related to the Presbyterian Church (U.S.A.) with an enrollment of over four hundred students. Founded on the belief that everyone deserves the opportunity of advancement through education, the college has an open admissions policy. Through the dedication of its professors and staff, students receive the kind of individual attention not often available at larger schools in order to build the knowledge and skills necessary to compete in today's world.

As is the case at most private colleges, tuition can no longer cover the entire cost of an education at Mary Holmes. The Presbyterian Church (U.S.A.) provides assistance to the college through the denomination's yearly Christmas Joy Offering, gifts from individual churches and members, and technical support. Even so, more financial assistance is needed, especially since Mary Holmes, like many other small colleges, has a limited pool of graduates available to support the future needs of the college through special gifts and endowments.

Above:
Under the leadership of Dr. Elvalee Banks, Mary Holmes College is continuing to provide personalized education for all.

Below:
Ms. B. McClendon of the registrar's office helps students with scheduling and financial aid.

Kelvin Ruth's goal is to be either an educator or a school administrator.

International student Mwiche "Diane" Sichilongo from Zambia is studying business management.

Below:
Jerricka Gardner excels in sports and is planning to complete his education at Stillman College.

Even with all its financial pressures, the mission of Mary Holmes College remains strong. According to school president Dr. Elvalee Banks, "This college has been instrumental in guiding its students to success. We have a tremendous number of successful doctors, lawyers, educators, and business people who started their college education here. Almost everywhere I travel to talk about Mary Holmes College, someone in the crowd will come up to me and say they either know someone who attended or attended themselves. This is very gratifying. It tells us how important this school is in the lives of its graduates."

Typical of many Mary Holmes students is Kelvin Ruth. Raised on his family's farm in Woodland, Mississippi, Kelvin always had plenty of chores to do. In addition to his work on the farm and in school, he was president of the local 4H Club and a member of the Future Farmers of America. But Kelvin's passion is education. "I'm an education major here at Mary Holmes College and my goal is to be an administrator for a school. After I leave here I plan to go to Stillman College and then go on from there and get an advanced degree."

To Kelvin, education and faith have always been at his core. "In church I've learned to be a more mature person and to use my faith to love others as I love myself. Here at Mary Holmes I've been encouraged by the teachers and administrators. They've built me up when I was down and motivated me to be the best I can be. This is a small Christian college where the atmosphere feels more like home and everyone knows you by name. It's been a great experience. My hope is to take this experience and use it in my career. There is a need for more African American educators who can encourage others to continue their educations."

Another student, Jerricka Gardner, remembers his life growing up. When he was seven, Jerricka's father abandoned the family, leaving his mother to care for his sister and two brothers. "When I was young I got in with a bad crowd and caused my mother some pain. But after I accepted Christ into my life, things began to turn around. My grades improved and I was able to graduate from high school. I enrolled at Mary Holmes because it's a good school with Christian values. Here I've made real friends and together with the teachers and staff, they are like a family to me."

After graduation from Mary Holmes, Jerricka plans to enroll at Stillman College in order to complete his bachelor's degree. A physical education major, he would like to join the football team at Stillman and become a professional football player if the opportunity comes. Otherwise, Jerricka would like to become a high school coach and work with young people. According to Jerricka, "Even though I haven't had a relationship with my father since he left, my dream is for him to come to my graduation. I know he probably won't come, but it would be great to see him. Either way, I'm proud of myself, and my mother is also proud. I know she'll be at my graduation."

Julius Mason has childhood memories of staying at his grandparents' house. "They had a wood stove, and in the morning my grandfather would get me up and we'd sit and talk while we got warm. He told me that some day I would make something of myself, and if he wasn't around to see it, he would be in heaven watching down on me. After he passed away I told my mother that I was going to go to college to honor him."

Born in rural Noxubee County, Mississippi, Julius was raised in a single-parent home with three brothers. After graduating from high school, he realized that his test scores weren't high enough to get him into a university. "Some people told me that I should join the workforce and forget about college. But I was determined to go to school, so when I heard that Mary Holmes College had an open admissions policy and would give everyone a chance regardless of grades, I applied and was accepted. My whole family was proud of me and soon I moved away to school. It was the first time I'd been away from home."

Julius has always been a determined person, and he says that the secret to success "is to have faith, pray regularly, and keep looking up to God no matter what anyone says to discourage you." A devoted son, he remembers having two jobs while in high school. "Each week I'd bring one of my checks home and give it to my mother. She asked why I was giving her the money, and I told her that it was to show her how much I appreciated all she did for me."

During summer breaks, Julius goes home and works in order to help with the household expenses. "I get to spend some time with my brothers, and I hope they can follow in my footsteps and go to college." Julius sees Mary Holmes College as his home away from home. "The students and teachers are like family. Everyone helps each other out."

Faith has always been a big part of Julius's life. "I was raised Baptist and was always involved in my church back home. This is a Presbyterian college, and at first I felt a little shaky about that. But after I got here I started going to the First Presbyterian Church with some other students, and I liked it and found it had a lot in common with my church back home."

Julius loves to cook and has won several trophies in competitions around the state. A counselor in high school told him about the Culinary Arts School for Great American Chefs in Paris. He applied, was awarded a scholarship, and will attend once he completes his college education. Needing extra income to help cover his costs at school, Julius was given permission to use the kitchen in his dorm at night to make food for the other students. "My specialties are fried chicken and barbecue. The secret to good barbecue is in the sauce, and I have my own recipe. I really enjoy making food for the other students, and having the opportunity to make them food and earn extra money is very satisfying." ■

Julius Mason loves to cook and plans to attend the Culinary Arts School for Great American Chefs in Paris after graduation.

Professor Pat Thomas, a graduate of Mary Holmes College, has returned to teach at the college.

"0 the depth of the riches and wisdom and knowledge of God!" (Romans 11:33a)

A PLACE FOR

Presbyterian Conference Centers

The Presbyterian Church (U.S.A.) maintains four national conference centers, each with its own character. Open to people of all faiths, the conference centers provide places for spiritual renewal, opportunities to meet others, and a variety of programs and activities aimed at the deepening of faith. In addition to the national centers, there are more than 165 local and regional Presbyterian-related camps and conference centers throughout the United States.

National conference centers provide a place for spiritual growth and renewal.

Someone long ago referred to Psalm 121, "I lift up my eyes to the hills," to describe Montreat. The Reverend Emily Enders Odom, director of public relations, says "You can't help but do that as you gaze up to the mountaintops from this glorious valley."

She recalls a recent experience when a television crew was at Montreat to film a news segment during a worship and music conference attended by fifteen hundred people. Emily says, "As I stood outside with the producer, two teens strutted by. They were walking arm in arm, singing as they passed. The producer turned to me and said, 'I don't think you'd see that anywhere else, teenagers smiling and singing together, voluntarily!' That's the kind of effect Montreat has on people. They come here from all over the country and within a short time, they are transformed by feelings of safety, spirituality, and community."

Montreat Conference Center President Emile Dieth adds, "Montreat was founded over one hundred years ago to allow people to have a Christian

REFLECTION

experience away from their everyday lives. That is our mission: to bring people close to Christ through the programs we offer." Surrounded by the Blue Ridge mountains of western North Carolina, Montreat is situated on four thousand acres of lush forest and mountainous terrain, two thirds of which is dedicated to wilderness. Along with the Montreat Conference Center, Montreat is home to Montreat College, over six hundred cottages, the Montreat Presbyterian Church, and the regional office of the Presbyterian Church (U.S.A.) Historical Society. Each year over thirty thousand guests attend a variety of conferences hosted by the center. These include conferences for youth, adults, families, educators, pastors, and church leaders. Conferences are held year round and cover a vast number of topics, including spirituality, worship and music, issues of Christian life, and development of ministry and mission skills.

"I know of no place else where the wonders of God's creation are so evident," says Ghost Ranch director of Educational Programming, the Reverend,

"The Chimney" stands above the expansive landscape of Ghost Ranch in New Mexico.

Dr. Jean Richardson. "This is a place that has been home to humans for twenty thousand years and where dinosaurs roamed the land 250 million years ago. It is also a place where things have pretty much remained the same for thousands of years. People come here to admire spectacular beauty, study ancient cultures, participate in archaeological digs, and get closer to God. Imagine going on a dig and holding a piece of an ancient culture in your hands. There is no better reminder that we are not alone in this world."

Ghost Ranch is located one hour north of Santa Fe and is comprised of over twenty-one thousand acres of mountainous terrain. A gift to the Presbyterian Church from Arthur and Phoebe Pack in the 1950s, Ghost Ranch offers a variety of programming in the arts, theology, spirituality, writing, creation, culture, history, archaeology, along with outdoor activities that include anything from rafting to horseback riding. Each year Ghost Ranch welcomes nearly forty thousand guests. The center has year-round programming, and the conference center can house up to 450 people. According to Jean Richardson, "We have over thirty-three square miles of space, the same size as Manhattan, yet all the housing is centralized. You can enjoy the fellowship of people, yet also find places for absolute solitude."

Located in the heart of central Santa Fe, New Mexico, Plaza Resolana has a sister relationship with Ghost Ranch and is within walking distance of the opera, museums, art galleries, restaurants, and shopping. According to conference planner Jim Baird, "Plaza Resolana is unique in that it is the only conference center located in an urban area. Our name is derived from the phrase *la resolana*, which is the space on the south side of a building, protected from the wind and warmed by the winter sun. It's the perfect name for a conference center because it reflects what the church needs to be in this city, a safe place of warmth and life. It's the light of Christian hospitality." It's where people gather to exchange ideas, have conversations, and share stories. The center has year-round programming and will also customize programs for participants. Jim says, "If a group wants to come and experience a pueblo, we will arrange to have them spend a day with an artist who lives and works in one, which is far more educational than just viewing one from afar."

Another conference center that has mission and hospitality at its heart is Stony Point. First opened as a refuge for missionaries who were home from abroad on furlough, the conference center has expanded its focus to provide a quiet place for nurture, education, and mission. Located just northwest of New York City, nestled in the scenic Hudson River Valley, Stony Point welcomes over eighteen thousand guests a year who come to its peaceful setting for retreats, training, and renewal. ■

The accommodations at Ghost Ranch provide a view of the spectacular mountains.

Works of art fill the lawn of Plaza Resolana in Santa Fe, New Mexico.

Plaza Resolana in Santa Fe, New Mexico, is the only Presbyterian conference center located in an urban environment.

". . . you, O LORD, have made me glad . . . at the works of your hands I sing for joy." (Psalm 92:4)

The Work of the Presbyteries

The Presbyterian Church is called a "connectional church" because local churches are not islands unto themselves but are linked together for greater service. The more than eleven thousand congregations in the Presbyterian Church (U.S.A.) are grouped into over 170 presbyteries, which are regional associations of ministers and congregations.

For example, the 117 Presbyterian congregations in the greater Chicago area form the Presbytery of Chicago, which is committed to building partnerships in ministry—church to church and people to people. One such partnership is the decade-long relationship between two Chicago area churches—the suburban, mostly anglo Hope Presbyterian Church of Wheaton and the inner-city, mostly African American Hope Presbyterian Church of Englewood. The two congregations, though quite different, engage in dialog, trust-building, and mutual ministry projects in an effort known as "Hope."

Face painting is one of the many activities at the annual picnic put on each year by the Hope congregations of Chicago and Wheaton, Illinois.

Two congregations form a partnership of faith and community.

When Lee Van Ham was called as pastor of Hope Presbyterian Church in the Chicago suburb of Wheaton, he asked Floyd Rhodes, an African American from the Chicago Presbytery office, to speak at the installation service. According to Lee, "When I arrived in Wheaton, I was surprised that my new call was to serve a mostly white, affluent suburban congregation, which didn't fit in with my view of justice in the world. I saw it as a divine call and an opportunity to find a way to bring diversity and witness into the life of our church."

That opportunity came when the mission committee of the church asked about the possibility of forming a partnership with an inner-city church. Lee called Floyd for advice, and Floyd suggested that the Hope Presbyterian Church in the Englewood neighborhood might be open to such a relationship. It seemed an obvious match: two congregations named Hope, one a suburban Anglo church and the other an urban African American church. Members of both congregations met, and the road to partnership began.

As Lee remembers, "During our first meeting, the Englewood Hope representatives were suspicious of the Wheaton Hope representatives' motives. One Englewood member who was leery asked point blank, 'What's in it for you?' I replied that I felt incomplete in our ministry. We need a much stronger sense that the body of Christ is multi-ethnic. For us to feel a part of God's salvation we needed a partnership with a city church."

Englewood Hope pastor, Leslie Sanders, had his own concerns. "This type of suburban-city partnership historically revolves around financial resources, with the suburban church sending its money to the city church. I wanted this partnership to be based on sharing and appreciating our cultural differences, not dollars-and-cents."

The partnership began in a small way, with groups from the two congregations getting together for dialog on issues of race, suburban-versus-city living, styles of worship, and social justice. During one conversation, the controversial verdict in the celebrity trial of O. J. Simpson came up. According to Leslie, "The people from the suburbs couldn't understand the jubilation in the African American community, and many didn't feel justice had been served. We explained that it was the first time anyone could remember an African American having the unlimited resources to defend himself well. It had nothing to do with our opinion of O. J. Simpson; we felt he had abandoned us years ago. The joy was about the justice system in general and how so many people in the past had been railroaded."

For over ten years the partnership has continued. Little by little the two churches have developed mutual trust and understanding. "Each of our churches has a different style of worship," Lee observes. "Ours is more traditional and not as openly emotive. Hope Chicago, on the other hand, practices Afro-centric worship with the presence of gospel, jazz, and blues praise music and a more charismatic style of preaching."

There are also many commonalities. "A friendship has developed between Lee and myself," Leslie states, "both as fellow pastors and as Christians. We speak to each other at least weekly." The members of the two churches have discovered that their life experiences are not always so different. "We found," Leslie notes, "that our families face similar challenges both at work and at home."

Lee and his wife, Juanita, took a new path in their faith journey in 1999 when they left the Wheaton church to begin a new ministry called Jubilee Economics Ministries (JEM). Based in Chicago, JEM is a ministry of economic justice that seeks to integrate faith and economics through experiential education, activism, and cross-cultural immersions. It brings together people separated by economic and ethnic divisions. In many ways, this new ministry grew out of Lee and Juanita's experiences through the partnership with the Englewood Hope congregation. ■

The annual picnic allows families from two congregations to come together in fellowship.

". . . together with all those who in every place call on the name of our Lord Jesus Christ . . ."
(1 Corinthians 1:2)

Pastor demonstrates a passion for church planting.

In 1966, Grady Allison was pastor of a Baptist church in Baytown, Texas, with an opportunity to serve a congregation in New York City. In order to be considered for the post, Grady needed to get letters of recommendation from pastors of other denominations in Baytown, and he asked Burt Dowler, the pastor of the local Presbyterian church, to write one of the letters. As Grady remembers, "Burt said he'd be happy to write a letter. Then he added, 'I don't want to upset you, but from the way you're talking, you sound more like a Presbyterian than a Baptist.' Since I'd only attended two Presbyterian worship services in my life, I disregarded what he said."

A few weeks later, Grady was home in bed with the flu when the phone rang. It was Burt saying that he was about to write the letter and didn't understand why Grady was interested in a church in New York City. "Why go to New York when there is an opportunity in Houston." Grady replied, "I'm interested in an American Baptist church and there aren't any in Houston, so I don't know what you mean." Burt explained that the church in Houston was Presbyterian, and Grady replied, "Burt, I'm sick and you're crazy, go ahead and recommend me for anything you want, just get off the phone and let me get back to bed."

The Reverend Grady Allison is the chairperson of the New Church Development Committee of the Presbytery of Western Colorado.

The Reverend Jim Patton and his wife, Charlene, members of the Rico Ministry Committee, look through the scrapbook that shows Rico's progress from its first meeting as a fellowship to the present-day church construction.

"The presbytery provided funding and the only instructions we received were that they didn't care what we did just so within three years the church was self-supporting."

A week later the presbytery office in Houston called and asked Grady to interview for an organizing pastor position for a new church. Grady was offered the position and accepted the call. Grady explains, "The presbytery provided funding and the only instructions we received were that they didn't care what we did just so within three years the church was self-supporting. It was a tall order; however by the grace of God three years later not only was the church supporting itself but we had enough in pledges to begin the construction of a sanctuary."

The Rico Presbyterian Church in Rico, Colorado,
is one of five new churches being organized by
members of the Presbytery of Western Colorado.

The mountains of western Colorado provide breathtaking views.

The Reverend Grady Allison stands in front of the historic Eckert Presbyterian Church in Eckert, Colorado.

Even after Grady retired, the Presbytery of Western Colorado asked Grady to chair its committee on new church development. The presbytery had the fewest number of congregations in the denomination, only fourteen, and more churches were needed. A plan was developed to build five new churches by the year 2006, an extremely aggressive plan given the size of the presbytery.

According to Grady, successfully starting new churches requires a presbytery that has a passion for building ministries along with the faith, the people, and the financial resources to carry it out. "We are blessed to have people in the presbytery who have the vision of evangelism and are willing to dedicate their time to new church development. Without these dedicated people we couldn't do it."

So far, three out of the five proposed new churches are well on their way to becoming a reality. Two churches, one in Ridgeway and the other in Grand Junction, have called organizing pastors and are worshiping weekly. Land for the Grand Junction church has been acquired. The Rico ministry is progressing while the Eagle project has been temporarily postponed. The fifth site is under study and should be announced well before the 2006 goal. "It is insane for a presbytery of our size to be starting this many new churches," Grady observes, "but we feel called by God to do it anyway. The leap of faith that the members of this presbytery have taken cannot be over emphasized. At first we had very heated discussions, but in our own western way, somebody finally said, 'Let's put up or shut up.' To people in these parts, those are fighting words. So, of course, we decided to go ahead and do it." ∎

"Ask . . . where the good way lies; and walk in it, and find rest for your souls." (Jeremiah 6:16)

Commissioned lay pastors serve through the special authority of the larger church.

Binh Thanh Nguyen, who grew up in Vietnam, was born into a non-Christian family but attended a Catholic school. Although not a Christian, Binh studied theology and law and became an instructor at the National Training Center, where he taught for seven years.

After the fall of Saigon in 1975, Binh, along with other educated Vietnam citizens, was placed in a government-run re-education camp in order to be assimilated into Vietnam's communist society. As Binh recalls, "During my six years in the re-education camp, I was not a model prisoner, so I was placed in an isolation cell for my last year and a half. During my time in isolation, I accepted Christ into my heart and felt the call to serve the Lord."

When Binh was later moved to a larger cell, he decided to speak about his faith with the other seven men in the same cell. However, it was against the law in Vietnam to share the Christian faith, an offense sometimes punishable by death, so Binh knew that he had to be careful. "I was never afraid to share my faith," he says. "Since I had accepted the call, my personal safety didn't matter. After all, if they killed me, I would go to my Father's house."

One day Binh asked if anyone else in the cell was Christian. To his amazement, five were. As he remembers, "This was a special time for me. It was the first time I had ever shared the gospel with others."

After his release from the prison camp, Binh and his family immigrated to the United States, arriving in Seattle in the early 1990s. In 1999, Binh was trained as a commissioned lay pastor and became the founding pastor of the Vietnamese Presbyterian Good News Church. According to Binh, "The Commissioned Lay Pastor program is perfect for those of us who are from other countries and feel called to serve the Lord. In my case, I probably wouldn't have been a good candidate for seminary because of my age. It would have taken four years of college plus three years of seminary to become a pastor. By that time it would have been too late to reach out to many of the Vietnamese who had moved to this country. The need for pastoral care is now. My English language may not be perfect, but my heart and mind are filled with the Holy Spirit. I feel blessed to be given this opportunity to serve our Lord."

Commissioned lay pastors are lay persons who are given special authority in the Presbyterian Church, usually for a year at a time, to lead worship and perform the sacraments of Baptism and the Lord's Supper. Many commissioned lay pastors are from other countries, and some are serving small rural congregations or are in specialized ministries. The Presbytery of Seattle has been in the forefront in commissioning lay pastors because it believes that the Commissioned Lay Pastor program is the best way to serve the many new residents who have moved to the Seattle area from other countries. ■

Commissioned lay pastor in training José Corado of Juntos Alcanzando Las Naciones, commissioned lay pastor Jonathan Kobayashi of the Japanese Presbyterian Church, and commissioned lay pastor Binh Thanh Nguyen of the Vietnamese Presbyterian Good News Church serve churches in Seattle.

Mansour Khajehpour and Esmaeil Goltapeh are commissioned lay pastors in training at the Persian Presbyterian Fellowship in Seattle.

"Think of us . . . as servants of Christ and stewards of God's mysteries." (1 Corinthians 4:1)

Photography:

W. Patrick Chambers

1, 5–11, 15–17, 27–28, 33–35, 39–44, 51–73, 80–89, 91, 94–101, 111–16, 118–28, 132–36, 144–45, 150–59, 164–77, 179–80, 181 (bottom), 182–83, 184 (top, center), 192, 194–97, 207–8, 212–14, 222–23, 227

John Fitzgerald

2–4, 12–14, 18–25, 29–32, 36–38, 45–50, 74–79, 102–10, 130–31, 137–43, 146–49, 160–63, 181 (top), 184 (bottom), 186–91, 193, 198–206, 209–11, 215 (center, bottom), 216–17, 224–26

Other Photo Credits

Endsheet map: copyrighted by Universal Map, 800-829-6277, and used with permission, 26: courtesy of Beulah Travis, 92-93: photo by Brook Kraft/Corbis Sygma, 215 (top): photo by Carlos Studio, 218-19: photos by John Warner, 220-21 (top): copyright ©1998 by Melinda Hess & Patricia Roberts of Convivial Design, Inc., 221 (center, bottom): courtesy of Sue Rundstrom

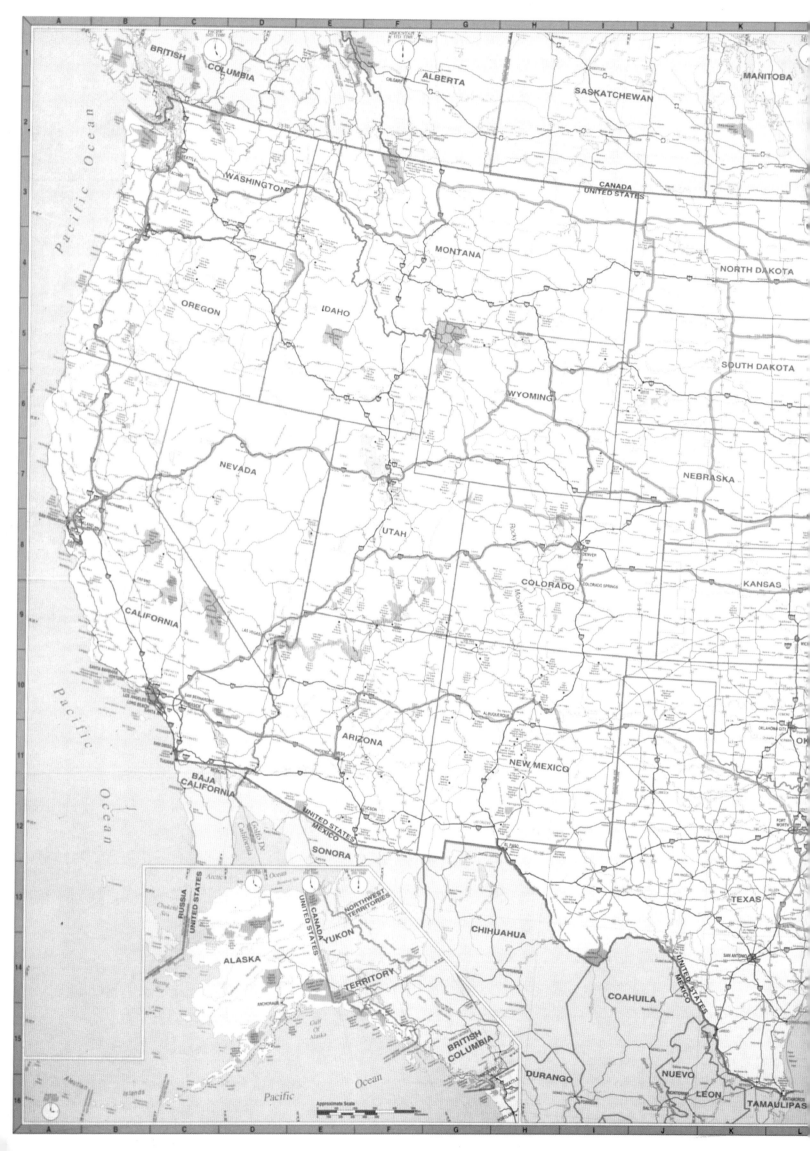